THE PRINTED BOOK

IN AMERICA

THE
PRINTED BOOK
IN AMERICA

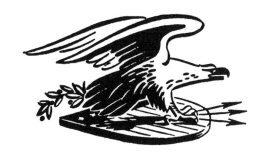

BY JOSEPH BLUMENTHAL

PUBLISHED FOR
THE DARTMOUTH COLLEGE LIBRARY
BY
UNIVERSITY PRESS OF NEW ENGLAND
HANOVER AND LONDON

THE PRINTED BOOK IN AMERICA
was prepared during Joseph Blumenthal's
incumbency as Bibliographical Associate of
the Dartmouth College Library, 1973–1977. A comple-
mentary provision was the creation by Mr. Blumenthal
of an exhibition of books featured in the plates section of
the present volume—an exhibit which opened at Dartmouth in May of 1977, with plans for its being shown
thereafter at other libraries across the United States.

Dartmouth and its Library here record their warm
gratification over the association between the College
and Mr. Blumenthal which has resulted in both this publication and the traveling exhibition.

EDWARD CONNERY LATHEM
Dean of Libraries and Librarian
of the College, Emeritus

PRINTED IN THE UNITED STATES OF AMERICA
∞
LIBRARY OF CONGRESS
CATALOGING-IN-PUBLICATION DATA

Blumenthal, Joseph, 1897–
The printed book in America.

Bibliography: p.
Includes index.
1. Books—United States—History. 2. Printing—United
States—History. 3. Book industries and trade—United
States—History. 4. Publishers and publishing—United
States—History. I. Title.
Z208.B56 1989   070.5'0973   88–40520
ISBN 0–87451–485–1
ISBN 0–87451–480–0 (pbk.)
5 4 3 2 1

The eagle on the preceding page
has been reproduced from a woodcut by
Fritz Kredel for the Spiral Press

TABLE OF CONTENTS

PREFACE

THE PURPOSE of this volume is to trace the main currents in the development of the printed book in America and to present its leading practitioners. Printing made its start in Cambridge, Massachusetts, in 1638. During the two decades following the landing of the Pilgrims, more than ten thousand Puritans settled in the new world. Unlike the adventurers from other nations who came to plunder, these resolute English immigrants came to build. Among them were artisans and farmers, merchants and schoolteachers, doctors and ministers—including more than one hundred graduates of Oxford and Cambridge. Despite the struggle for survival, the Massachusetts Bay Colony made provision for the establishment in 1636 of an academy of learning, soon to be named after John Harvard. Two years later the new college provided working space and supervision for the first printing press in a British-American colony. (The first press in the Western Hemisphere, sponsored by the Spanish church, had been set up almost a century earlier in Mexico.) During the seventeenth and eighteenth centuries, new printers established their shops in the expanding American colonies where they printed the almanacs and newspapers and the laws of the colonial assemblies.

The growth of industrialism during the nineteenth century and the enormous economic expansion after the Civil War gave rise, for the first time in the United States, to a society with the means and the leisure to enjoy some of the amenities of older civilizations. The 1870's brought the opening of the Metropolitan Museum of Art in New York and the Museum of Fine Arts in Boston. In 1884 a group of dedicated book collectors founded the Grolier Club of New York for "the literary study and promotion of the arts entering into the production of books." With similar aims, the Club of Odd Volumes in Boston soon followed, as did other organizations concerned with printing and the graphic arts.

The arts and crafts which burgeoned during the late decades of the nineteenth century found their counterpart in an extraordinary gathering of typographic genius in New England—an heroic generation of designers and printers whose work has properly been called a renaissance of fine printing in America.

What is fine printing? Fine printing involves an esthetic dedication. It is an expression of the human spirit which, through the arrangement and presentation of the printed word, reaches toward order and harmony and beauty. Fine printing implies scholarship, artistry, and craftsmanship at the command of the practitioner, whether in printing houses, at private presses, or in workshops of college art departments—whether on automatic machinery or on hand equipment. Such are the criteria by which the books discussed and reproduced in this volume have been chosen. The author, who has made the selections, is alone responsible for any sins of omission and commission. The anthologist who chooses, and necessarily also rejects, is acutely aware of his own fallibility and knows only too well that he will not please all.

The ancient method of setting type and printing by direct impression (known as letterpress) dominates this volume. Dictated by the limitations of time and space, newer trends, such as photographic books and books planned for electronic type composition, have not been included. Neither have the technology and the commerce of printing. Footnotes are not provided in the essay form that follows, since most sources are identified in the text itself and related to the bibliography.

ACKNOWLEDGMENTS

As I look back over the several years during which this volume has been in preparation, it becomes a great pleasure and privilege to acknowledge, with gratitude, the friendly help, so freely given, of so many men and women engaged in the small world of fine book production. John Dreyfus, eminent English typographic scholar, has read much of the manuscript. Professors James D. Hart and Rollo G. Silver have read regional portions. Individual biographical sections have been read by Frederic B. Adams, Jr., Edna Beilenson, Daniel B. Bianchi, J. M. Edelstein, Carolyn Reading Hammer, and Lawrence Siegfried. Help in many ways was given by Charles Antin, Herman Cohen, William Glick, Sinclair H. Hitchings, Harold Hugo, C. Freeman Keith, Sandra Kirshenbaum, Joe W. Kraus, Mike Parker, Caroline Rollins, Philip Sperling, Jake Zeitlin, and many others along the way. Extraordinary courtesies were extended by librarians and their staffs. Special thanks are offered to Mrs. Maud D. Cole at the New York Public Library; Marcus A. McCorison, the American Antiquarian Society; Kenneth Nesheim, the Beinecke

Library at Yale; Kenneth A. Lohf, Columbia University Library; Robert Nikirk, the Grolier Club; P. W. Filby, the Maryland Historical Society; Jean Peters, the Frederic W. Melcher Library; and, of course, to Walter W. Wright and the many other persons at the home base, the Dartmouth College Library. Edward Connery Lathem, Dean of Libraries at Dartmouth, has been from the start the wise and generous sponsor who has, with patience and good will, guided this undertaking to its present completion. And finally my deepest thanks go to my wife, constant companion during uncounted hours devoted to this book and, indeed, through a half-century of the vagaries of a typographic career.

J. B.

West Cornwall, Connecticut
March 1977

LIST OF THE PLATES

xvi

THE

PRINTED BOOK

IN AMERICA

DURING THE SUMMER of 1638 the Reverend Jose Glover, a non-conformist British minister, sailed from England on the ship *John of London* with his wife, five children, servants, and a printing press. He also brought a supply of type and a stock of paper. The destination was Massachusetts. The purpose was to establish a press in the infant colony to serve church and a theocratic state. The Glover family was accompanied by Stephen Daye, a locksmith engaged to set up the press, and by Daye's wife and their two grown sons. The Reverend Glover, a man of some wealth who had previously made a voyage to Massachusetts, headed for the new academy in whose planning he is believed already to have had some share. Unfortunately, the minister died during the transatlantic voyage. Ownership of the printing equipment passed to his wife, who proceeded to Cambridge as planned and saw the establishment of the press on the grounds of Harvard College and under its protection. Locksmith Daye was not an educated man. His work needed direction and this was supplied by Henry Dunster, the first president of Harvard College, who in 1641 married Mrs. Glover.

Stephen Daye's name is enshrined as America's first printer. But he was not a printer by trade, and documents in later court cases show him to be barely literate. It must be assumed that his eighteen-year-old son, Matthew, had been apprenticed to printing as a young man before leaving England and that it was Matthew who was primarily responsible for the Cambridge production. Stephen Daye's name was never included on any of the title pages. Matthew Day's name (without the terminal "e") appears as printer on an almanac of 1647 (plate 2) "to be solde by Hez. Usher at Boston," America's first bookseller. Clearly, neither Daye, father or son, was a trained craftsman. Their workman-

THE
COLONIAL
PERIOD

THE
CAMBRIDGE
PRESS

STEPHEN
DAYE

MATTHEW
DAY

1

THE

COLONIAL

PERIOD

THE

CAMBRIDGE

PRESS

THE

BAY PSALM

BOOK

SAMUEL

GREEN

ship was poor. This could hardly have been otherwise, since printing, due to the restrictive acts imposed by the British Crown, was at a very low ebb in the England from which the Dayes had come. Nevertheless, considering the primitive conditions in the new country only twenty years after the first landings in Massachusetts, and the extreme limitations of a tiny, crude, candlelit, one-press shop, profound respect must be acknowledged for work that was finally accomplished. The first printed items, in 1638–39, as recorded by Governor Winthrop, were a freeman's oath (probably a one-sheet broadside) and an almanac of perhaps some eight pages. Neither has survived. The next year, 1640, saw the completion of *The Whole Booke of Psalmes Faithfully Translated into English Metre* (plate 1), the first book to have been printed in British America.

The *Booke of Psalmes*, or the "Bay Psalm Book," as it is generally known, is a metrical translation of the Psalms from the Hebrew into English. The preface and the translations are the work of John Cotton and other colonial clergymen, including Richard Mather, first of the famous family of ministers and scholars. The Bay Psalm Book, considering the hazards of its time and place, is a commendable work of 296 pages, despite its poor presswork and its numerous typographic errors. The original page was probably about 5 by 7½ inches. Existing copies vary in size owing to the trimming by different binders. The edition was 1700 copies. Eleven copies of this most precious of American books are known to have survived the hard usage of a faithful church-going and psalm-singing population. An excellent complete facsimile reprint, with a companion volume, *The Enigma of the Bay Psalm Book* by Zoltan Haraszti, was issued by the University of Chicago Press in a two-volume set in 1956.

Matthew Daye died in 1649. That same year a successor, Samuel Green, took over operation of the press in Cambridge. Stephen Daye remained only as a workman. Samuel Green, who carried on until the press was dissolved in 1692, was born in England and had crossed with his parents in 1633 at age eighteen. He was not a trained printer and at first added little to the workmanship of the press, although the books had fewer errors than in the Daye years. As Green gained experience the work improved, especially after he was joined by a newcomer from England. The Green family name was honorably perpetuated in printing for almost two hundred years by descendants in Massachusetts,

2

Connecticut, Maryland, and Virginia. Gregory Dexter, an English printer who became an associate of Roger Williams in Rhode Island, was called on for occasional help at the Cambridge press. Isaiah Thomas quoted from the manuscript papers of Ezra Stiles, President of Yale: "It is said that after Samuel Green began printing at Cambridge, Dexter went there, annually, for several years, to assist him in printing an Almanack."

The most extraordinary volume of the Cambridge press, and indeed of the whole colonial period, was the Eliot Indian Bible (plate 3). John Eliot (1604–1690), known as the apostle to the Indians, was born in England, educated at Cambridge, came to America in 1631, and held a pastorate in Roxbury, Massachusetts. His mission, as he conceived it, was to convert the Indians to Christianity, that, he vowed, "they may be the Lord's people, ruled by Him alone in all things." Eliot mastered the Indians' speech and preached to them in their own tongue. In order to make the holy scriptures known to his wards, he translated the entire Bible into the local Algonkian language, expressed in roman type. Its complete title was *Mamusse Wunneetupanatamwe Up-Biblum God, Naneeswe Nukkone Testament, Kah Wonk Wusku Testament.*

Eliot induced the English Society for Propagating the Gospel among the Indians to finance the printing and publication of the Bible. To make production possible, the Society sent a new press to Cambridge, together with new type and, on a three-year contract, a young printer, Marmaduke Johnson, to assist Green with the work; Eliot himself provided an Indian convert, called James Printer, to aid in the menial duties. Isaiah Thomas in his notable *The History of Printing in America* (Worcester, Mass., 1810) expressed his admiration: "Green now began printing the Bible in the Indian language, which, even at this day, would be thought a work of labor, and must, at that early period of the settlement of the country, have been considered a business difficult to accomplish, and of great magnitude. It was a work of so much consequence as to arrest the attention of the nobility and gentry of England, as well as that of king Charles, to whom it was dedicated. The press of Harvard college, in Cambridge, Massachusetts, was, for a time, as celebrated as the presses of the universities of Oxford and Cambridge, in England."

Printed on two wooden handpresses, the edition of the Indian Bible realized a remarkable production of fifteen hundred copies, completed in 1663, almost twelve hundred pages, 5½ by 7⅛ inches. As to the "praying Indians" who had been converted in the several settlements in which Reverend Eliot preached, one may hope they were well received in some Christian heaven where all souls enjoyed the same color of skin. Here on this earth many were exterminated by their own kind in King Philip's War.

According to Robert F. Roden in *The Cambridge Press, 1638–1692*, some 192 items were printed and issued in Cambridge during those fifty-four years. Not all have survived. In any event, for forty years this press under the supervision and editorial direction of Harvard College produced the only printed matter in the colonies. Lawrence C. Wroth, the pre-eminent scholar in colonial-American printing, states in *The Book in America*: "No other press of the whole colonial period partook to the same degree of the qualities of the learned presses of Europe, or maintained so successfully the great traditions of the craft as an intellectual force in the midst of a new and rude environment. Its inability to show the production of any work of imaginative secular literature was not an item in its discredit. In New England, and elsewhere in a country of laborious living, that particular flower of the spirit came to blossom only in the relative leisure of the next century. Nor did that press concern itself to any extent with the material affairs of the people, with the farming, fishing, buying, selling, and building by which they lived. It had been established, Edward Johnson wrote in 1654, to advance the work of church and commonwealth. Within that limitation it was a successful concern, surpassing, it may be, the expectations of its founder."

Censorship plagued the colonial printers. The same fears that provoked the government in England to impose severe restrictions in the homeland worked against the press in the new world. According to Isaiah Thomas: "The fathers of Massachusetts kept a watchful eye on the press; and in neither a religious nor civil point of view, were they disposed to give it much liberty. Both the civil and ecclesiastical rulers were fearful that if it was not under wholesome restraints, contentions and heresies would arise among the people." In 1662 the government of Massachusetts appointed licensors of the press, and in 1665 approved a law that "no printing should be allowed in any town . . . except in Cambridge, nor should anything be printed but what the government permitted." In 1695 the Governor of New York received instructions from

4

the British Crown "that noe person keep any press for printing, nor that any book, pamphlet or other matters whatsoever bee printed without your leave and license first obtained."

Permission to establish a press in Boston, the first outside of Cambridge, was secured in 1674 by Marmaduke Johnson. However, Johnson died before he could put his press into operation and was succeeded by John Foster, a Harvard graduate. In 1690 Boston briefly saw America's first newspaper. It was an abortive attempt from the press of Richard Pierce (for Benjamin Harris) because of prompt suppression by the Governor and Council. Not until 1704 was a newspaper finally established in Boston, printed by Bartholomew Green, that would sustain some continuous publication. The harassment of local printers proved a spur to the spread of the press outside Massachusetts. In 1709 officials of Connecticut invited Thomas Short of Boston to settle in New London. Rather than yield to official restraints, James Franklin, elder brother of Benjamin, moved his press and his newspaper from Boston to Newport, Rhode Island, in 1727. In 1755 James Parker in New Haven began the first newspaper in Connecticut. Interference from Massachusetts authorities drove Daniel Fowle to New Hampshire, and presses appeared in what is now Vermont, in 1780, and in Maine, in 1784, to complete the coverage of New England.

Although the history of newspaper publication is not within the province of the present essay, it should be noted that newspapers were often the financial mainstay of the colonial printer. Royal authority had reason enough to be reluctant about allowing liberties to the press. Newspapers became powerful, unifying forces in the growth of American colonial society. In their weekly issues, many courageous printer-publishers provided the most effective instrument for the expression of an aroused public opinion and, ultimately, a powerful voice in the rebellion against the mother country. Indeed, the colonial press became a vigorous rival of the pulpit in the spread of thought.

The primary position in printing passed from Boston to Philadelphia during the eighteenth century. Unlike the homogeneous English immigration that had built an aristocratic theocracy in New England, the commonwealth of Pennsylvania opened its doors to English, Scottish, German, Dutch, and Swedish settlers. The rapid and vigorous development of this colony may well be attributed to its mixed population, to greater tolerance in government and religion, to freedom from strife

5

with the Indians, and to improved means of communication in an expanding economy. Here was a new, more democratic society. Its citizens were, according to Parrington in *Main Currents in American Thought* (New York, 1927–30), "part of that emerging humanitarian movement which, during the last half of the eighteenth century, was creating a new sense of social responsibility."

WILLIAM BRADFORD (1663–1752)

The first printer in Philadelphia, William Bradford, had crossed the ocean in 1682 with William Penn. He set up his press in 1685 and opened a bookstore in 1688. He was handicapped, as were other colonial printers, by lack of equipment. In his first issue, an almanac for the year 1686, entitled *Kalendarium Pennsilvaniense, or America's Messenger*, he dutifully addressed the reader: "Hereby understand that after great Charge and Trouble, I have brought that great Art and Mystery of Printing into this part of America, believing it may be of great service to you in several respects, hoping to find Encouragement, not only in this Almanack, but what else I shall enter upon for the use and service of the Inhabitants of these Parts. Some Irregularities, there be in this Diary, which I desire you to pass by this year; for being lately come hither, my Matereals were Misplaced, and out of order, whereupon I was forced to use Figures & Letters of various sizes . . . and by the next (as I find encouragement) shall endeavour to have things compleat. . . ."

In 1690 Bradford with Samuel Carpenter and William Rittenhouse established the first American paper mill, near Germantown, where the Rittenhouse family continued for several generations to make paper. In 1692 Bradford came into conflict with the Quaker hierarchy and was brought to trial for printing a pamphlet they found offensive. However, Governor Fletcher of New York, temporarily with jurisdiction over Pennsylvania, stepped in and took Bradford to New York. In 1693 he became Royal Printer to the colony (plate 4), and there his career flourished for the next fifty years. He printed the first legislative proceedings issued in the colonies, became official printer also to New Jersey, and in 1725 began publication of the *New-York Gazette*. His son Andrew later returned to Philadelphia and there reestablished the Bradford imprint.

BENJAMIN FRANKLIN (1706–1790)

At seventeen years of age Benjamin Franklin escaped from his apprenticeship in printing to his older brother in Boston and made his way to New York where he applied to William Bradford for work. Unsuccessful, he proceeded to Philadelphia, where in 1723 he found employment with Samuel Keimer, whose shop consisted of an old damaged press and a small supply of worn type. Soon thereafter Franklin spent two years in England as a journeyman compositor in two of London's leading printing houses. Returning to Philadelphia, and only briefly to Keimer, he set up, in 1728, in a partnership with Hugh Meredith whose father financed the acquisition of a new press and equipment brought from England. A year later Franklin became sole owner. In 1730, when only twenty-four years of age, he was the proprietor, editor, and publisher of the *Pennsylvania Gazette*, which soon enjoyed the largest newspaper circulation in the colonies. His *Poor Richard's Almanack*, printed annually in editions of more than ten thousand copies from 1732 to 1757, brought fame and fortune, as did other almanacs he published, including one in German. Franklin became official printer to Pennsylvania and Delaware. Printing the laws and proceedings of the colonial assemblies was sustaining and profitable work for those printers fortunate to be chosen. It was, also, the most provocative, with its sense of participation in great current events.

Franklin was Philadelphia's first bookseller and a very successful merchant. He financed partnerships with employees who were capable of managing printing shops. Such alliances were set up in Philadelphia and Lancaster in Pennsylvania; Charleston, South Carolina; and in Antigua and Kingston in the West Indies. A designated printer of money, he branched out into the printing and publishing of literature. When still in his mid-forties, after twenty years in commerce, Franklin's financial successes, together with an agreement for an annual retainer made with his Philadelphia partnership, Franklin and Hall, enabled him to retire from the daily demands of a printing house and to devote his life to a larger stage, as a scientist, diplomat, and citizen of the world.

Although Franklin's workmanship as a printer was essentially practical to its purposes and to its market, he did rise occasionally to special production efforts. His best-known book typographically, said to have been his own favorite, is Cicero's *Cato Major* (plate 7), in Caslon type with a two-color title page, printed and published in 1744. The translation was by the Chief Justice of Pennsylvania. In his foreword, Franklin concludes with: "... my hearty Wish, that this first Translation of a *Classic* in this *Western World*, may be followed with many others, performed with equal Judgment and Success; and be a happy Omen, that *Philadelphia* shall become the Seat of the *American* Muses." The present writer's favorites among the Franklin opus are his printing in 1740 of *A Collection of Charters and Other Publick Acts relating to the Province of Pennsylvania* (plate 6) and the first of the famous thirteen treaties with the Indians. The full title of the latter is *A Treaty of Friendship Held With the Chiefs of the Six Nations, at Philadelphia, in September and October 1736.* (The bearing and dignity of the Indian leaders at the meetings with the Pennsylvania and Delaware delegates, and the nobility of their speech, led Carl Van Doren to observe that "life seems to have made itself almost unaided into literature.") Franklin rose to the historic occasions with excellent pamphlet-bound, folio-size documents of the complete proceedings. The thirteen treaties have been reproduced in facsimile in a folio volume issued by the Historical Society of Pennsylvania in 1938, with an introduction by Carl Van Doren and an historical commentary by Julian P. Boyd.

Franklin appreciated the subtleties of fine printing. He corresponded with the European masters Baskerville and Bodoni and bought their books. The Infante Don Gabriel Antonio de Bourbon of Spain presented Franklin with the monumental four-volume *Don Quixote* printed by Ibarra in Madrid. While in Paris, Franklin placed his grandson as an apprentice with the great French printer and typefounder François Ambroise Didot. And in the late years of his life Franklin turned back to the work of his youth at his private press in Passy, where he entertained himself and charmed his ladies with the bagatelles he wrote and printed between more serious duties at the French court.

THE EPHRATA PRESS

Several presses came out of the large German population in Pennsylvania. A group of German Baptists, popularly called Dunkers, settled a brotherhood in 1732 in Ephrata, near Lancaster. They were educated, peaceable, and hard-working. In order to provide free religious books for the poor Germans in America, the Brethren in Germany sent over a press and equipment. With the German typesetters and pressmen who emigrated to Ephrata, the press turned out more than forty publications. Their most prodigious single work and the largest publication of colonial times is *Der Blutige Schau-Platz* (plate 9), a history of the Mennonite martyrs who bled and died for their religious beliefs. It is a ponderous and unattractive folio of 1512 pages, completed in 1748. About 1200 copies were printed on paper made by the Brethren at a paper mill they themselves built, in a German gothic font imported from the homeland. The presswork was above the average of the times, albeit the typography shows a heavy Teutonic hand.

CHRISTOPHER SOWER, AND SON

The other German press of consequence was that of Christopher Sower who came to America in 1724. He was skillful in many trades and became a printer only because the Brethren needed help at Ephrata, where his technical ingenuities enabled him to master typographic processes. He gave up his other trades and set up his own press in Germantown in 1738; then later built a paper mill and a book bindery. He issued a newspaper, almanacs, hymn books, prayer books, etc., all in the German language; also a quarto Bible in German, in 1743 (plate 8), the first Bible in the colonies since the Eliot Indian translation of 1663. His work was neat and his presswork good. Sower died in 1758 and was succeeded by his son, who inherited his father's mechanical gifts.

Christopher Sower II continued his father's press and bindery. He printed and published almost entirely in German. He supervised the building of his own presses, established a paper mill on the Schuylkill River where he manufactured and sold writing and printing papers, and made and sold printing ink. In 1772 he cast type using moulds and matrices imported from Germany. Two of his employees, Justus Fox and Jacob Bay, developed sufficient skills to cut punches and to cast enough German (Fraktur) type to enable Sower to print a Bible in German and keep the type standing. Fox acquired the Sower foundry, made and sold type. Jacob Bay later established a foundry of his own from which he provided roman and italic type for contemporary printers.

Because Sower was pro-British during the Revolution, he was stripped by court action of his properties. As a member of the Baptist Dunker sect opposed to legal conflict, he did not contest the court decision. His sons went over to the British side, and the Sower press came to an end.

9

COLONIAL PRINTERS
OF TYPOGRAPHIC IMPORTANCE

THE
COLONIAL
PERIOD

There were more pressing problems in colonial America than the pursuit of typographic niceties. Nevertheless, a few printers in Boston, New York, Philadelphia, Maryland, and Virginia produced work that showed an instinct for order and design and special devotion to craft. The printing of James Parker, John Green, William Parks, Jonas Green, and William Goddard was much superior to the utilitarian average of their contemporaries.

JAMES
PARKER

James Parker served his apprenticeship with William Bradford in New York and later succeeded him as the printer of official documents. He was also involved with partnerships in Connecticut and New Jersey. As James Parker & Company in New Haven, he published the *Connecticut Gazette* in 1755, its first newspaper. In 1754 in New York he produced a noteworthy publication, *The Charter of the College of New-York, in America* (plate 10), done with W. Weyman "at the New Printing-Office in *Beaver-Street*." Columbia University, long known as King's College, was thus founded by grant of George II. This charter has an excellent title page, good text pages, and interesting woodcuts for a coat of arms and several decorative tailpieces. The presswork is poor by today's standards, but the overall result shows typographic effort and achieves some distinction.

JOHN
GREEN

John Green (a great-grandson of the pioneer Samuel Green of the Cambridge press, printer of the Indian Bible) in partnership with J. Russell is best remembered for an attractive quarto volume, *Pietas et Gratulatio* (plate 11), produced in Boston in 1761. The book is a ceremonial poem written and addressed by Harvard College dignitaries to George III on his accession to the English throne. The roman type, equivalent to today's 24-point, was well composed and generously spaced, with ample margins. The several stanzas of Greek were set in a font that belonged to Harvard College and was lost when its library burned in 1764.

WILLIAM
PARKS

William Parks was an English printer of substance who crossed the ocean with his printing equipment in 1725–1726 and settled in Annapolis as Public Printer to the Maryland Assembly. He printed and published books of general and literary interest. He issued Maryland's first newspaper, the *Maryland Gazette*, in 1727, set up as a bookseller and bookbinder, and built the first paper mill south of Pennsylvania. In *Men of Letters in Colonial Maryland*, Leo Lemay wrote: "By encouraging and printing the literature of Maryland and Virginia from 1726 to his death in 1750, William Parks performed an important service for the culture of early America. In view of the high literary quality of the extant newspapers, broadsides, and pamphlets printed by Parks, every student of American literature must regret that so few of his imprints have survived." Wroth called Parks "a man of excellent public spirit, who possessed as well a pretty taste in *belles-lettres*." The Parks printing at Annapolis in 1731 of the *Laws of Maryland* shows considerable typographic competence.

In 1730 William Parks also opened an office in Williamsburg, Virginia, where he established the first permanent press in that colony. (An abortive attempt to establish a press in Virginia had been made in 1682 by William Nuthead. Perhaps because of Nuthead's indiscretion in printing certain Assembly papers without permission, his press was prohibited from further work. But Virginia was officially inhospitable to printing in the seventeenth century. Its royal governor, Sir William Berkeley, is quoted as having said, "I thank God, we have not free schools nor printing, and I hope we shall not have these hundred years; for learning has brought disobedience and heresy, and sects into the world, and printing has divulged them. . . . God keep us from both!") For a few years Parks acted as printer to both Maryland and Virginia, but in 1737 he gave up his press in Maryland. As Public Printer to Virginia he spent all his time in Williamsburg and produced a substantial body of work. His editions of the *Laws of Virginia* (plate 5) and the 1736 *Charter . . . of the College of William and Mary* are outstanding. Parks is also remembered for having printed *Typographia, An Ode, on Printing* by John Markland in 1730, a stilted poem but the first American contribution to the literature of typography. Only one copy, at the John Carter Brown Library, has survived.

Jonas Green, perhaps the best colonial printer, was born in Boston. He, too, was a great-grandson of forebear Samuel. After serving an apprenticeship with his father in New London, he began his career in Boston, then spent several years in Philadelphia in the printing houses of Andrew Bradford and Benjamin Franklin. When the government of Maryland offered him the appointment as printer to the colony to succeed William Parks, he moved to Annapolis and there set up his printing shop in 1739–1740. Isaiah Thomas, never given overmuch to praise, wrote of Jonas Green: "His printing was correct, and few, if any, in the colonies exceeded him in the neatness of his work. Green possessed handsome talents, was respected for his conduct in private life, and, in the circle of his acquaintance, was celebrated for his wit and urbanity."

Green's printing of Bacon's *Laws of Maryland* (plates 12 and 13), a large folio volume of more than 700 pages, completed in 1765, was a conspicuous achievement. The difficult composition, with marginal notes, was handled with skill. The Caslon type, imported from England, was apparently new and well printed for its time and place. Total production is said to have required four years. The reader must remember that during the eighteenth century only limited amounts of type were available. Only a section or two of eight or sixteen pages could be hand-set and printed, to be followed by type distribution, further setting, printing and distribution—and so continued throughout the work to be done. With leather inkballs and wooden handpresses, a volume such as Bacon's *Laws* was an immense undertaking.

William Goddard was an able and colorful, if difficult and contentious, printer and newspaper editor. After apprenticeship with James Parker in New York, aided by his mother, Sarah Updike Goddard, he founded the first press and newspaper in Providence, Rhode Island, in 1762 (plate 14). In 1766 he moved to Philadelphia, where he formed a partnership with the primary purpose of setting up and publishing the *Pennsylvania Chronicle*. This became the third Philadelphia newspaper and one of the best in the colonies. However, after six unhappy years of financial, editorial, and personal misunderstanding, during which he battled for the freedom of the press, as well as for his own, the partnership foundered and Goddard was jailed for failure to meet his debts. In 1773 Goddard moved to Baltimore, again to set up a general printing office, and to publish the *Maryland Journal*. But his consuming interest, and what he saw as his patriotic duty, was the need to establish a new continental postal system to replace the outmoded British system. For this he traveled on horseback throughout the country. His plan was ultimately put into practice with Benjamin Franklin as Postmaster-General, but Goddard received neither the honorary nor the financial rewards to which he was probably entitled, which his belligerence and his animosity to Franklin doubtless prevented.

COLONIAL WOMEN IN PRINTING

The early colonial printing shop was small, usually part of the family household, together with a stationery and book store. It was, therefore, only natural that some members of the family should help with type-setting and other details of the workshop. At a time when death often struck at an early age, widows kept the business afloat for its necessary income until a son would be ready to take over, or until a partner were brought in by a new marriage.

The first woman involved with printing in America was Mrs. Jose Glover, who carried out her minister-husband's intentions when she saw to the setting up of the press in Cambridge in 1638. The first woman to be licensed to print in America was Dinah Nuthead in Maryland, widow of the printer William Nuthead. She succeeded to the estate of her husband in 1694–95, involving "a printing press and letters" and accounts receivable amounting to about nine thousand pounds of to-bacco, then a medium of exchange. Since Dinah signed her bond with a cross it is clear she was unable to write. Her printed matter, if any exists, has never been clearly identified.

Among the many sturdy women who kept open the printing house doors, a few should be singled out for special mention. In Rhode Island, Anne Franklin, widow of James, operated the family business from 1735 to 1763. She was aided by her two daughters who were, wrote Isaiah Thomas, "correct and quick compositors at case." Elizabeth Timothy of South Carolina has been immortalized in Benjamin Franklin's *Autobiography*. He wrote that the widow "managed the business with such success that she not only brought up reputably a family of children but at the expiration of the term was able to purchase of me the printing house and establish her son in it."

On Jonas Green's death in Annapolis in 1767, his widow, Anne Cath-arine Green, took over her husband's printing office. She was succeeded in 1775 by her son Frederick, who was later joined by his brother Samuel. They continued as printers to the government; they kept the post office; and they issued the *Maryland Gazette*, which remained in the family until 1839. They were the fifth generation of printers descended from patriarch Samuel—the only such dynasty in American typo-graphic history.

Two women became printers in their own right. Mary Katherine

Goddard had supported her brother William throughout his erratic career. During his absence in Baltimore, from 1774 to 1784, she took over complete direction of the printing house and produced the general printed matter, almanacs, and the newspaper. When her brother returned in 1784 Katherine stepped out but continued with her bookstore and as Baltimore's postmistress. Jane Aitken, daughter of the printer of the first American Bible in English, had, according to Isaiah Thomas, "a printing house in Philadelphia; and printed *Thompson's Translation of the Bible* [1808], in four volumes, octavo. The printing was well and handsomely executed."

There were more than twenty-five printers at work in Philadelphia when that city had become the central seat of American government and the country's main commercial center. Among them was Robert

Aitken, who in 1782 completed the printing of the first American Bible in English (plate 15). (Prior to the Revolution, British laws prohibited the production of an English-language Bible in the colonies.) The Aitken Bible was pocket-size. It received the endorsement of the Congress of the new United States as a "pious and laudable undertaking . . . as well as an instance of the progress of arts in this country. . . ." Aitken, born in Scotland, was apprenticed in Edinburgh to bookbinding. On arrival in Philadelphia he established himself in 1771 as a bookseller and pursued his trade as a highly respected binder. In 1774 he set up as a printer and so continued until his death in 1802. Another Philadelphia printer, John Dunlap, earned his place in history when, late into the night of the fourth of July, 1776, he completed the first printing of the Declaration of Independence.

The close of the American Revolution marks the approximate point at which colonial printers began to be relatively self-sufficient. Presses, type, and paper were being manufactured in several of the larger centers before the end of the century. Nevertheless, methods of production were here, as everywhere in the world, still primitive, with little fundamental change from the years of the invention of movable type three and a half centuries earlier.

PRESSES

The first American to manufacture presses for sale was Isaac Doolittle of New Haven in 1769. By 1775, presses were being made in

Philadelphia and Hartford, and soon thereafter in other centers. During the first decade of the nineteenth century, presses made of Honduras mahogany, with some refinements but still employing the torsion-screw principle, were well received from the maker, Adam Ramage of Philadelphia. Meanwhile, the first all-iron press had been made in England by Lord Stanhope. With its increased weight and strength and greater ease of operation it achieved much greater productivity. In 1814–1816 George Clymer of Philadelphia built an iron lever press, with a platen large enough to cover and print a newspaper page in one pull. Called the Columbian, the press was only a partial success in the United States. Soon thereafter Clymer took his press to the larger markets of England and the Continent, where he was more successful. Further improvements and simplifications came in a press by John Wells, in 1818, which introduced a novel form of toggle joint for greater impressional strength. Finally came the best and the last of the iron handpresses. Samuel Rust built an iron press, heavier and stronger than the Wells press. Known as the Washington Press, it was taken over about 1835 by the manufacturer (later to become large and famous) of printing presses, Robert Hoe and Company, where eventually more than six thousand were produced. Other printing press manufacturers produced rather similar models. These presses were in common use throughout the United States and remained so in country printing houses until long after presses driven by horses, then by steam, then by electricity, had ushered in the Industrial Revolution.

TYPE

The first roman and italic types used in the colonies were of Dutch and English manufacture, nondescript in design. By the middle of the eighteenth century Caslon type was the main import, and it has the distinction of having been used for the original printing of the Declaration of Independence. The first type to be cut and cast in America was the work of Abel Buell of Killingsworth, Connecticut, in 1769. It was a crude cutting, as may be seen in a surviving fragment at the Yale Beinecke Library. Despite some financial aid from the Connecticut Assembly, Buell, apparently of unstable reputation, realized production of only a few fonts of long primer (approximately 10-point) type.

The first independent foundries were established, as mentioned above, by Justus Fox and by Jacob Bay. John Baine, who had been associated with Alexander Wilson in Glasgow, set up in Philadelphia with his grandson. During their years of survival they cast type for several important publications, including Mathew Carey's Bible and Thomas Dobson's encyclopedia (plate 18). Adam Gerard Mappa, a Dutch type-founder, settled in New York in 1789. He brought foundry equipment and established himself in business, but unfortunately his workmanship was not satisfactory. He was unable to continue and sold out in 1794. Benjamin Franklin bought foundry equipment in France, which he set up in Philadelphia for his grandson Benjamin Franklin Bache. This proposed foundry, too, was never successful, and in 1806 the equipment was bought by Binny and Ronaldson.

Two Scots, Archibald Binny and James Ronaldson, established a foundry in Philadelphia in 1796 that sustained a long and honorable life. In 1809 they issued their first type specimen, which consisted solely of type ornaments, French in spirit and much of it attractive. In 1812 they issued a *Specimen of Printing Types from the Foundery of Binny & Ronaldson, Philadelphia* (plate 21). This was a thoroughly professional performance, entirely free of provincialism. There were several romans and italics in a full range of sizes, also black letter, Fraktur, Hebrew, Greek, and an assortment of printers' flowers. Daniel Berkeley Updike wrote in his *Printing Types, Their History, Forms, and Use*: "Of the larger sizes of type shown in this specimen, the French Canon roman and its italic is a really handsome letter. The rest of the larger sizes are of the heavy face then fashionable. The transitional forms of smaller roman and italic shown are delightful." This "transitional" type had apparently been cut by Archibald Binny. The pica size was used by Isaiah Thomas in his *History of Printing in America* (1810). These matrices were preserved and eventually used for casting by the American Type Founders Company, in the 1890's, after the new company had absorbed the remaining offshoot of the original Binny and Ronaldson partnership. The type was called Oxford and enjoyed the distinction of purchase and use by both Daniel Berkeley Updike and Bruce Rogers, and was extensively favored by the Grabhorn Press in San Francisco for many of their handsome books. The Binny design was chosen in 1946 as the basis for a typeface produced by the Mergenthaler Linotype Company for the Princeton University Press edition of the Thomas Jefferson Papers, appropriately named Monticello. The Binny and Ronaldson great primer roman (approximately 18-point) appeared in Joel Barlow's *Columbiad* (1807), an impressive quarto (plate 20) excellently printed by Fry and Kammerer in Philadelphia. This volume, patterned after the Bulmer books in England, is the first American attempt to produce a substantial deluxe edition.

PAPER

With the end of the Revolution, almost a century after Rittenhouse had built the first American mill, papermaking had become an established American industry. In 1787, according to Wroth, some eighty or ninety mills were in operation. In 1810 Isaiah Thomas acknowledged 195 mills. With sixty mills within its borders, Pennsylvania held first place, as it had throughout colonial times. Paper was still being made much as it had been when first introduced into Europe in the thirteenth century. Each sheet of paper was formed one at a time by dipping a wire mould into a vat containing beaten pulp suspended in water. In order to achieve a fine, rich, textured sheet of paper, it would have been necessary to have perfect control of a clear, abundant water supply, a continuous stock of clean, white cotton and linen rags, and highly developed manual skills in forming and finishing the paper. The workers' dexterities grew out of generations of craftsmanship in papermaking centers in Europe and Asia. The colonial paper manufacturer was not well equipped. Nevertheless, he made paper adequate to the needs of his contemporaries, and because the content of all paper was cotton and linen rags, the paper, made well or not, was permanent. The books and pamphlets of that period not worn to shreds by use may be seen today in our great libraries.

A society preoccupied with religion, politics, and physical survival had scant opportunity for the enjoyment of books. The local printers supplied the general reading public with newspapers, magazines, and almanacs, and, in New England, a substantial number of sermons by their eminent clergymen. Nevertheless, the literary classics and copies of contemporary English writing, imported by American booksellers, found their way into many colonial homes. In the middle and southern colonies, where life was less severe, wealthy plantation owners sent their sons to school in England where direct relations were often made with English bookshops. The most famous library in eighteenth-century America contained the thirty-five hundred volumes that graced the ancestral home of William Byrd in Virginia. Important too was the three-thousand-volume library of Cotton Mather in Boston. Wroth, writing of libraries in *The Colonial Printer*, states that ". . . whatever the components of these collections may have been, their possession was not confined to the individuals of any one section of the country. No one whose way has led him to the examination of wills and inventories in various colonies has failed to be impressed by the presence in them of collections of books, itemized or otherwise, standing up bravely in the lists of more material possessions."

The hundred and sixty-one years from 1638 to 1799 mark the growth from primitive beginnings in Massachusetts and the printing of the crude Bay Psalm Book to the closing years of the eighteenth century with the completion in Philadelphia by Thomas Dobson of a monumental eighteen-volume encyclopedia (plate 18) containing more than five hundred full-page engravings. With the colonial period drawn to its close, a new epoch opens into the nineteenth century.

ISAIAH THOMAS (1749–1831)

Isaiah Thomas was the first major figure in American printing. Printer, binder, papermaker, publisher, and bookseller, he was, too, a colonial patriot, an historian, and a public benefactor. His long life witnessed the transition from provincial commonwealths to an established nation, from primitive manual working conditions to an early industrialism.

Isaiah's ancestors, he stated, were among the early settlers from England. His grandfather was a merchant in Boston, but his father squandered an inheritance and abandoned his family. Isaiah's mother, unable to support all her children, arranged through the Overseers of the Poor for an apprenticeship for him at six years of age with Zechariah Fowle, a childless printer in Boston, who took the lad into his home and agreed to provide board, room, and clothing, to instruct him in reading, writing, and cyphering, and to teach him the art and mystery of printing. The indenture, dated June 4, 1756, a printed form characteristic of the period, provided in part that

... the said Apprentice, his said Master and mistress, well and faithfully shall Serve, their Secrets he shall keep close, their Commandments lawful and honest every where he shall gladly obey: he shall do no Damage to his said Master, etc., nor suffer it to be done by others, without letting or giving seasonable Notice thereof to his said Master, etc.: he shall not waste the Goods of his said Master, etc., nor lend them unlawfully to any: At Cards, Dice, or any other unlawful Game or Games he shall not play: Fornication he shall not commit: Matrimony during the said Term he shall not contract: Taverns, Ale-Houses, or Places of Gaming he shall not haunt or frequent: From the Service of his said Master, etc., by Day nor Night he shall not absent himself; but in all things and at all Times, he shall carry and behave himself towards his said Master, etc., and all theirs as a good and faithful Apprentice ought to do. . . .

In an autobiographical fragment Thomas relates: "After I was bound and he [Zechariah Fowle] had absolute power over me, he put me to all the servile employments in his family that I could perform, and when business of that kind was wanting, he placed me at the type cases. In order that I might reach the boxes of both capitals and lower case he had a bench made of sufficient heighth, and of the length of a double frame, that I might traverse when necessary from Roman to Italic and from Italic to Roman. I soon learned the type boxes. The first Essay I made was on a ballad called The Lawyer's Pedigree. I set the types which were double Pica, for this ballad in two days, tho' I then knew only the letters, but had never been taught to put them together and spell."

From the beginning Isaiah showed remarkable aptitude. Having set some type at seven years of age, by the time he was twelve he was said to have been a better workman than his not very competent master. Without schooling, Isaiah's education depended on what he could pick up. The Fowle shop consisted of only one wooden handpress and a few worn fonts of type. The main source of income were popular ballads which the young apprentice was sent into the streets to sell, and for which, later, he was to cut type-metal illustrations. During a few succeeding years when Fowle took in Samuel Draper, a trained printer, as partner, several larger jobs were undertaken, such as a *New England Primer* and a spelling book, *The Youth's Instructor in the English Tongue*. From Draper and the journeymen who came and went, Thomas learned his trade.

At sixteen years of age, having absorbed all he could at the Fowle shop, he yearned to get to London. As a hopeful first step, although his indenture was not to expire until his twenty-first birthday, he escaped to Halifax in 1765 after a five-day voyage by sea. Isaiah found work with Anthony Henry, the only local printer, at three dollars per month, plus board and washing. Because his employer wanted time for fishing, and because he found he could lean on the capacities of the sixteen-year-old from Boston, Isaiah was entrusted with production of the *Halifax Gazette*, the only newspaper in the province. He immediately improved its appearance. Given editorial freedom, he aired his anti-British feelings and his hatred of the recently imposed Stamp Act. This enraged the local government officials and embroiled the publisher to such an extent that, after a half year, Isaiah was forced to leave. He next arrived by ship at Portsmouth, New Hampshire, where he obtained employment with Furber and Russell, publishers of the *Portsmouth Mercury*. After only a few months he returned to Boston and Zechariah Fowle. Following a bitter quarrel Thomas again left and tried to reach London, this time by way of the southern colonies and the West Indies. After several misadventures that thwarted his good intentions, he landed in Charleston, South Carolina, where he worked for Robert Wells, who also owned a well-stocked bookstore which gave Thomas his first opportunity for wide reading. At Charleston he made a disastrous first marriage. With new responsibilities, after five years as a wandering journeyman printer, he returned again to his early master, Fowle, who now took his former apprentice into partnership. Here Isaiah faced his future during the turbulent pre-Revolutionary years when every citizen had to take his stand for or against independence. Isaiah Thomas had long since made his choice.

In 1770 when the twenty-one-year-old Thomas had the temerity to enter the newspaper field with a paper he called the *Massachusetts Spy*, there were four other newspapers published in Boston: the *News-Letter*, the *Evening-Post*, the *Post-Boy*, and the *Gazette*, all weeklies. The *Spy* was first issued as a tri-weekly single sheet, 9 by 12 inches in size, directed to artisans and shopkeepers—the less-privileged class from which Thomas came. Within a few months the format was changed to folio size, the largest in Boston, four pages issued weekly for a wider audience. It was an attractive paper with well-designed, engraved headings and, thanks to much improved presswork, more readable than its poorly printed competitors. Its editorial policy was bold and vigorous and politically radical. It is not surprising that the *Spy* soon outstripped its rivals, with a circulation of thirty-five hundred copies, the largest in New England. When Thomas and his colleagues attacked Governor Hutchinson and the royal government, he was called to appear before the Council but refused. He escaped arrest and prosecution, thanks to the strength of the following the *Spy* represented, and perhaps because Hutchinson remembered that an earlier royal governor had been defeated in court when the trial of John Peter Zenger, a New York printer, had established the principle of freedom of the press in America.

With backing from John Hancock, Thomas took possession of the Fowle shop by a rental agreement; then by assuming Fowle's outstanding debts, he became sole owner. Along with production of the *Spy*, Thomas enlarged general printing and publishing activities with schoolbooks, almanacs, etc. In 1774 he launched the *Royal American Magazine*, with illustrations engraved by Paul Revere and Joseph Callender. It did not survive the war.

With the approach of military hostilities, it became imperative for Thomas to leave Boston where both his person and his press (known as the "sedition factory") would have been seized by the British army. Because of the *Spy*'s importance to the patriot cause, and because printing facilities would be needed by the Provincial Congress, Hancock and other Revolutionary leaders urged Thomas to remove to Worcester. On the night of April 16, 1775, the press was dismantled and secretly transported. Thomas arrived in Worcester on the twentieth, where he would remain through life. Within two weeks he was again publishing the *Massachusetts Spy*, but, with the exception of the official account of the battles of Lexington and Concord, he did no printing for the Provincial Congress.

The war years brought the usual chaotic conditions. Paper was almost unobtainable. The *Spy* was reduced to a half sheet or less, circulation fell off, much of it unpaid, and general printing all but disappeared. But with the war over, the Thomas star rose rapidly. Paper was again in good supply. Thomas ordered several new presses made in America and bought large quantities of type from Caslon, Fry, and Wilson in Britain. This type, including a complete range of Caslon, with Greek and Hebrew, mathematical characters, and printers' flowers, was shown in a type specimen booklet he printed in 1785 in Worcester. In the 1780's Thomas put up new buildings that housed his presses, the bindery, and a bookstore, with one corner for the post office of which he was postmaster. He also built a "mansion" where he later entertained George Washington and other eminent contemporaries.

From 1784 to 1802 Thomas built a flourishing chain of partnership-branches for the printing, publishing, and selling of books. Clifford K.

Shipton, in his admirable brief biography of Thomas, wrote that "A great part of the American people learned their letters from his primers, got their news from his papers, sang from his hymnals, ordered their lives by his almanacs, and read his novels and Bibles." Seven handpresses were kept busy in Worcester and five in the early years of Thomas and Andrews, his Boston branch. Partnerships were also established in New-buryport and Springfield in Massachusetts, Albany and Troy in New York, Windsor and Rutland in Vermont, Walpole, New Hampshire, and Baltimore, Maryland.

The Thomas publishing program reached phenomenal proportions for his time. His *New England Almanac* reached an annual circulation of 30,000 copies. A speller by William Perry of Edinburgh University, published to compete with Noah Webster's books, sold 20,000 copies per year, while the same author's *Royal Standard Dictionary* found 54,000 buyers in four editions. Finally, Thomas and Andrews negotiated a con-tract with Noah Webster and sold 300,000 copies of his famous speller in a decade. Printed and published, also, were geographies, enchant-ing small illustrated children's classics, medical and scientific books, history, music, and general literature (plate 17). Editions of the Bible were issued in several formats, including the two-volume folio in 1791 (plate 16) with fifty full-page copperplate engravings. Typical other publications were Millot's *Elements of General History* in five volumes, Blackstone in four, Bell's *Surgery* in three, and the first American novel, Brown's *Power of Sympathy*. Ultimately, Thomas added a paper mill which produced about fourteen hundred pounds of paper weekly, em-ployed eleven girls and ten men, among them Zenas Crane who later built his own mill at Dalton, Massachusetts. Altogether at the height of the Thomas activities, he gave work to about one hundred and fifty people in Worcester, not counting the branches. The former appren-tice, with never-failing love for his craft, had become one of the most important purveyors of books on either side of the Atlantic. The poor lad who had had no schooling received two honorary college degrees and donated his substantial wealth to scholarship and the endowment of education.

In order that he might spend his later, but still energetic, years in public-spirited activities, after 1802 Thomas gradually withdrew from printing and publishing. Of the many interests to which he then gave time and money, the two most important and the most permanent

were his history of printing and the founding of the American Antiquarian Society, which still thrives as a vigorous national institution.
He was the Society's first president and its active head until his death.
He gave the site, the funds ($20,000) for its first building, and his own
library of eight thousand volumes (including his extensive collection of
colonial printing) as the foundation for the Society's library. Thomas
spent many years on the history of the craft which had so handsomely
repaid his lifetime of devotion. Published in 1810 in two volumes, its full
title is properly descriptive: *The History of Printing in America with a Biog-*
raphy of Printers and an Account of Newspapers, to which is pre-fixed a Concise
View of the Discovery and Progress of the Art in other Parts of the World. Because Thomas himself had been a part of colonial printing, he was able
to record with authority its origins and development, and to discuss the
men and women who established and operated the presses. The Thomas
history is a prime source for any study of the production of early American ephemera, books, and newspapers.

In evaluating the typographic standards of Thomas' work, one should
take into consideration his many outside interests and responsibilities.
He displayed a sense of craftsmanship and a pride of workmanship
above and beyond the needs of commercial success. The work turned
out under his immediate supervision in Worcester was produced with
care, as may still be seen in the neatness of much of the Thomas output.
Although Benjamin Franklin called him the Baskerville of America,
and a visiting Frenchman compared him to Didot, Thomas was not a
professional designer, nor was he an innovative typographer. Neither
was there any place in the America of that time for such work. Thomas
was an intuitive humanist who honored his craft and his fellow man.

When Thomas was seventy-six years of age he was invited by the
Franklin Typographical Society of Philadelphia to be their guest of
honor. In declining, he wrote: "Although I cannot take to myself all the
merit you are pleased to allow me, for my endeavors, long since, to
establish our Art in this extensive continent, on a more respectable foot-
ing than it then was, yet, so far as my efforts for that purpose produced
any good effect and have met with the approbation of the Typographic
Family it will ever afford me high satisfaction.... My attachment to the
art, of which we are professors, is not diminished. Could I live my life
over again and choose my employment it would be that of Printer."

MATHEW CAREY (1760–1839)

Mathew Carey began as a printer, but his fame rests on his later achievement as a publisher. In his "Autobiographical Sketches," written for the *New England Magazine* in 1833 and 1834, Carey notes his birth in Dublin of parents in financially comfortable circumstances. At age fifteen, with a limited education, contrary to his father's wishes he sought and found an apprenticeship in printing and bookselling. With a passionate nature, zealous for the rights of the underprivileged, Carey at nineteen wrote a strongly pro-Irish, anti-British pamphlet, which brought a threatened official reaction from which he fled to France. He was employed for a few months by Benjamin Franklin at his private press in Passy, where Carey met Lafayette—who wanted data concerning Ireland in anticipation of a proposed French invasion. A job with the famous Didot printing house in Paris followed. When Mathew returned to Ireland, then twenty-four years of age, his father provided him with funds to establish a paper, the *Volunteer's Journal*. Young Carey again attacked the British Prime Minister and Parliament, and this time landed in Newgate prison for a month. On release, but threatened with further prosecution, he escaped in disguise to a ship bound for America. He chose Philadelphia, the seat of United States government and the most active center for printing and publishing.

Lafayette was then (1784) on a visit to the new nation. After a fortuitous meeting with Carey he sent the young immigrant a gift (later repaid) of four hundred dollars which Carey used to buy some second-hand press equipment and to establish a newspaper, the *Pennsylvania Herald*. The *Herald* lasted until 1787, when Carey started the *American Museum* which drew praise from George Washington. In 1792 Carey gave up periodical publishing and devoted his entire energies to the printing and publishing of books (plate 19). He succeeded Isaiah Thomas as the publisher who most successfully fed the countrywide hunger for educational books and the growing demand for literature. Carey was among the first users of the newly invented stereotype process which made possible the reprinting of books without the heavy costs of standing type. He rushed the works of Charles Dickens and Walter Scott into print ahead of other American printer-publishers at a time when foreign authors had no copyright protection in the United States. Among his most successful ventures were the *Encyclopedia Americana* in thirteen vol-

24

umes, said to have sold 100,000 sets, and the Carey Family Bible on whose flyleaves were solemnly written the names and dates of generations of rural American families. In addition to the usual bookstore channels of distribution, Carey, like other publishers, employed itinerant travelers who sold on commission throughout the countryside. Approximately two hundred wagons fitted with portable bookcases are said to have been on the roads. Best remembered among the itinerant book salesmen is Mason Locke Weems, known as "Parson Weems," who covered southern territory, and who, himself an author of a biography of George Washington, provided that cherished bit of Americana, the cherry tree legend.

Carey's work as a printer is undistinguished. When his publishing activities became countrywide he gave up his own plant. As a successful entrepreneur whose books were produced for him in many printing houses, his imprint reflected nothing better, typographically, than the mediocre average prevalent in England and in America during the first half of the nineteenth century. His importance to the present history lies in the impetus he provided for the reading habits of a growing population. It has been said of him that he brought literature to the people.

Carey plunged into American life, an ardent and voluminous pamphleteer. He believed in trade and tariff protectionism. Ultimately a man of considerable property, he worked for renewal of the charter of the Bank of the United States. Through his most influential treatise, *The Olive Branch*, he hoped to unite Republicans and Federalists in support of the War of 1812. He helped to establish an association of American booksellers. He remained a loyal and fighting Irishman and wrote in Ireland's defense. He worked for the emancipation of the slaves, aid for indigent immigrants and needy soldiers, adequate wages for working women, and other worthy causes.

Isaiah Thomas and Mathew Carey were among the last printers whose beginnings were in the eighteenth century, with its productive economy and patterns of life dependent on human energy. The whole length of the nineteenth century lay ahead, with the enormous transformations in living and working conditions brought about by the Industrial Revolution, by the transition from sail to steam, from the covered wagon to the railroad, and by the final conquest of a continent. Of the first years of the new century, Rollo Silver writes pertinently in his book *The American*

25

Printer, 1787–1825: "In the first quarter of the nineteenth century, the application of new technical and scientific knowledge to the efficiency of the printing process marks the beginnings of industrialization. The wooden press became an iron press, rollers instead of balls inked the type, horse power and steam power were substituted for human energy, stereotyping became a normal procedure, lithography began to be used for illustrations. In these twenty-five years the equipment of the shop changed more than in all the past three and a half centuries put together."

THE HOUSE OF HARPER

In March of 1817 two young men, brothers, twenty-two and twenty years of age, both already accomplished in the trade of printing, set up their own shop in New York. With meager savings backed by their father's offer to mortgage the family farm if needed, James and John Harper bought two used Ramage handpresses and a few fonts of type, rented a small space in a building on the corner of Front and Dover Streets, and hung out their sign: "J. & J. Harper, Printers." New York was then a city of one hundred and twenty thousand inhabitants. The nation had grown to nine million. Lumbering stage coaches carried travelers and mails to other cities over rough dirt roads. Sloops on the Hudson River were the only direct means of communication between Manhattan Island and Albany. During the next eight years of American expansion, the two founding Harpers were joined by their two capable younger brothers to make a formidable business partnership that laid the foundation for a long-lived printing and publishing dynasty that became an important part of American literary history.

Within a year after their start, James and John Harper published their first book, Locke's *Essay Concerning Human Understanding*, and thereafter as their program grew rapidly, they were and would remain primarily publishers, with a printing plant to serve their needs. In 1825 they took over a four-story building on Cliff Street, installed ten presses and employed fifty workers, then the largest printing establishment in New York. In 1827 they introduced cloth binding. In 1833 newly invented steam presses built by Daniel Treadwell of Boston replaced the faithful white horse that had for many years walked a circular path harnessed to a beam attached at right angles to a perpendicular shaft that furnished power to the ten presses on the floor above. (The horse

26

had earned his rest and was taken to the family farm where his retirement has become part of the Harper legend. Turned out to pasture, the old horse frolicked on the fresh grass for a few days, then went to a solitary tree in the middle of the field and walked round and round and round from morning until evening and took an hour's rest only at midday.)

In December of 1853 the Harper complex of buildings was gutted by fire. Plans were immediately made to build two large six-story fireproof buildings divided for publishing and printing. The new printing plant housed all the latest technological advances and established an early industrial assembly line. The basement contained steam boilers and space for the storage of paper, with facilities also for dampening paper for printing. The ground floor held twenty-eight new steam-driven Adams bed-and-platen presses, each of which could produce 600 to 900 hand-fed sheets per hour. On the second floor the printed sheets were dried and pressed. The next three floors were given over to folding, gathering, sewing, and completion of bound books. The top floor, with maximum light, was used for hand composition of type and for stereotyping. (The Linotype, the first practical means of mechanical type composition, was not invented until 1884.) According to Eugene Exman in *The House of Harper: One Hundred and Fifty Years of Publishing* (New York, 1967), "They had at that time an establishment that in the numerical strength of its operation outranked any other publishing house in the world."

Typographically, Harper books of the nineteenth century were representative of the average output of their contemporaries in publishing and printing in America and Europe. In other words, they were commercially acceptable during a period when the proprietors of the new machinery devoted their energies to larger editions at lower prices for a constantly growing reading public. The available types were nondescript "moderns" or transitional faces, stemming from Bodoni and Didot but debased in the transition. There was neither capacity nor inclination for the niceties, finesse, and attention to detail required for fine bookmaking. Any recognition of the art of the book would have been expected to come from illustration (plate 22). The three Harper magazines, with immense readership—*Harper's Weekly, Harper's Monthly,* and *Harper's Bazaar*—provided excellent graphic forums for some of the best American artists then at work. Winslow Homer (at the front for *Harper's*

27

Weekly in the Civil War), Edwin Austin Abbey, A. B. Frost, Frederic Remington, and Howard Pyle, among others, made drawings which were cut on wood by skillful staff engravers for printing in these publications.

JOEL MUNSELL (1808–1880)

Joel Munsell was humbly born in the small town of Northfield in Massachusetts and served his apprenticeship in printing at the newspaper office of *The Franklin Post and Christian Freeman* in nearby Greenfield. At nineteen years of age he moved to Albany, the thriving capital of the State of New York. He sustained himself there as a bookstore clerk and journeyman compositor until he was able to establish his own plant in Albany in 1836. Munsell's work was good during a typographically bleak period. It was well received, and in due course he prospered and became a loyal son of his adopted city. His typographic design was orderly, if now rather dated.

Munsell is remembered because he was dedicated to the best principles of his craft, because he read widely and wrote about its historical background, and because he took an intense antiquarian interest in local history. He gathered the many articles about printing history and shop practices that he had written for trade papers, magazines, and local newspapers, into a potpourri which he printed and published in 1850 under the title *The Typographical Miscellany*. He also issued *A Chronology of Paper and Papermaking* in 1856, and in *Bibliotheca Munselliana* he listed and briefly described the more than two thousand books and pamphlets he had produced. His life and work are covered in much detail in a book by David S. Edelstein, *Joel Munsell: Printer and Antiquarian*, published by the Columbia University Press in 1950.

THEODORE LOW DE VINNE (1828–1914)

Theodore Low De Vinne, together with Isaiah Thomas before him and Daniel Berkeley Updike who soon followed, is of first rank in American typographic history. Each of these printers enriched the literature of his craft and demonstrated mastery of its practice. Each owned and in his own style directed a successful printing office and gave it stature. Each began life with limited schooling and later received academic recognition as a scholar in his chosen field.

De Vinne was born in Stamford, Connecticut. His father, who had come from Ireland of Dutch ancestry, was a cultivated schoolteacher and preacher, a Methodist circuit rider, and a friend of the Methodist printer James Harper. When Theodore was seven years of age he was taken to New York to visit the Harper plant on Cliff Street. There can be little doubt that the family friendship influenced four De Vinne boys to choose printing as their careers, one of whom was apprenticed in the Harper establishment. Two other sons chose bookbinding. Theodore at fourteen was engaged as an apprentice in the newspaper shop of the Newburgh (New York) *Gazette*. In an interview at age seventy-five, De Vinne spoke of his early years: "I began my experience as a printer in 1843–'44 in an office which was not as big as one floor of a small dwelling-house. It had only one old-fashioned Washington hand press and no steam press. The newspapers even did not have steam-presses . . . one or two newspapers only had them. The New York *Sun*, established by Benjamin H. Day, was printed on a hand press. He was a job-printer and as he did not get enough work to do, he conceived the idea of making up a paper and selling it for a cent. The circulation ran up so rapidly he could not print enough. He engaged three pressmen, and each one worked about twenty minutes and pulled like a horse at the hand press until he was played out, and then another took his place. They got out four hundred or five hundred copies an hour. The *Sun* was afterward sold to Moses Y. Beach, who put in a cylinder press."

THE
NINETEENTH
CENTURY

THEODORE
LOW
DE VINNE

The rigorous discipline of setting type by hand and running presses by brawn inspired the young De Vinne with understanding, competence, and respect for the basic and historic elements of printing. These he never lost during his career of more than sixty years which spanned a complete revolution in shop methods and the mechanics of production. In 1848 he left Newburgh for the wider horizons of New York City, to work in several printing establishments, newspaper composing rooms, and a stereotype foundry. In 1850 he was employed as a journeyman compositor by Francis Hart, who had earlier advertised his plant for sale. Hart, who wished to withdraw from the arduous duties of managing a printing office, soon recognized his new employee's ability and made him foreman. In 1858 De Vinne became a partner and gradually took over complete management. In 1877 Hart died and by the provisions of his will De Vinne was able to assume complete ownership in 1883 and to change the company name to Theodore L. De Vinne & Company. When De Vinne first entered the Hart plant in 1850 the equipment consisted of a Hoe cylinder press operated by a hand wheel, and three handpresses, with accompanying type and appurtenances. The workroom was illuminated by five camphene lamps and twenty candlesticks. During the second half of the century De Vinne embraced all the extraordinary technological changes that came on in rapid succession and used them to maximum advantage. Before he retired in 1908, type was mechanically set on Linotype machines; high-speed cylinder and rotary presses operated by electrical push-buttons had been installed in the especially built seven-story De Vinne Press building on Lafayette Street in New York, with more than three hundred employees.

THE
NINETEENTH
CENTURY

THEODORE
LOW
DE VINNE

Contrary to Hart's timid advice, De Vinne took on, in 1873, the printing of the very popular juvenile magazine *St. Nicholas,* whose performance of literary and artistic excellence was then unsurpassed. This was soon followed by *Scribner's Monthly* which became *The Century Illustrated Magazine.* Illustrated literary magazines were a primary source for home entertainment in the years before radio and television. The *Century* magazine reached a circulation of over 227,000 copies in the 1880's.

The handpress had become obsolete. De Vinne's sense of craft, his experienced eye for type composition, and his concern for fine presswork led the way toward coping with the new problems imposed by long runs on automatic presses. It was no longer necessary to dampen paper for the vastly greater strength of cylinder press printing. De Vinne replaced the soft impression used for dampened paper on the handpress with a hard packing for printing on dry paper. "Overlays" were perfected—a means of building up the solids and bringing out the full quality of wood engravings, then the chief medium for magazine illustration. And, of the greatest importance, De Vinne spent unlimited press time to achieve sensitive control of ink and paper, and the coordination of delicate adjustments on automatic machinery that alone produce even depth of impression of type on good paper. Fine presswork is a subtle achievement at the heart of the craft. De Vinne wrote in some detail about these problems in an essay, "The Growth of Wood-Cut Printing." The invention of photoengraving brought more fundamental changes. Wood engravings were supplanted by "linecuts" and "halftones." Drawings, paintings, and photographs became subject to mechanical reproduction. De Vinne added his own technical ingenuity

30

in collaboration with photoengravers and paper manufacturers, and worked with his friend Robert Hoe, press manufacturer, to obtain the best results possible with the new, faster, cheaper methods and machines, without a wasted backward look to "the good old days," gone beyond recall.

NINETEENTH
INTO THE
TWENTIETH
CENTURY

THEODORE
LOW
DE VINNE

In the normal cycles of changing taste, De Vinne and the publishers of the *Century Magazine* decided to replace the old-style type which they had been using with a new, more vigorous, and hopefully more legible, face. A new type was therefore designed and cut under De Vinne's immediate supervision. Because he believed hairlines in existing types were too sharp for dry printing, he began by increasing their weight; the lowercase was slightly increased in width; and the serifs were slightly modified. These changes were enough to transform the overall appearance of the printed page. The magazine was well received when it appeared with the new type. But "Century Roman," as the type became known, and the Century family of types, as well as two other faces in which De Vinne was involved, seem not to have weathered the tests of fickle time. Type design is the most minute of the typographic minutiae. There have been relatively few great type designers in the five centuries of the printed book. De Vinne, with all his gifts, is not one of the elect. De Vinne described the reasoning that called forth the new Century type and the steps toward its achievement in a characteristically lucid and informative essay, "The Century's Printer on the Century's Type," that appeared in the first issue of the magazine in its new dress in March of 1896. This, with other papers by and about De Vinne, including that on the printing of woodcuts mentioned above, and a full list of his writings are included in an excellent small-format, two-volume edition, *Theodore Low De Vinne*, issued by The Typophiles, New York, in 1968.

The Century dictionary and encyclopedia (plate 24), published in ten volumes from 1889 to 1906, is De Vinne's most workmanlike achievement. It represents mastery of the processes of type composition and printing of a compendious, complicated undertaking. The volumes are nine by twelve inches, three columns to the page, in eight-point and six-point "modern" roman type. Carl Purington Rollins, the eminent Printer to Yale University, wrote in 1950: "In this matter of presswork alone the *Century Dictionary* outranks any other dictionary of its time, and I believe that for compactness, legibility, convenience of arrangement of definitions it is the most successful of our dictionaries."

NINETEENTH
INTO THE
TWENTIETH
CENTURY

THEODORE
LOW
DE VINNE

De Vinne felt a great sense of obligation to the printing industry and participated with fellow printers in its problems. He worked to improve and stabilize apprenticeship rules, labor relations, and shop standards. He was active throughout his career in local and national employer groups and served a term as president of the United Typothetae of America, which he had helped to establish and whose code of ethics he had written.

Nine men of affairs—printers, publishers, bankers, and others—gathered in 1884 at the home of Robert Hoe, Jr., press builder and a great book collector, in response to an invitation to organize a club "for the literary study and promotion of the arts entering into the production of books." The Grolier Club which they founded still enjoys a vigorous life in its own fine building in New York, with an international membership of six hundred amateurs and professionals of the book in its many aspects. The Club has a continuing policy of historical, literary, bibliographic, and typographic exhibitions and a concurrent program of publications. De Vinne was one of the founding members, an early president, an active organizer and occasional speaker at exhibition openings, and its chief printer. Of the fifty-five Club publications issued before his death in 1914, forty-five came from the De Vinne Press. The first such publication was a reprint of the English *Decree of Star Chamber* of 1637 which placed severe censorship and other restrictions on seventeenth-century printers and their output. De Vinne was the author as well as the printer of several volumes issued by the Club, including *Christopher Plantin and the Plantin-Moretus Museum at Antwerp*, the story of a reverential visit in 1888; *Title-Pages as Seen by a Printer* in 1901; and *Notable Printers of Italy during the Fifteenth Century* in 1910. Although these forty-five Grolier Club books are but a small portion of the work that came from the large De Vinne plant, they are the books to which De Vinne must have given his best efforts. They form a considerable memorial. He used the best paper available, with two copies of each title on vellum. Presswork was excellent. They are luxurious books in small editions for Club membership, lively and varied. He was not seduced by the phenomenon of William Morris, whose influence can be seen in the work of almost every other practitioner of the period. He admired Morris for his extraordinary craftsmanship, but he believed that Morris retreated into the past. Nor did De Vinne succumb to the overdecorated effulgence of the Arts and Crafts Movement.

De Vinne wrote voluminously. His first published works were *The Profits of Book Composition* in 1864 and *The Printer's Price List: A Manual for the Use of Clerks and Book-Keepers in Job Printing Offices* in 1869. He continued with instructional manuals and informative articles for the trade. Most useful for its period, and still of historical interest, were four comprehensive, illustrated volumes, with a series title *The Practice of Typography*, issued from 1900 to 1904. De Vinne also contributed pieces on cultural aspects of his craft to general magazines such as *The Century*, *The Nation*, and *The Outlook*. His most lasting monument is, and will continue to be, his full-length historical study *The Invention of Printing*, published in 1876 by Francis Hart and Company.

De Vinne had learned Latin from his father. In order to read the large body of authoritative volumes needed for his researches, he taught himself French, Italian, and German. The scope of *The Invention of Printing*, which, the English scholar Stanley Morison wrote in 1963, "has still to be superseded," may briefly be described by quoting the subtitle: *A Collection of Facts and Opinions Descriptive of Early Prints and Playing Cards, the Block-Books of the Fifteenth Century, the Legend of Lourens Janszoon Coster, of Haarlem, and the Work of John Gutenberg and His Associates. Illustrated with Fac-Similes of Early Types and Woodcuts.* It is a volume of 557 pages, a book of original research about the origins and early years of printing, by a practical scholar-printer. De Vinne cut through the bibliographers' controversies about the invention of printing by pointing to the adjustable type mould as the heart of the invention and the key to its solution. He wrote of Gutenberg: "He was not the first to make printed books; it is not certain that he made the first printing press; it is not probable that he was the first to think of movable types. His merits rest on a securer basis. While others dreamed and thought, and, no doubt, made experiments, he was the first to do practical and useful work—the first to make types that could be used—the first to demonstrate the utility of typography. The first practical typographer, but not the first printer, he was really at the end of a long line of unknown workmen whose knowledge and experience in ruder forms of printing were important contributions toward the invention of the perfect method."

Theodore Low De Vinne was a rare phenomenon in American society. He was a very successful business entrepreneur, a technician in his craft, a scholar who contributed to stature in his field and who built a printing house that participated in the cultural life of its time. He collected a specialized library of six thousand volumes, received honorary degrees from Columbia and Yale universities, and smoothed the way ahead for a triumphant period in the arts of the book.

AN HISTORICAL RETROSPECTIVE

The invention of the Linotype machine in the 1880's (by Ottmar Mergenthaler, a German-American at work in Baltimore), which gradually replaced hand composition, and the accelerating development of high-speed presses completed the change in printing from a handcraft to a highly mechanized industry—all within the span of the nineteenth century. The responsibilities and expenses of automatic machinery in an increasingly complex society, with soaring costs of maintenance and labor, brought about the final separation of printing and publishing, and, also, of plant management and typographic design. Before the 1890's, typographic design, when it could be called design, was done in the printing shop by the proprietor or by his foreman. Beginning with the 1890's, a wholly new awareness of the esthetics of bookmaking could be seen in the ventures of several young publishers who designed or commissioned their own attractive books; in the rise of a number of private presses; in the appearance of the professional independent typographic designer; and in the existence of a few small printing offices conducted by scholar-printers committed to the production of fine books and ephemera. It is well worth the effort to try to understand the historical background and the contemporary influences that brought about this surge of adventure in the production of fine printing.

Let us look back in very brief outline to the origins and growth of estheticism and industrialism in the history of the printed book. These forces, at first closely parallel, later diverged but never became wholly independent. Printing is not a studio art. When pursued as an articulated craft, the printed book must involve scholarship correlated with men and machines. The handpress was (and still is) a machine, operated by human muscle, to be sure, but a machine nonetheless. The designers and printers who achieved artistry in their bookmaking, by hand or on automatic machinery, worked within the framework of scholarship joined to craftsmanship, whether in presses established for livelihood or by royal or private subsidy. The major share of the important

34

advances in the art and craft of printing, and its finest masterpieces, have come from the professionals in their workshops. Nevertheless, a number of inspired amateurs have issued glorious books from private presses which have stimulated collecting and spread the gospel of superior workmanship.

Movable type, Gutenberg's legacy to civilization, and his magnificent Bible were both achievements of the middle of the fifteenth century. During the next hundred years the printer, of necessity in a new and developing craft, was responsible under his own roof for all the processes of production, from type design and type casting to type setting, inkmaking, printing, and binding. He was, too, the publisher and bookseller. Despite those manifold commitments, the first golden century, 1450 to 1550, yielded many of the brightest names in the typographic constellation: Gutenberg, Jenson, Aldus, Tory, Estienne, among others, to whom society owes its debt. The printed volumes of the fifteenth century (the most notable were German and Italian) were patterned on the illuminated manuscripts that the new invention soon made obsolete. During the first half of the sixteenth century Paris and Lyons became the seminal typographic centers where, in the high tide of the French Renaissance, the physical book evolved into the form with which we are now familiar. Many of these volumes are among the finest ever produced. New books came from busy shops whose proprietors and employees operated presses for their livelihoods. The books were articles of commerce made for sale to churches, scholars, and to the emerging literate merchant class. The largest percentage of published works were inexpensive books in small format. These books were not all typographic gems. On the contrary, from the output of the many hundreds of early presses and their millions of volumes, only a handful of books are honored today for their physical beauty, and only a few printers are remembered. The outstanding examples from these early years of great bookmaking were not made as "collectors' items." They were made by the few great printers who enjoyed extraordinary skills of design and craftsmanship joined closely to scholarship and combined with the astuteness necessary to meet the demands of the marketplace. Commerce and typographic devotion had not yet gone their separate ways. Specialization arrived one hundred years after Gutenberg, when two independent French type designers, Claude Garamond (1480–1561) and Robert Granjon (d. 1579), offered printers their superbly designed fonts. As European commerce expanded and its markets became more complex, the varied phases of bookmaking and book distribution naturally became independent, or interdependent, operations.

The first influential press whose primary purpose was the making of beautiful books of liturgical and classical texts was established by Cardinal Richelieu in 1640 for the greater glory of the French Crown. Since the years when François I had appointed his *Imprimeurs du Roi* (the King's Printers) and had protected them from harassment by the Catholic theologians of the Sorbonne, the French monarchy has supported national typographic aspirations. Many of the aristocracy, including Madame de Pompadour, played at their private presses. Richelieu, having rebuilt the Sorbonne and having founded the Académie Française, persuaded Louis XIII to establish the *Imprimerie Royale*. Here, under royal subsidy, during its first ten years more than a hundred imposing titles came from seven handpresses, including a monumental folio Bible in eight volumes and the superb, profusely illustrated edition of Buffon's *Natural History*.

Except for the lavish *editions de luxe* of the *Imprimerie Royale* and the neat little books of the Elzevirs in Holland, the seventeenth century was a bleak typographic period. Governments, as well as the church, had learned to fear the power of the printing press and severely restricted its output. The eighteenth century, on the other hand, witnessed a great resurgence throughout Europe in new type and book design. During this century, the last to permit princely extravagance, a few especially esteemed printers were beneficiaries of private or royal subsidies. Their work, if not "art for art's sake," was, certainly, printing for printing's sake. Because the wealthy aristocrats of Europe were a receptive audience for opulent books, sumptuous folios graced the library shelves of English manor houses and decorated the rococo tables of the French nobility.

An English writing master, John Baskerville (1706–1775), having made a fortune in japanned metals, devoted his fortune and the last twenty years of his life to the design of a new, crisp typeface (the first "modern" face); to improvements of papermaking; and to the mechanics of printing. He completed the publication of a handsome series of quarto volumes and a great folio Bible. These books, unlike the extravagant volumes of the Continent, were forthright in design, free of ornamental ostentation.

36

Giambattista Bodoni (1740–1813) was born in the north of Italy and after an apprenticeship in printing and type cutting was invited by the Duke of Parma to establish a ducal press patterned after the French *Imprimerie Royale*. Bodoni rose to the occasion and soon produced exalted printing for pomp and circumstance, free from the usual mortal concern for costs. He continued to design and cut brilliant roman and italic types from the smallest to monumental sizes, and in innumerable foreign alphabets. Permitted also to publish on his own, he issued several Greek and Latin classics in giant folio editions. Although the scholarship was not impeccable, the bold, austere (if glacial) conception, the perfection of type composition, superb paper, and sparkling presswork dazzled his contemporaries. Bodoni became a European personage, collected by wealthy bibliophiles, pensioned by kings, and honored by Napoleon. He was, beyond question, one of the great printers. His types, copied, but unfortunately debased, are still in use.

Perhaps the most lavish book ever printed and certainly one of the most beautiful is the edition of the Racine *Oeuvres* produced in Paris in three large folio volumes by Pierre Didot, completed in 1801, with engraved illustrations by several eminent French artists. A set on vellum, breathtaking to a modern practitioner, may be seen in the Yale Beinecke Library in New Haven. The Didot folios were similar in grandeur and expertness to the Bodoni classics, but the Didot books gained from gallic charm, appropriate decoration, and thorough scholarship. The several generations of the Didot family of typefounders, printers, papermakers, and publishers was the third dynasty (after Estienne and Fournier) to contribute their varied talents to the sustained leadership of Paris in the arts of the book. The Didots' extensive publications included small, popular-priced texts as well as sumptuous volumes. Louis XVI and his brother the Comte d'Artois upheld French tradition by their patronage of special Didot editions, the last of the royal subsidies.

The pendulum swung back during the nineteenth century. In 1814 the London *Times* was first printed on a cylinder press, a clear omen of what lay ahead. The introduction of machinery, and the consequent disruption of society brought on by the Industrial Revolution, produced a long period of degraded taste. To many in the privileged classes and artistic circles in England, this spelled the end of certain cherished amenities. The rapid growth of the factories and the decline of workmanship found its most eloquent antagonist in John Ruskin. Dissatis-

37

faction among British artists, architects, and craftsmen coalesced into the Arts and Crafts Movement in the 1880's and continued with missionary zeal to the end of the century. In addition to the craftsmen most directly involved, many men of arts and letters were actively sympathetic: Rossetti, Burne-Jones, Oscar Wilde, Whistler, and Aubrey Beardsley. The movement found its greatest protagonist in the person of William Morris. Morris was a writer, painter, designer and decorator, and a manufacturer of wallpapers, tapestries, stained glass, etc. He was a romantic who turned to medievalism in art. At the same time, he embraced socialism with the hope that a return to the handcrafts would provide the working classes with some joy in their labor and less injustice in their daily lives. In 1890 he founded the Kelmscott Press, and during the remaining six years of his life, he produced a procession of magnificent books, crowned by the monumental Chaucer in 1896. Paradoxically, Morris, who looked to the past, exerted enormous influence on the future, not only in book production, but also in the wider fields of industrial design where Morris' respect for materials and workmanship were profound stimuli. His passionate search for beauty and his majestic craftsmanship ignited a fifty-year renaissance of bookmaking in England, on the Continent, and in the United States. His example gave rise to a notable private press tradition and to a generation of amateurs and collectors of fine printing. The man who loathed the machine was, nevertheless, an inspiration to professional practitioners who would make peace with power-driven machinery and learn to direct it intelligently and adventurously.

Groundswells of cultural promise appeared in the United States in the several decades before the "explosion" of the Arts and Crafts Movement in the 1890's. The ferment was at work in the Philadelphia Centennial Exposition of 1876; in the warm reception and the large audiences that greeted Oscar Wilde during his American lecture tour in 1882; in the founding of craft societies, book clubs, libraries, and museums, all across the nation; and by way of further example, among others, in the indigenous architecture of H. H. Richardson, of Louis Sullivan, and, only a little later, of Frank Lloyd Wright. Rich young Americans read Carlyle and Ruskin and traveled in Europe. In the last decades of the century, Boston and Cambridge, which had harbored the first colonial printers three hundred years earlier, again became the center for a group of scholars, editors, designers, printers, and publishers, who found significance in their craft. The young men who were there drawn together became leading actors in a renaissance of printing that gradually spread, over the years ahead, to receptive persons in other parts of the country. The same yeast was at work on both sides of the Atlantic. For the first time, Americans would exert an innovative influence on the international course of the finely printed book, and two American practitioners would find place among its immortals.

The reader of these pages should realize that in the 1890's and during the early years of the present century, fine workmanship was still closely tied to the hand and eye, with control of rather easily comprehended and manageable machines. Mechanical type composition and huge presses had become current only in newspaper offices and in plants concerned with mass production. The most superb handmade and mouldmade papers were readily available from fine European mills. Letterpress—direct, impressional printing—was the sole book process. Lithography and gravure were supplementary. Offset printing, photo-composition, computers, forbidding costs, even the income tax and burdensome government forms, were all in an unforeseeable future.

BOSTON, 1860 TO THE 1890's

Professor Ray Nash in his book *Printing as an Art*, prepared for the fiftieth anniversary, in 1955, of the Boston Society of Printers, describes the men and the conditions that led to the "revival" of printing in that city. From the 1860's, Henry O. Houghton, who had been apprenticed in Burlington, Vermont, and who had studied early masterpieces of printing, brought his capabilities to the publishing firm of Houghton, Mifflin Company and set high standards for the Riverside Press, owned by the publishers. "He was," writes Nash, "instrumental in laying down foundations for the best American bookmaking achievement of the late nineteenth and early twentieth centuries." Other dedicated men soon followed. A printer from Glasgow, John Wilson, and his son settled in Cambridge soon after the Civil War. Ten years later the younger Wilson, in partnership with Charles E. Wentworth, acquired the University Press, a well-set-up shop, not an official part of Harvard, but in the college's good graces and of typographic importance in the community. A young German immigrant in the employ of John Wilson became a key figure in Cambridge. He was Carl Heintzemann, the son of a German

39

schoolmaster, who had been reared in a home devoted to books and the arts. Although young Heintzemann was an accomplished pianist, at age twenty-five he established his own first-rate printing shop which became a meeting place for artists and writers and a haven for promising young men for whom a typographic career was the heart's desire. Bertram Grosvenor Goodhue, an architect who was to become deeply involved in book decoration, who designed a typeface for The Merrymount Press, and, later, the very successful face Cheltenham, was employed by Heintzemann to design his office. There was, too, Henry Lewis Johnson, who became the editor of *Printing Art*, a printing journal that has rarely received adequate recognition for its share in the history of fine printing. Johnson was the moving spirit in the establishment of the Boston Society of Arts and Crafts. Carl Purington Rollins, later the distinguished Printer to Yale University, left Harvard to serve an apprenticeship with Heintzemann.

Clubs were organized to talk about books and printing and esthetics, about collecting and exhibitions. The Tavern Club was brought together under the friendly, scholarly, and avuncular wing of Charles Eliot Norton, Professor of Fine Arts at Harvard, who was deeply committed to furthering the handcrafts. In 1897 he served as founding president of the Boston Society of Arts and Crafts. In 1887 bibliophiles organized to found the Club of Odd Volumes which is still a lively association of aficionados. From 1892 to 1894 a group of amateurs and professionals—artists, architects, and writers—banded together and achieved publication of four issues of a handsome magazine, *The Knight Errant* (plate 23), an impressive quarto on handmade paper, printed by the Elzevir Press in Boston. Its participating sponsors included Ralph Adams Cram, Bertram Grosvenor Goodhue, Herbert Copeland, Fred Holland Day (who conducted a column, "Regarding Recent Books and Bookmaking"), and Francis Watts Lee, with Bernard Berenson, Louise Imogen Guiney, Brander Matthews, and others among its contributors. In 1893 Daniel Berkeley Updike established The Merrymount Press. In 1895 Joseph M. Bowles came from Indianapolis with his then avantgarde magazine *Modern Art*, soon followed by his friend from Indiana, Bruce Rogers. Will Bradley, a native Bostonian who had made a reputation in Chicago, returned and soon set up the Wayside Press in Springfield, Massachusetts. Well-attended lectures on typography were given at the Boston Public Library. Meantime, Stone and Kimball, Copeland

and Day, and Way and Williams announced themselves as publishers. These were serious, esthetic, well-born, and financially privileged young men, some of them still Harvard undergraduates, who were devoted to the best in literature and committed to producing books in elegant typographic dress. Men and events crowded these productive Boston years.

THOMAS BIRD MOSHER (1852–1923)

Thomas Bird Mosher of Portland, Maine, was not a participant in the Boston-Cambridge burst of typographic fervor. Neither was he touched by the tidal wave from Kelmscott. He is the first American to have established and sustained a program, over thirty-two years, of splendid literary output in consistently felicitous typographic form. From 1891 to 1923 his books included much of the best English poetry of the time, and he drew on the riches of the past, convinced, in his own words, "that in literature alone is to be found and cherished the element which brings together vanished past and living present." The Mosher books were small, modest, and inexpensive. They never aspired to grandeur and never achieved the competitive recognition of the auction room. They were bought by thousands of literate men and women whose pleasure in reading was enhanced by fine paper, good workmanship, and an unassuming and quiet typographic elegance.

Mosher was born in Biddeford, Maine, and received a grammar school education in Boston. His father was a New England sea captain who, as was the occasional custom among Yankee skippers, brought a member of the family on the long ocean voyages. At fourteen years of age, young Tom went to sea with his father and read before the mast for the next four years. During a European stopover, Captain Mosher bought books for his son's education and enjoyment. Picked up in a second-hand bookstore in Hamburg were the thirty-four eighteenmo volumes of *Bell's British Theatre* which unlocked for the impressionable lad, in his own words, "the treasure-trove of English literature." Mosher wrote much later: "I shall never again read books as I once read them in my early seafaring when all the world was young, when the days were of tropic splendour, and the long evenings were passed with my books in a lonely cabin dimly lighted by a primitive oil lamp, while the ship was ploughing through the boundless ocean on its weary course around Cape Horn."

After a few years of youthful wandering on land, Mosher settled in

NINETEENTH
INTO THE
TWENTIETH
CENTURY

THOMAS
BIRD
MOSHER

Portland, in a law-stationer's office. Next he filled a junior partnership in a law book publishing firm where he picked up knowledge of paper, printing, and binding. At thirty-nine years of age he began his career as an independent provincial publisher, where he could hope to fulfill his expressed desire that someday he would publish books "of literary distinction that would be truly beautiful as well as within the reach of those who appreciate beauty but who cannot possess it at exorbitant rates."

Mosher's first book, *Modern Love* by George Meredith, was issued in the autumn of 1891. The first of the dramatic Kelmscott volumes, *The Glittering Plain*, had been completed a few months earlier. The books were as different in conception as their makers were different in character. During the many years of Mosher's publishing, he produced more than four hundred books, chosen with his unerring taste for the written and the printed word. From 1895 to 1914 he issued a small-format magazine, *The Bibelot*, which reprinted poetry and prose, largely from scarce editions and unusual sources. Mosher's typographic style was consistent, simple, literate, and of sufficient distinction to be easily recognized as his personal expression (plate 31). The books were usually well printed in local shops in Portland to Mosher's design and under his immediate supervision. He asked Bruce Rogers to design a title page and some ornaments for *Homeward Songs by the Way* in 1895, but this was a rare exception. Type in the Mosher books was usually an Old Style from the Dickinson letter foundry in Boston. Caslon was often used in his later books. The paper was usually Van Gelder, handmade in Holland, with a few copies of special editions on "Japan vellum."

At a time when United States copyright laws did not, unfortunately, protect foreign writers, several American publishing houses issued books without royalties. Mosher was one of the transgressors, but he justified himself to the English authors whose texts he printed by claiming that he rescued their work from neglect by American readers. Some writers called him a pirate; others had reason to be pleased. In a letter of March 1892, now in the collection of Norman H. Strouse, George Meredith wrote to Mosher: "Sir, a handsome pirate is always half pardoned, and in this case he has broken only the upper laws. I shall receive with pleasure the copy of 'Modern Love' which you propose to send. I have it much at heart that works of mine should be read by Americans." Robert Frost, who much later claimed that he was the best-printed

American author, had hoped (in vain) to be printed and published by the Portland pirate.

Two recent books about Mosher have, appropriately, been printed by special presses in small editions, eloquent tributes to a former worker in the same vineyard. Norman H. Strouse, ardent collector of Mosher books, wrote a biography, *The Passionate Pirate*, that was printed in 1964 at the Bird and Bull Press in North Hills, Pennsylvania, on paper made by hand by the printer, Henry Morris, in his cellar. *A Check List of the Publications of Thomas Bird Mosher* was compiled and edited by Benton L. Hatch, with a biographical essay by Ray Nash, and printed in 1966 at the Gehenna Press by Leonard Baskin, for the University of Massachusetts Press in Amherst.

Mosher visited in England and was well received by some of the authors whose works he had printed. But for the most part he led a retiring life in Portland in his own world of books and among friends of his own critical choosing. Mosher was a member of the Grolier Club of New York, but he was more comfortable in his Maine house where he had gathered together a library of eight thousand volumes. Just as he had united literature and typography in the books he edited and published, he chose similarly among the books he possessed and cherished. At the sale of his library at auction in 1948, in addition to the many books of general literature, those inscribed to him by contemporary authors, and the special collection of Walt Whitman to whom Mosher was devoted, there were books by American designers and a fine choice of the masterpieces of the great English private presses, including, among others, Kelmscott, Doves, and Ashendene.

STONE & KIMBALL, 1893–1897
HERBERT S. STONE & CO., 1896–1906

Herbert Stuart Stone (1871–1915) and Hannibal Ingalls Kimball (1874–1933) were friends and undergraduates at Harvard College, class of 1894. In their sophomore year they decided to become publishers. In their junior year they issued their first books. From the start their commitment to well-designed and well-made books drew to the youthful Stone & Kimball imprint a surprising number of prominent contemporary American and English authors. Stone, son of a wealthy Chicago newspaper publisher, was already well grounded in foreign languages and literature, an editor of the Harvard *Crimson*, and himself

NINETEENTH
INTO THE
TWENTIETH
CENTURY

STONE
& KIMBALL

an artist of some competence. Kimball, who had entered Harvard at age sixteen, also enjoyed the privileges of good background and was also drawn to the arts. He was business manager of the *Crimson* where he showed considerable financial ingenuity. In their partnership Stone was primarily the editor, Kimball the business manager. Their first publication was a guide to the Chicago World's Fair in 1893, followed by *First Editions of American Authors: A Manual for Booklovers*, compiled by Stone, with an introduction by Eugene Field. Then during the next four years came one hundred six books of poetry and prose by an extraordinary list of authors, among them Hamlin Garland (plate 26), Eugene Field, Bliss Carman, George Santayana, Robert Louis Stevenson, William Butler Yeats, Maeterlinck, Ibsen, and others, with a definitive edition of Edgar Allan Poe in ten volumes. It is not surprising that these youngsters attracted and held so many eminent writers. The Stone & Kimball books delighted the authors as they pleased their readers at a time when books were the companions of long winter evenings and leisurely summer afternoons, without telephones, automobiles, movies, radio or television.

Most of the books were designed by Herbert Stone and very well printed at the John Wilson and Son University Press in Cambridge. Type was usually modernized Old Style and only occasionally Caslon. After the firm moved to Chicago, Donnelley's Lakeside Press was the most frequent printer, with Caslon type predominant. Books were cloth-bound and stamped on the front cover, frequently in floral designs with the title in type or hand-lettered, many of them designed by Bruce Rogers and Will Bradley (plate 27). Almost all were twelvemos (c. 4¼ by 6¾ inches), rarely smaller, with larger formats and handmade papers only for special limited editions. They were light, modest, attractive, and pleasant to handle. Typography was spirited but simple and forthright, with clarity and ease of reading the primary objectives. The Stone & Kimball books possessed the elusive quality of typographic warmth that comes from a love of literature joined to skill in handling type.

In 1894 Stone and Kimball launched *The Chap-Book*. Sidney Kramer wrote in his excellent full-length study, *A History of Stone & Kimball and Herbert S. Stone & Co.* (Chicago, 1940): "When on May 15, 1894, the first number of *The Chap-Book* was issued from Cambridge, Stone and Kimball had the means to move from the limited, however interesting, circle of family and friends into the mainstream of American life. As one looks back, the four years of the magazine is seen as part of an historical movement in arts and letters with antecedents and parallels in this country and others, and an influence of its own, manifested by swarms of imitators." Issues were, usually, thirty-two to forty pages, $4\frac{1}{2}$ by $7\frac{1}{2}$ inches, published semimonthly at five cents per copy, later changed to ten cents. The printers were, successively, Graves and Henry in Cambridge, the Camelot Press (F. W. Goudy), and the Lakeside Press in Chicago. Circulation had reached 14,500 by 1898 when *The Chap-Book* was merged into *The Dial*. *The Chap-Book* was a literary magazine that represented the best writing of its time, aided and abetted by the best contemporary graphic artists. An extraordinary index of authors for the four years of the magazine's existence shows almost three hundred contributors: Thomas Bailey Aldrich, Stephen Crane, Ellen Glasgow, Lincoln Steffens, Anatole France, Kenneth Grahame, H. G. Wells, Paul Verlaine, and many others. Artists for decorative covers, illustrations in the text, and posters included Aubrey Beardsley, Max Beerbohm, Will Bradley, Charles Dana Gibson, Bertram Grosvenor Goodhue, Lucien Pissarro, Charles Ricketts, and Henri de Toulouse-Lautrec.

An avocation that had grown into a demanding business forced the young publishers to leave Cambridge. They moved their headquarters to Stone's home city of Chicago where they soon became a vital part of that city's growing literary activities. *The Chap-Book* continued to thrive and their publishing grew beyond all expectations. Kimball went to New York to set up a sales office. Meanwhile, the rapid expansion of the firm began to worry its backers, especially Herbert Stone's father, who urged the young partners to reduce their investments and commitments. Kimball disagreed, and in a quixotic gesture made an offer to buy Stone's share. Stone accepted. Kimball borrowed the necessary money and was sustained for a while by his suppliers. However, he was unable to carry on alone, and in 1899 the business was dissolved. At the liquidation sale Stone bought back much of the list.

The new firm of Herbert S. Stone & Company, which had begun to publish in 1896 in Chicago with Herbert's younger brother as a junior partner, continued with spectacular success. Between 1896 and 1905 they published more than two hundred books, as well as the magazine *The House Beautiful*, of which Herbert Stone was both the editor and publisher. The literary and typographic standards set in Cambridge were continued. George Bernard Shaw's first American books appeared over the Stone imprint. Among other highlights, Stone published George Ade's *Fables in Slang*, George Moore's *Esther*, books by Henry James, Ibsen, and Maeterlinck, as well as George Barr McCutcheon's best seller, *Graustark*. But by 1906 the meteoric career had burned itself out, and the Stone list was bought by New York publishers. Nine years later Herbert Stuart Stone was among those who lost their lives in the sinking of the *Lusitania*.

After the liquidation of the partnership Kimball remained in New York, where he established a respected printing house, the Cheltenham Press. He preserved the Stone & Kimball good taste in his printed matter and advertising. Kimball was responsible for the appearance of Cheltenham type, perhaps the fastest-selling typeface ever produced. Its conception was Kimball's, although he induced his friend Bertram Grosvenor Goodhue to make the drawings.

COPELAND & DAY, 1893–1899

Fred Holland Day and Herbert Copeland were two of the dedicated young men who had been responsible in 1892 for *The Knight Errant* (plate 23), the handsomely produced magazine already mentioned. The publication was to be, stated the editors in the first number, "not only an expression of the most advanced thought of our time, but, as well, a model of perfect typography and the printer's art." This crusading spirit in literature and the arts fired the Harvard undergraduates who gathered over ale and talk, and called themselves the Visionists, the Pewter Mug Associates, or the Procrastinorium. "Its members," wrote Ralph Adams Cram in his memoirs, "included that original and vivacious group of individuals that, for ten years between 1890 and 1900 made life for me so notably worth living." The Copeland and Day partnership was formed to publish books that would further those high ideals. Day was the financial backer and the artistic spirit. His father was a successful merchant who had endowed his son with the means to allow a life in pursuit of the arts. Fred Day was an eccentric in manner and in dress, and a dilettante in the best sense of the word. He had been associated for five years with the Boston branch of a New York publisher. He was, too, an amateur photographer and a serious bibliophile with a notable Keats collection. Foreign travel and friendships brought about a professional relationship with the publishers Elkin Mathews and

John Lane at the Bodley Head in London that made possible the importation, with a joint imprint, of many of the first year's attractive books of Copeland and Day.

Herbert Copeland, less picturesque than his partner, with sound literary judgment, attended Harvard when Herbert Stone and Ingalls Kimball were also at college. Other enthusiastic undergraduates who also became publishers were Herbert Small, later Small, Maynard & Company, and W. B. Wolffe, later Lamson, Wolffe & Company. These budding publishers, together with Way & Williams in Chicago and R. H. Russell & Son in New York, had much in common. They were all young; they were amateurs and idealists who committed themselves to literary and typographic excellence. Their books looked much alike, and several authors appeared on more than one list. And none (except Small, Maynard for a while) remained in publishing for more than a few years past the turn of the century. Bigness, mass production, problems of distribution had arrived in publishing as it had in other areas of less cultural importance. Inevitably the small publishers yielded to the facts of economic survival.

From their start Copeland & Day were agents for *The Yellow Book* magazine, and together with the English publishers they put their imprint on the poetry of Richard Le Gallienne, Alice Meynell, Francis Thompson, Lionel Johnson, and on Oscar Wilde's *Salomé* with its daring drawings by Aubrey Beardsley. The American lists included many young writers who received first publication from Copeland & Day. Among the ninety-six books issued during their six years as publishers was the work of Bliss Carman and Richard Hovey, Gelett Burgess, Josephine Prescott Peabody, Stephen Crane, M. A. De Wolfe Howe, Louise Imogen Guiney, and the successful juvenile, Gertrude Smith's *Arabella and Araminta*.

Many of the books were designed and decorated by Bertram Grosvenor Goodhue with borders and floriated initial letters directly in the spirit of the Kelmscott Press. One of the most successful is Rossetti's *House of Life* (plate 25), an octavo on handmade paper, printed in Cambridge by John Wilson & Son in a regular edition of five hundred copies, with fifty special copies, rubricated. Tom B. Meteyard and Will Bradley were also called on for embellishment. But most of the books were planned by Fred Day with production supervised at the Wilson plant by William Dana Orcutt. After the florid Kelmscott influence had worn

NINETEENTH
INTO THE
TWENTIETH
CENTURY

COPELAND
& DAY

off, a simple, well-balanced, well-produced typography became standard practice. Among the artists commissioned to illustrate the texts and make posters were Will Bradley, Maxfield Parrish, John Sloan, T. B. Hapgood, and others.

Alice Brown, one of Day's authors and a friend, wrote of him to Mr. Joe Walker Kraus, who has done valuable research among these publishers: "... I think he would have liked to write, but realized he hadn't quite the touch, and he gave all his time in one way or another to books. Good printing—that was a religion with him. . . ." A publishing house so personal in its expression could hardly be expected to have had a long life. In 1899 the Copeland & Day list was offered for sale and was purchased by Small, Maynard & Company and by Houghton, Mifflin Company.

WAY & WILLIAMS, 1895–1898

Chicago in the 1890's supported a literary life of considerable proportions. *The Dial* magazine had been started in 1880 and there were several literary and book collecting groups, amateur and professional, including the Saints and Sinners Corner whose meeting place was McClurg's Wabash Avenue bookshop. Among the professionals were Melville Stone and his son Herbert, Eugene Field, Finley Peter Dunne, George Ade, Brand Whitlock, Loredo Taft, Hamlin Garland, Harriet Monroe, and the two men (somewhat less than professionals) who established a new publishing house, Way & Williams. W. Irving Way was born on a farm in Canada. During a railroading career that brought him to the United States, Way showed a pronounced inclination for fine printing and book collecting. He joined the Grolier Club in New York at its inception in 1884; he was one of the founders of the Caxton Club in 1895 in Chicago, and much later (1928) he aided in the founding of the Zamorano Club in Los Angeles. He made a vocation of his avocation when he turned to selling magazines and books for publishing houses in New York and Philadelphia. His partner in the new firm, Chauncey L. Williams, came from a wealthy midwestern family. After ten years of his boyhood had been spent in London, Williams returned to the United States to inherit a substantial fortune, to marry, and to commission Frank Lloyd Wright to build his River Forest home which became a meeting place for Chicago literati. His interest in fine printing showed in an 1894 Christmas booklet, Rossetti's *Blessed Damozel*, printed by the De Vinne Press. In 1895 Williams and his neighbor, William H. Winslow, set up the Auvergne Press, at first in Williams' attic, later in Winslow's basement. There, on their handpress they produced Keats' *Eve of St. Agnes*, designed by Frank Lloyd Wright who joined in the labor of printing. Then came *The House Beautiful* by William C. Gannet, whose title page all in capital letters reads: "The House Beautiful in a Setting Designed by Frank Lloyd Wright and Printed by Hand by William Herman Winslow and Frank Lloyd Wright during the Winter Months of the Years Eighteen Hundred Ninety-six and Seven." Wright's book design was decorative and architectural, and, as would be expected, completely unconventional.

The first Way & Williams publication was *Volunteer Grain* by Francis F. Browne, issued in 1895 in a limited edition of one hundred sixty copies. Way's own words in an interview shortly before his death give the flavor of the Way & Williams output: "Among the things we published was *Plato's Banquet*, for which Bruce Rogers made the designs, as he also did for the *Compleat Angler*, technically and spiritually the first of the series of our small books, each representing a period and no two alike in design. . . . Our first move, however, was my trip to England to arrange with William Morris for a small Kelmscott Press edition of Rossetti's *Hand and Soul*, a very pleasant experience which gave our firm an auspicious start. On the same trip I met Andrew Lang, with whom I visited at Oxford and arranged for the translation and publication of *The Miracles of Madame Saint Katherine of Fierbois*, a very beautiful book printed at the De Vinne Press, with an initial by Selwyn Image." Of the sixty books finally issued by Way & Williams, nineteen were of British origin and manufacture. Among American writers, William Allen White's first work of fiction, *The Real Issue*, a book of Kansas stories, was often reprinted. Another author who later became well known was Edgar Lee Masters, although his *Book of Verses* was caught in the firm's dissolution, printed but never published.

Late in 1896 W. Irving Way withdrew from the partnership. Williams continued with primary emphasis on western authors and regional fiction. During the first Way & Williams' years the English books were of considerable typographic interest. For the books made in this country (most of them printed by R. R. Donnelley's Lakeside Press) Frank Hazenplug, Will Bradley, and Bruce Rogers were called on for design and decoration. Several prominent illustrators were engaged, among them Maxfield Parrish and J. C. Leyendecker. Good intentions tempered with inexperience do not, alone, sustain a publishing program. In 1898 Williams decided not to continue, and it was announced that Herbert S. Stone & Company had purchased the entire stock and goodwill of Messrs. Way & Williams.

More than one critic and historian has looked back with nostalgia to the "delectable twelvemos" produced by the young men of the nineties. It was a springtime for the flourishing interest in typography whose seed bore rich fruit in succeeding years. In September of 1949 Carl Purington Rollins wrote in *The New Colophon*: "Between the founding of the Kelmscott Press and the outbreak of the First World War American printing became conscious and creative. . . . In the short quarter century from 1890 to 1914 the spirit of adventure seized the printers. It was not that they endeavored to imitate Morris so much as that his dynamic work stimulated the imagination and loosed the restrictions of conventional typography. There was ferment in the air, not all of it imported from Europe. . . . The printers of those days had no such repertory of type faces as are now available, but they made good use of what they had. And they had what is of at least equal importance, a respect for solid impression, and a wide range of book papers unequaled today. The result was a richness in the final product which gives to the printing of the time a solid quality comparable to the best hand-press work of the eighteenth century."

ELBERT HUBBARD (1856–1915)

A multitude of Americans from 1895 to 1915 enjoyed the flowery prose of Elbert Hubbard and the flamboyance of his printed matter. More than two hundred thousand subscribers read his monthly magazine, *The Philistine*, most of which Hubbard wrote himself, and by his own report, many millions of copies were printed of his most famous pamphlet, *A Message to Garcia*. Thousands of summer-vacationing pilgrims flocked to the Roycroft grounds at East Aurora, New York, where Hubbard had built a compound consisting of a hotel and gardens, a printing plant and bindery, workshops for weaving, metalwork, leather novelties, cabinetmaking, stained glass, and more, even a bank. The community building had a John Ruskin room and a William Morris room. Dard Hunter, who later became a distinguished historian of early papermaking, went to East Aurora as a young man to learn about printing. He stayed nine years. Looking back, many years later, Hunter wrote: "Just as Hubbard had once inundated the country with soap premiums, so he now undertook to place limp-leather bindings on the golden oak tables of every sitting room in America. Books in their window-cleaner [chamois] covers were turned out in mass production; the dozen or more Roycroft presses were kept humming night and day; hand-made paper was imported by the thousands of reams; red and black ink was purchased by the barrel, and every goat in the world was a potential limp binding. . . . Those were flourishing days at the Roycroft shop and Elbert Hubbard gave employment to more than five hundred workers; to countless thousands he gave inspiration." Hubbard was widely regarded in his own time, from adoration to contempt, cultural messiah or, to the solemn young men at Harvard, a charlatan with "the delicacy of a hippopotamus on a tight-rope."

Elbert Hubbard was born in Hudson, Illinois. At thirty-nine years of age he ended a successful business career in soap and sold his interest for a modest fortune. He then enrolled in Harvard College in 1893 but soon found the situation untenable. In 1894 he visited William Morris (at the Kelmscott Press) and others he would later include in his very successful inspirational series, Little Journeys to the Homes of the Great (plate 29). On his return to America, Hubbard set up the Roycroft Press in East Aurora with the Kelmscott Press as exemplary objective. However, the instincts of a successful soap salesman took over, and the undertaking soon became a thriving business. The first books were set by hand and printed on a Washington handpress, but these methods soon proved inadequate and were replaced by mechanical composition and automatic power presses. The typography was wholly unsophisticated and inelegant. Heavy, eccentric types were used, with crude art-nouveau borders and ornaments. Paper was thick, with rough deckled edges. Books were frequently bound in the chamois leather known in the trade as "limp ooze," printed or stamped and embossed. The workmen, with only a few exceptions, were untrained country lads of the neighboring small towns. The range of titles for Hubbard's books and pamphlets, other than his own inspirational writings, was large and widely chosen, from Shakespeare to Ralph Waldo Emerson and Rudyard Kipling. They were available to those who came to East Aurora in person, or sent by mail to his more remote and grateful subscribers.

NINETEENTH
INTO THE
TWENTIETH
CENTURY

ELBERT
HUBBARD

It is fashionable to scoff at Hubbard. But it is a measure of the contribution to his period that many distinguished men and women made the journey to East Aurora. Dard Hunter mentions Gutzon Borglum, sculptor; Brand Whitlock, diplomat; Eugene Debs, labor leader; John Burroughs, naturalist; Clarence Darrow, lawyer; Richard Le Gallienne, English poet; and many others. Booker T. Washington, the Negro teacher and leader, was an invited guest. Well-known speakers and musicians were engaged for the educational programs and for concerts given at the Roycroft Inn or in the chapel.

Hubbard and his wife were among those who drowned when the *Lusitania* was lost to a submarine in the First World War. He was not a person of academic scholarship, nor, inherently, a craftsman. Nevertheless, a contemporary could say of him that he had translated a great vision into terms of the vernacular, and had brought beauty into the lives of thousands who would never have seen or understood the message in any other form.

THE PRIVATE PRESS

Private presses appeared in the United States before and after the turn of the century, although no American work compared favorably with the several great British private presses that followed the Kelmscott Press and produced some of the most beautiful books in typographic history. The five noble volumes of the Doves Press Bible (London, 1903–05) and the sumptuous illustrated Ashendene Press folio Dante (London, 1909) are conspicuous examples of typographic grandeur. Such books can be made only in a highly cultured society, at a time of civilized leisure, when designers and printers are free to plan them, and when appreciative collectors exist with the inclination and the means to buy them. However, the private press has no defined lines of demarcation and has been operated on many levels, from the amusement of kings to more modest proportions. Normally, the private press that survives for some years is a substantial, scholarly, and esthetically dedicated undertaking, set up as an avocation for the serious pleasure of its owner. Its profitless purpose is, always, the printing and publishing of small editions of fine books. The private press often overlaps and is easily confused with its less affluent relation the hobby press which provides enjoyment on occasional evenings and Sunday afternoons in the cellar. The private press movement has been very well documented in books by Will Ransom and Roderick Cave. Both bibliographers have been generous in their inclusions.

THE ELSTON PRESS

The Elston Press of New Rochelle, New York, was probably the best of the American private presses of the period, with some twenty books issued from 1900 to 1904. The work was expertly produced by Clarke Conwell and illustrated by his wife, Helen M. O'Kane. Their first publication was *Sonnets from the Portuguese* by Elizabeth Barrett Browning, that darling of the private presses. The Elston editions of the *Sonnets* and of Rossetti's *The House of Life*, another favorite of small fine printers, contained elaborate full-page borders by O'Kane, touched by the Kelmscott effulgence and with pronounced elements of the sinuous and flowing lines of art nouveau. These quartos were striking accomplishments during the highly ornamental era of the Arts and Crafts Movement (plate 30). The early Elston books were printed in Jenson and the eccentric Satanic types from the American Type Founders Company. Thereafter Conwell imported Caslon's Old Roman type from England, an archaic face of some distinction. The later Elston books, most of them octavos and quartos in editions of approximately one hundred fifty copies, occasionally illustrated, were less decorative, more dependent on pure typography, and on excellent paper with good presswork. Conwell, whose books were produced on handpresses, wrote in an Elston prospectus: "The advantage of hand-press work does not, then, after all, lie in the hand, but in the head, which is here allowed to direct each step of the work, humoring the refractory sheet of hand-made paper in a thousand ways which are impossible when printed by other means."

WALTER GILLISS (1855–1925)

In his *Recollections of the Gilliss Press*, published by the Grolier Club in 1926, Walter Gilliss tells the story of the fifty years of his press, from 1869 to 1919. When he was a growing boy, Walter's father gave him and his brother a small "Novelty" press with a six-by-nine-inch chase. The press was big enough to print business cards and the young lads earned pocket money by soliciting orders from neighborhood merchants. This early success was the forerunner of a rather large, well-organized printing plant in New York City, and a lifetime's devotion to excellent workmanship. Miscellaneous printed matter was produced for many of New York's cultural institutions, including Columbia University and the Metropolitan Museum of Art. The friendship of Arthur B. Turnure, editor of the magazine *Art Age*, brought Gilliss to the Grolier Club where he became an active member and officer. His best work was done in a dozen books for the Club and for several prominent collectors, including J. Pierpont Morgan, Robert Hoe, and especially William Loring Andrews. Among his best books are *New Amsterdam, New Orange and New York* (1897) and *New York as Washington Knew It* (plate 32). Gillis adorned these, as well as many other volumes, with copper engravings. He used Modernized Old Style, Elzevir, and Caslon types. His presswork was excellent. Books on handmade papers with the Gilliss press mark were expertly done in wholly conservative and safely elegant taste. Without doubt they were highly pleasing to the wealthy collectors who were his friends and patrons.

DANIEL BERKELEY UPDIKE (1860–1941)

Daniel Berkeley Updike established The Merrymount Press in 1893 and directed its operations during the next forty-eight years. A printer who succeeded with great style, he gave stature, scholarship, and a lofty excellence to his press which ranks high among the great printing houses of the past. Updike's solid workmanship produced a large body of superbly designed books and occasional printed matter. Of great importance to his craft, his written works in the history and scholarship of printing are primary sources for its understanding and appreciation. Nevertheless, Updike was not a printer by intuitive choice or passion. The mastery he achieved was not made in heaven. It came from a highly developed sense of order and grace, and a determined and disciplined and cultivated mind. The paradox in the successful career of this complex personality may be discovered in part in a prefatory note he contributed to a vocational manual of printing issued by the Boy Scouts of America in 1920 when Updike was sixty years of age and at the peak of his career. He wrote for young men about to enter their trade: ". . . starting with no education, not much health, little money, and a generally poor and unpractical training for life, and being pushed by necessity into printing, a work that I hated, by studying that work and persistently keeping at it, I have succeeded in it better than some men, and, in spite of many handicaps, made myself over through it. . . .

54

The trick is to fall in with Fate; and disarm her by fully agreeing with her plans! . . . I became a printer by accident. If I have become a good printer—not more—it is through intention and determination, and the intention has got hold of me to such an extent that printing has become to me—with one exception—the most interesting thing in the world. . . ."

The exception was Updike's deeply felt religion and his lifelong devotion to the Episcopalian Church of his forefathers. Updike and Stanley Morison, the English typographic scholar, were friends who shared profound (if not denominationally the same) theological beliefs and typographic convictions. After Updike's death, Morison wrote of his friend and mentor: "Having chosen printing as his work, he performed it as he thought it should be performed and paid for. His business was never a hobby with him, though dining out and writing were. He was a charming and solicitous host, a witty talker and an amusing and stylish writer. To be all these things was more important to him than printing. That was his business, his occupation. He felt no need for taking it sufficiently seriously. But there was in him something more fundamental to his personality. Religion underlay his life and his business; his typographical expression was not at variance with it. . . . The task of living the kind of life he was determined to live did not permit him to shirk difficulties, spiritual, intellectual and other, inherent in that life-long struggle which is the lot of men who take upon themselves, under the grace of God, the burden of self-discipline."

In Updike's *Notes on the Press and Its Work*, published by the Harvard University Press in 1934, he wrote of his beginnings, of the establishment of The Merrymount Press, about the books there printed, and about the attitudes that regulated his working hours.

Daniel Berkeley Updike was born in 1860 in Providence, Rhode Island, in a family that had owned land in that state for more than two hundred years. Ministers of the Anglican faith, none of them Puritans, were among Updike's ancestors. His father, who had been presiding officer of the Rhode Island House of Representatives during the first two years of the Civil War, died suddenly in 1878 without funds to send his eighteen-year-old son to college. However, Updike's mother was a studious and intellectual woman, widely read, with a thorough knowledge of French and English literature. She guided Daniel's early reading, as well as his character, and gave him, together with a strong sense of personal discipline, an easy familiarity with books and literature.

THE
RENAISSANCE
IN
AMERICAN
PRINTING

DANIEL
BERKELEY
UPDIKE

THE

RENAISSANCE

IN

AMERICAN

PRINTING

DANIEL

BERKELEY

UPDIKE

Mother and son were devoted and almost inseparable companions.

Daniel's first position was temporary employment in the library of the Providence Athenaeum, which gave him access to the library of Brown University and, when in Newport, to the books of the Redwood Library. What next? A bank job was offered and, fortunately, refused by the young man who then, and later, said he could hardly add a column of figures. A telegram from a relative in Boston paved the way for a position with the publishing firm of Houghton, Mifflin & Company, then publishers of many of the most important books in American literature. The assignment turned out to be that of errand boy, where, he was told, everyone started. Updike wrote of that period: "The *personnel* of the office was unattractive, the hours were long, the duties new and wearisome . . . by summer I was so tired that at the end of two weeks' holiday, after much searching of heart, I gave up the place. Four days later a letter arrived. The firm was so pleased with my efforts and saw in me (God only knows why!) so much promise that I could return on shorter time. That was enough to arouse an already uneasy conscience."

Soon after, he was moved up to assist the advertising manager. He wrote copy and arranged the advertisements for magazines and newspapers. Without thought to the future, Updike, then in his twenties, began to familiarize himself with type. House catalogues followed. These were set and printed at the firm's own Riverside Press where Updike made his first direct contact with a printing plant. In the preparation of layouts and instructions to the compositors, and in efforts to make type achieve, in his own words, "some uniformity of arrangement and harmony of style," an articulate typographic designer had been born. Updike spent two years at the Riverside Press where its owners, Henry O. Houghton and George H. Mifflin, exercised genuine interest in good bookmaking. After twelve years in the employ of these paternalistic gentlemen, Updike was ready to step out on his own.

His position in an important publishing house, fortified by his own family background, brought Updike lasting friends, many of whom later became staunch supporters of The Merrymount Press. Among the literary personages who were still living in Boston in that extraordinary period, he met Henry Wadsworth Longfellow, Harriet Beecher Stowe, William Dean Howells, Thomas Bailey Aldrich, Oliver Wendell Holmes, Charles Eliot Norton, and others of lesser fame. Updike could remember

Miss Ellen Emerson "conducting her father to a desk whereon lay a visitor's book in which the old man tremulously signed his name." These were good years for a young man with literary and typographic aspirations to be at work in Boston and, with the interest in fine printing at floodtide, an auspicious time for the establishment of a new press.

In the summer of 1892, during his last year at the Riverside Press, Updike was offered a free-lance commission to redesign a *Book of Common Prayer*, with certain conditions imposed by the sponsors. The fee was attractive and Updike reluctantly accepted. It was the first of his many assignments in liturgical printing to which he brought a high degree of both theological and typographic expertness. The completed volume, with decorations by Bertram Grosvenor Goodhue, was enthusiastically received, but Updike was unhappy with the result. This experience taught him in good time that final decisions concerning suitability and good taste must conform to high standards established in the printing house by a designer-printer who himself embodies those principles and on which he must stand or fail.

In 1893 Updike rented rooms for a studio in Boston, furnished them attractively, and faced the future as an independent typographic designer. Excellent support was provided by his close friend Harold Brown, who shared religious convictions and affiliations with Updike, through a proposal to finance a new *Altar Book* for the Episcopal Church "to be as fine a piece of work" as Updike could make. The first step was to commission a new typeface and decorations, for which Goodhue was again chosen. Illustrations were made by Anning Bell in England. After the new type, called Merrymount, was finally cut and cast, a separate workshop was set up for type composition and page makeup, a proof press acquired, and a proofreader employed. The pages were shipped to New York for printing by the De Vinne Press. Completed after being in work for three years, the volume was a "monumental quarto," meticulously designed and produced, completely in the Kelmscott medieval manner. Updike soon came out from under the William Morris influence. Other books designed during these early years show his shift toward the simplicity and clarity that would remain firm objectives throughout his career. As his familiarity with historical backgrounds deepened, Updike showed the influence of the great figures of the classic past. Jenson and Aldus of the fifteenth century, Tory, Estienne, and others of the French Renaissance became his mentors; but the strongest

THE
RENAISSANCE
IN
AMERICAN
PRINTING

DANIEL
BERKELEY
UPDIKE

and most lasting tie was to English work of the eighteenth century, notably Bulmer. He was also impressed by the forthright workmanship in the books turned out nearer to his own time in London by Pickering and the Chiswick Press.

THE
RENAISSANCE
IN
AMERICAN
PRINTING

DANIEL
BERKELEY
UPDIKE

With the *Altar Book* as a valuable backlog, Updike obtained commissions for some eighteen books between 1893 and 1896. These he designed, then supervised production at excellent outside plants. But he soon found this procedure unproductive and unprofitable. Only direct, constant, and absolute control by the designer-printer can produce fine printing. Thus, taught by experience, according to Updike's *Notes*, "I was forced to invest, most unwillingly, in a small amount of type and ornaments, and by this tortuous path I arrived where most printers begin. Perhaps the reason that I survived, in spite of mistakes, was that a simple idea had got hold of me—to make work better for its purpose than was commonly thought worth while, and by having one's own establishment, to be free to do so." This hesitant beginning grew, in the following decades, into a substantial printing house, with a superlative collection of type and typesetting equipment including Monotype machines, three cylinder and two job presses, and with thirty-five employees. From the start in 1893 Updike had the great good fortune, and judgment, to find John Bianchi who was his first employee and typesetter, later to become plant foreman and, in 1915, Updike's partner. Bianchi was responsible for production and estimating because Updike had no understanding of machinery, and declared himself unable, or perhaps unwilling, to cope with arithmetic. Bianchi set up the firm's cost system after studying law and accounting at night. During Updike's trips abroad, he was in sole control, including designing. The forty-eight-year relationship between these two men was harmonious and fruitful. In complete agreement with the aims of the Press, Bianchi was an essential participant in its success.

The Press took its name, wrote Updike, "from the fancy that one could work hard and have a good time." The press mark (when used) was the famous Maypole of Merrymount. A banner flying from its top carries the Updike family motto, *Optimum Vix Satis* (the best is hardly enough). Six young people dance demurely round the pole. It is difficult to relate this seemingly innocent gambol to the original Maypole of the notorious adventurer Thomas Morton and his band of Anglican revelers who scandalized the Puritans.

From the beginning Updike set a clear course of scholarship and craftsmanship. If he "hated" printing and became a printer by accident, as he had said, he showed great aptitude in its production. When his duties at Houghton, Mifflin required him to clip their advertising from newspapers and magazines, he could at once identify the different publications by recognizing their type. His friend Rudolph Ruzicka observed: "In *In the Day's Work* and elsewhere Updike said all he cared to say and perhaps all that need be said about his approach to the designing of a piece of printing. What he did not describe, though amply demonstrated, was the quality of his amazing knowledge of the intellectual and artistic tools of his profession. I have often seen him identify at a glance the precise style and size of a type, the subject immediately dismissed with an abrupt comment on the artistic values involved in its use. This knowledge appeared instinctive; there was never the slightest suggestion of the erudite drudge—his perception had the quality of genius."

THE
RENAISSANCE
IN
AMERICAN
PRINTING

DANIEL
BERKELEY
UPDIKE

The clientele that was drawn to The Merrymount Press consisted of individuals and institutions with cultural interests. Updike produced books for publishers, book clubs, and booksellers; libraries and museums; privately printed genealogies, memorials, and family histories; liturgical works for the church; and ephemeral printing for occasions of all kinds, such as announcements, invitations, bookplates, Christmas cards, dinner menus, etc., etc. Professionals, The Merrymount Press welcomed any work that was to be done well: "Over and over again we have said that all kinds of work are done here and no piece of printing, however small, is neglected—much less despised." Every designer who obeys the strict and confining rules of book design enjoys the opportunity ephemeral printing frequently offers for levity, gaiety, and informality. It is also welcomed in the printing shop as grist for the grinding of the economic mill. Updike's occasional printing is always of interest.

Among the most important assets of the Press was a superb selection of typefaces and a carefully chosen body of printers' ornaments, gathered during a period when good type was not easily available. No other printing house at that time had a comparable collection. Two types were especially commissioned. Merrymount, made for the *Altar Book*, was a large heavy cutting, rarely used thereafter. In 1904 Herbert Horne, an English designer, completed Montallegro (Italian equivalent

59

THE
RENAISSANCE
IN
AMERICAN
PRINTING

DANIEL
BERKELEY
UPDIKE

of Merrymount). Horne stipulated that the first volume in which the type appeared was to be designed by him. This was accomplished in *The Life of Michelagnolo Buonarroti*. The type is a mannered, anachronistic face which Updike used in the volumes of the Humanist's Library. Updike's first purchase (in 1896) was his well-loved Caslon, to which he ever remained faithful. While in Europe he purchased interesting ornament, an Old English black letter, and French pointed gothic types (*lettres bâtardes*) adapted from sixteenth-century Books of Hours. These were used sparingly and, of course, only where appropriate. Then between 1897 and 1906 he added the faces which, with the Caslon, he used most frequently: Scotch Roman, Janson (used in the 1930 *Book of Common Prayer*), Mountjoye (later identified as the type cut for John Bell in the eighteenth century), and Oxford, a transitional face which originated in the Binny & Ronaldson foundry a century earlier, used in Updike's *Printing Types*. Later he added a Bodoni, Poliphilus and Blado, and Jan Van Krimpen's Lutetia. On the Monotype he had the English-produced Caslon, Scotch Roman, Baskerville, and Bulmer.

At the turn of the century Updike's reputation had arrived on solid ground. In 1899 his friend Edith Wharton required her publishers in New York, Charles Scribner's Sons, to employ The Merrymount Press to print *The Greater Inclination*, her first book of short stories. Her subsequent books and other Scribner publications developed into an active relationship. "Nothing could have helped the Press more, just then, than the Scribner connection," wrote Updike, "for it showed we were not amateurs but could hold our own with larger printing houses." Books for other trade publishers followed: T. Y. Crowell; Dodd, Mead; Appleton; L. C. Page; Longmans, Green; Doubleday, Page; and others. But this did not last. In 1902 the Press produced forty-one books of which nineteen were for trade publishers. In 1914, of twenty books printed, only one was a trade publication. During these few years publishers turned, by economic necessity, to manufacturing printers with Linotype composition and large high-speed presses. The general quality of bookmaking suffered. The Merrymount Press did not. Its production capacity was absorbed by books, catalogues, reports, and ephemera for semipublic, nonprofit institutions, such as the John Carter Brown Library (plate 34), Brown University, and the Carnegie Foundation for the Advancement of Learning. Updike had earlier attempted some publishing himself with eight titles issued in the Humanist's Library, before it was abandoned. Limited editions came along and provided Updike with the opportunity to use finer papers, larger formats, and other indulgences not permitted in day-to-day printing. Some of his most attractive books were done for Goodspeed's Bookshop and the Club of Odd Volumes in Boston, and, among others, the Grolier Club in New York.

Rudolph Ruzicka contributed illustrations for several of Updike's beautiful books. Notable among them is a small-format, three-volume Grolier Club edition in 1921 of Washington Irving's *Notes and Journal of Travel in Europe, 1804–1805*, executed in aquatint and watercolor; and wood engravings in several colors for a tall volume, *Newark* (plate 33), for the Carteret Book Club of that city. One of the rewards of the long, close friendship between artist and printer was a famous series of Ruzicka's wood engravings of views of Boston, sent each New Year's from 1912, until 1942, as a holiday Press keepsake. Two other artists, who were themselves independent book designers with much printing experience, lent their considerable talents to some of the Merrymount books. The collaboration and friendship with T. M. Cleland started in 1903, that with W. A. Dwiggins in 1908.

The high point of Updike's career as a designer and printer was the completion in 1930 of *The Book of Common Prayer . . . According to the Use of the Protestant Episcopal Church in the United States of America* (plate 35). His specimen pages were chosen, from among those invited from four printers, by the Church's Commission on Revision. The whole undertaking was financed by J. Pierpont Morgan. "It was an enormous task," wrote Updike, "and one which taxed our resources in many different directions, but in which what knowledge I had of the history of a Church to which my family have been for nearly three hundred years adherents, and of the liturgical requirements and practical use of the Prayer Book stood me in good stead. . . . The book was begun in 1928 and was finished in the autumn of 1930." Without decoration, except a typographic leaf, initial letters, and rubrication, this is an austere and handsome quarto. Five copies were printed on vellum. The edition is a superb example of American craftsmanship and an abiding tribute to all concerned in its production.

Updike's greatest contribution to his profession is his invaluable, two-volume publication, *Printing Types: Their History, Forms, and Use*. First issued by the Harvard University Press in 1922, it has been reprinted several times. The book's origin was a series of lectures Updike

THE
RENAISSANCE
IN
AMERICAN
PRINTING

DANIEL
BERKELEY
UPDIKE

had been invited to give ten years before at the Harvard School of Business Administration. When proposed that the lectures be put into book form, a decade was involved in transforming relatively informal talks into written form, and for the necessary research to select a multitude of relevant illustrations. With type as the core, the text is a historical review of printing, with emphasis on its survival as craft. A portion of the Harvard lectures not included in *Printing Types* was combined with discourse on the conduct of a printing house under the title *In the Day's Work*. Updike's scholarship is thorough and perceptive, his style is urbane and witty.

Updike's printing was honored in its own time. Major exhibitions were held at the American Institute of Graphic Arts in New York in 1928, at the Boston Public Library in 1935, and jointly by the A.I.G.A. and the Grolier Club in 1940, with an impressive opening reception a year before Updike's death. The addresses of the evening were printed by Elmer Adler at the Pynson Printers and published by the Institute. The Huntington Library in California, which houses a very extensive collection of Merrymount work, held an exhibition in 1942, with a descriptive catalogue by Gregg Anderson. "The Updike Collection," which includes Updike's bequeathed personal library of type specimen books, is housed in the Providence Public Library. Many, perhaps most, of the major college and institutional libraries have, in their special collections, substantial holdings of Merrymount books. Updike was given honorary degrees by Harvard and Brown universities. He was elected to membership in the Massachusetts Historical Society and as an honorary member of the Phi Beta Kappa Society. From the members of his craft he received the medal of the American Institute of Graphic Arts.

Daniel Berkeley Updike was an eminently practical man. He shunned preciosity and sham. Clarity, scholarship, restraint, tradition, workmanship, good taste, good manners were all inherent in everything he said, or wrote, or printed. He was blessed with an observant and retentive mind that allowed him to assemble a remarkable repertory of type and ornament. His craftsmanship was of the highest quality. He attracted people of substance and succeeded in business. With all of these admirable traits it would have been surprising if Updike had also been an original and innovative designer. His typographic design was a lively and cultivated intellectual exercise that embraced only sound traditional virtues and escaped the seductive pitfalls of novelty.

Updike's own informative but too-diffident closing lines in his *Notes* summed up the picture as he saw it: "Nearly fourteen thousand pieces of printing of all sorts have been turned out here, and each of them has had the personal supervision of my partner or myself; and not one but every page of each book has come under our inspection. This means labour, and constant labour; and to such effort—which is within the power of any man—the success of the Press is chiefly due. Add to this a love of order, a wish to make good, and, as a by-product, the desire to demonstrate that a trade can be profitably practised in the spirit of a profession, and one has the whole story. None of these characteristics or desires has, necessarily, a connection with printing: each is applicable to other occupations. In this case, through force of circumstances, I happened to apply them to printing, for which I had little taste when I began, nor ever the kind of fervour that is stated (in improving books) to be essential to success."

BRUCE ROGERS (1870–1957)

The forces that converged to produce an American typographic renaissance found its finest realization in the work of Bruce Rogers, a young artist out of the Indiana corn belt. The career that first flourished in Boston reached its culmination on both sides of the Atlantic. Rogers' first books were made when the crafts were within the province of the hand; his long life witnessed the startling advances of technology and industrialism. Rogers' earliest masterpieces among the Riverside Press editions were set by hand and printed sheet by sheet on dampened handmade papers. His ultimate triumph, the Oxford Lectern Bible, was entirely a product of the machine, set in type and printed at the Oxford University Press in England. Bruce Rogers' genius was doubly clear in his ability to have crossed over from the frontier of handcraftsmanship to control of the machine, and to have retained artistry and finesse in the transition. His greatness lay in the felicity of his brilliant manipulation of type and ornament, in his command of all the basic processes and their consummation in beautiful books—noble books that can be read with pleasure and owned with pride—not *objets d'art* to be stored behind glass. One of the present century's immortals of the printed book, Sir Francis Meynell, producer of the superb procession of Nonesuch Press volumes, made the carefully considered statement that Bruce Rogers "was the greatest artificer of the book who ever lived."

63

Artful devices, subtle stratagems, delicate maneuvers—these are the uses of the artificer, joined under this designer's hand to originality and ingenuity. Add endless variety, novelty, dexterity, and, yes, humor and *jeu d'esprit.*

THE
RENAISSANCE
IN
AMERICAN
PRINTING

BRUCE
ROGERS

Bruce Rogers was born of English Yorkshire stock in 1870 in Lafayette, Indiana. His ancestors had come overland from Virginia; a grandfather had been captain of a stern-wheeler on the Wabash. Bruce's father encouraged his son to develop an inborn talent for drawing and penmanship. While still in high school the lad showed his predestination by hand-lettering a single copy of William Cullen Bryant's "Forest Hymn," with illustrations in watercolors and simulated etchings by his own hand. He pressed the plate marks for the "etchings" into the paper with a hot iron in his mother's kitchen. It was his first and most limited edition. At age sixteen he entered Purdue University in Indiana and promptly enrolled in the art class at a time when art was considered a poor thing for rising young Americans. In a group of female students, he and John T. McCutcheon, who later became a famous cartoonist, were the only men. While in Purdue, Rogers' inclination toward matters typographic rose to the surface. He made covers, initial letters, and drawings for several Purdue publications and lettered one or two title-pages for Mosher. After graduation in 1890, Bruce (or Bert, as he was then known) became a newspaper artist in Indianapolis with assignments that involved quick pictorial reporting of fires, visits to jail, and even to the local morgue. The newspaper days did not last long; neither did a period of landscape painting. Book design, waiting in the wings and about to take the stage, would stay out front for the next sixty-two years. While still in Indianapolis, Rogers saw the early Kelmscott books, imported by his friend J. M. Bowles, who ran an art store and edited a small magazine, *Modern Art.* Upon seeing Morris' printing Rogers said that his whole interest in book production became rationalized and intensified. He abandoned the idea that a book could be made beautiful through the work of an illustrator alone and determined instead to use that curiosity he had always felt as to type and paper toward a study of the physical form of printed books.

Rogers' professional life in book design began in 1895 with decorations for a Mosher publication, A.E.'s *Homeward Songs by the Way,* and the typography and decoration for *Notes: Critical & Biographical* by R. B. Gruelle, The Collection of W. T. Walters, Indianapolis. Meanwhile,

64

J. M. Bowles and his magazine were carried off to Boston by L. Prang and Company. Soon there was need for a part-time typographic designer. Prang offered fifty cents an hour with a guarantee of $10.00 per week. Editor Bowles offered the job to his friend from Indianapolis. It was accepted at once and Rogers came east. Bowles has written that "Rogers would work for a few hours, then go to the cashier, get his money and walk in the beautiful Massachusetts country for two or three days." At this time he also completed some free-lance book and cover designs for Stone & Kimball and Way & Williams.

THE
RENAISSANCE
IN
AMERICAN
PRINTING

BRUCE
ROGERS

In 1896 Rogers joined the Riverside Press where he designed trade books and advertisements for the next four years. In 1900, after planning and urging by Rogers, a special department was established by George H. Mifflin, the senior partner, for the design and production of limited editions for sale to collectors. An American printing office thus placed its resources, with funds for experiments, and without pressures of time, at the disposal of a young practitioner, with full editorial responsibility. What a fortunate meeting of personalities and potentialities this was. The proprietor of a solid, conservative business in Cambridge, Massachusetts, giving his support to a relatively untried designer out of the midwest, who at the beginning of a new century had a wholly new and original approach to the making of books.

During the next twelve years (1900–1912), B.R., as he came to be known to his friends, broke new ground with the completion of sixty limited editions. These were the first fine books to escape from the private press tradition of a proprietary typeface, a uniform house style, and limp vellum binding with ties. Each of the Rogers books was different in size, type, paper, decoration, and binding. Succeeding books were adventures down new paths for the designer as they were, certainly, for the collectors who bought them. Always within the limits of readability and good sense, these books had (and still have) charm, assurance, and an elusive luster difficult to analyze. They were a revelation to those who had to do with books and printing. At least a dozen of the Riverside Press editions can be chosen as small masterpieces. One might name, among others, Ronsard's *Songs and Sonnets* (1903) (plate 36); Boccaccio's *Life of Dante* (1904); *The Song of Roland* (1906); *The Banquet of Plato* (1908); Walton's *The Compleat Angler* (1909); Wordsworth's *Sonnets* (1910); *Ecclesiastes or the Preacher* (1911).

Rogers designed his first type for the printing of a three-volume folio

65

THE

RENAISSANCE

IN

AMERICAN

PRINTING

BRUCE

ROGERS

edition, *The Essays of Montaigne*, in work for three years, 1902 to 1904. The type, appropriately named Montaigne, was cast in a sixteen-point size for the large page. Rogers used the type occasionally thereafter but was never wholly pleased with the cutting. The Montaigne was based on the fifteenth-century Jenson letter. Rogers used the same model for his second type, the Centaur, cut a dozen years later but this time eminently satisfactory. Centaur is a beautiful type, delicate and subtle, which was made available on Monotype composition. It has never been widely popular in the trade, but has been used with elegant effect by sensitive typographic designers. At the Riverside Press Rogers used a wide range of typefaces including, chiefly, Caslon, Brimmer, Scotch Roman, and Oxford. During the Rudge period (1920–1928) he welcomed the newly produced Garamond, also Bodoni and several Goudy faces among others.

Neither Rogers nor his friend Updike found an adequate American tradition of design and craftsmanship on which to build. The aristocratic Updike leaned logically on Anglo-Saxon influences. Rogers' blithe spirit found itself more in sympathy with the clarity of fifteenth-century Venice and the sophistication of sixteenth-century France. Rogers has been charged with being derivative. He has also been called the master of allusive book design. In his early work, both these trends came from a serious and thorough historical study of the art of the book. Historical perspective and a lively mind probably furthered his tendency toward eclecticism and away from tiresome repetition. Inevitably, a subtle personal style developed. In his later masterpieces he was neither allusive nor derivative, except as any work of art must derive, in part at least, from the sum total of the experience of the past.

After sixteen years at the Riverside Press, Rogers became restive. He said that he had "always looked forward to living, for a term of years at least, either in England or the Continent. . . . My present agreement with the Riverside Press expires next year. . . . They pay me very well but they give me no leisure except two weeks vacation yearly. And now leisure for my own pursuits has come to mean more than money to me." He made the choice to become a free-lance artist with its freedoms (as well as the insecurities which he more than once regretted) and so remained throughout his life. He never allowed himself to become involved in any situation or employment, administrative or financial, which might intrude on his complete absorption with the work in hand.

66

However, he enjoyed friendly and helpful relationships with the compositors and pressmen who produced his work and who respected his skills.

Rogers spent the summer of 1912 in England. Unable to make acceptable working arrangements that would also provide a living, he returned to four lean years in the United States. Nevertheless, this period saw the completion of the Centaur type, one of his most brilliant achievements. The Centaur is based closely on the Jenson letter in the Eusebius of 1470, but with considerable freedom in the redrawing. The undertaking was sponsored, with some proprietary rights, by Henry Watson Kent, then Secretary of the Metropolitan Museum of Art in New York, where he had established an excellent press in the Museum basement for announcements, posters, labels, etc. The type's first book appearance was in Maurice de Guerin's *The Centaur* (plate 37) which gave the type its name and which has become one of the most sought-after of the B.R. books. Hand-set by Mrs. Rogers, it was printed in an edition of 135 copies at Carl P. Rollins' lively and idealistic Montague Press at the Dyke Mill in Massachusetts.

In 1916 Emery Walker, who had been a close associate of William Morris and T. J. Cobden-Sanderson, invited Rogers to come to England to form a partnership for the production of fine books in the spirit of the Kelmscott and Doves presses. In a long letter Rogers expressed his acceptance with pleasure. It revealed, at age forty-six, a sense of inadequacy that was to remain with him, even in the later years of international acclaim. He wrote: "For five or six years, now, I have struggled against a growing sense of despondency and discouragement. . . . I have felt that I was accomplishing nothing worthy of the encouraging start I had made at Riverside . . . and the prospect of an outlet for the many ideas that still bubble up within me seem definitely closed." And further on: "I still have dreams of doing something finer in a fully developed style of my own than has yet been accomplished. I do not, for an instant, think that I can ever surpass Morris or Sanderson or Hornby on their own grounds—but my own ideal book is still far from being a realization and I must keep working toward it, however slowly and painfully." The Rogers family—B.R. himself, his wife Ann, and daughter Elizabeth—sailed for England in December to settle in a cold flat in Hammersmith in the midst of wartime London. He had in his pocket a commission from the Grolier Club to reprint that part of Dürer's *Geom-*

THE
RENAISSANCE
IN
AMERICAN
PRINTING

BRUCE
ROGERS

etry that deals with the design of letters for inscriptions. Entitled *On the Just Shaping of Letters*, the edition was completed late in 1917 under formidably trying conditions. Walker's last pressman, who had run only the first two sheets, was called up by the army. Consequently, in Rogers' own words, "the only thing to do was to volunteer for the job myself. I'd never run a press of any kind, but with a little instruction I found it simple enough. . . . There is of course no heat anywhere and I have to dampen the Kelmscott hand-made paper in the converted kitchen. Both my hands and feet have developed chilblains."

The partnership with Emery Walker did not work out. Then followed a depressing month in a boarding house. The Rogers family was about to return to the United States when Sydney Cockerell, Director of the Fitzwilliam Museum in Cambridge, determined to hold Rogers in England and to secure his services for the University Press. Typography was important to Cockerell, who had been secretary to William Morris at the Kelmscott Press and an associate of Emery Walker. Despite the gravity of the war, the Syndics requested Rogers to become Adviser to the Press and to give four days per week to survey existing conditions and to recommend changes. Within a few months Rogers turned in a very lengthy, detailed statement which included the blunt comment: "I cannot believe that any other printing house of equal standing can have gone on for so many years with such inferior equipment of types. . . . They are in my opinion beyond belief." To the credit of the Syndics, the report was accepted and implemented as war and postwar conditions allowed. In later retrospect the Director of the Press, Brooke Crutchley, wrote in 1950 that it was the example of Bruce Rogers' "painstaking quest for perfection as much as the report itself that was to put new life into the University Press, and it is a pleasure, thirty-three years later, to acknowledge once more the debt that Cambridge, as indeed the whole world, owes to a great craftsman and artist." In less than two years at Cambridge, Rogers was given rights to use the dons' parlor in Emmanuel College, he made firm friends among prominent figures in the English book world, he punted on the river Cam, and he roamed the English countryside to which he was profoundly attached. But a vital element was missing: there was no opportunity to make fine books. A postwar boom in the United States offered some hope. In the summer of 1919 the family returned home. It was a fortunate move.

On arrival Rogers was offered appointment as Printing Adviser to the Harvard University Press. With a much-needed retainer, this association continued for sixteen years. David Pottinger tells in a Typophile publication, *B.R. Marks & Remarks* (1946), that in an already well-staffed and well-equipped organization, what they asked from Rogers were creative suggestions from an outsider to prevent staleness of treatment, and to improve the output of the Press. B.R. designed some thirty books himself, and, Pottinger continues, "he gave each of his thirty or so run-of-the-mill Harvard books more detailed attention than most typographers would ever dream of giving to their prized items. . . . It was, however, Mr. Rogers' own presence in the shop [the Harvard printing office] that did most of it."

Many years had slipped by since Rogers had done the kind of work that could nourish his soul. The opportunity presented itself in the person and the plant of William Edwin Rudge and in the prosperity of the 1920's. After a fortuitous luncheon meeting, Rudge proposed some form of collaboration. After Rogers' visit to the Rudge plant, then in downtown New York near the Brooklyn Bridge, B.R. wrote: "At first glance it looked like the ordinary establishment of that period, a confusion of type stands, presses, paper cutters, and all the other usual equipment. But as we walked about I sensed something out of the ordinary; it was partly in the character of the men themselves and partly in the manifest understanding between them and their employer." After a few months in Boston on Harvard University Press duties, Rogers returned and found Rudge in his handsome new low stone building in Mount Vernon which he developed into the finest printing house in the United States. "The prospect of working in such agreeable surroundings," continued Rogers, "helped on my decision to accept his proposition . . . before long I was spending almost every day at Mount Vernon, whether engaged on the work of the press, or on my own commissions; in fact there was never any strict accounting on either his part or mine . . . all in all I spent eight productive years working with Rudge, and no collaboration could have been happier for me. He left me an entirely free hand and unhesitatingly backed up nobly even my most unpromising projects with new types, papers, equipment—everything—whether they were likely to prove profitable or the reverse."

These ideal working conditions made possible about a hundred books. Rogers' new enthusiasm for printers' type ornaments for decoration, rather than pictorial illustration, flowered (almost literally) in Ernest

THE
RENAISSANCE
IN
AMERICAN
PRINTING

BRUCE
ROGERS

THE

RENAISSANCE

IN

AMERICAN

PRINTING

BRUCE

ROGERS

Dowson's *Pierrot of the Minute*, a small, exquisite book for the Grolier Club in 1923. There is marvelous dexterity in the makeup of the delicate, intricate rose design into enchanting pages for this romantic little poem. Among other memorable books of the Rudge period are *The Journal of Madame Knight* (1920); Thoreau's *Night and Moonlight* (1921); Aiken's *Priapus and the Pool* (1922); Kenyon's *Ancient Books and Modern Discoveries* (1927) (plate 38); Tory's *Champ Fleury* (1927), and, of course, many others. These titles are among thirty books—and only thirty!—that Rogers himself considered "successful" from the seven hundred books in his complete opus. These chosen thirty are listed on page 119 of *Paragraphs on Printing*. Of the thirty, nine were from his youthful Riverside editions. Space does not permit discussion of the making of the Rogers books. Neither should one try. Even B.R. refrained from telling how book design is done. At an exhibition opening he said, "I don't know. And even though I may have theories on the subject I have usually kept them to myself. If you do that you can change them as often as you like, and no one is the wiser." However, there are windows into B.R.'s thought processes. At the Rudge plant B.R. found in the type compositor assigned to him a young Shakespearean actor, James Hendrickson, who became a lifelong associate and friend. The relationship bore rich fruit in the publication *Paragraphs on Printing* (1943), subtitled "Elicited from Bruce Rogers in Talks with James Hendrickson on the Functions of the Book Designer." In this superb book "we are hearing [B.R.] himself talk for a time as he works." And the actor quotes from *Hamlet*: "And thus do we . . . by indirections find directions out."

While still in Mount Vernon, Rogers began to stir the ingredients that became one of his most magnificent books. On reading Lawrence's *Seven Pillars of Wisdom*, Rogers became convinced that T. E. Shaw (Lawrence) was the man to make a new translation of *The Odyssey*, "a man who could make Homer live again—a man of action who was also a scholar & who could write swift and graphic English." Rogers found Aircraftsman Shaw, who finally accepted the proposal but with serious doubts that his own ability to translate Homer would be worthy of Bruce Rogers' bookmaking. Rogers also found the sponsor, Colonel Ralph Isham, who made the undertaking possible. With *The Odyssey* translation under way, the urge again came over B.R. to visit his British friends, to walk the English countryside he knew so well and where he had made his drawings and watercolors. Besides, the English Monotype

70

people wished to cut his Centaur type under his personal supervision, and he had decided to set and print and publish *The Odyssey* in London with Emery Walker. Yale University gave Rogers an honorary degree in 1928. Then the family sailed to Europe, only this time a grandson took the place of a daughter who had died. Mrs. Rogers herself was ailing. Nevertheless, during the next four years in England Rogers would produce his finest work.

The present writer cherishes the remembrance when, in 1930, as a young man and a beginning printer, he enjoyed a few days with Bruce Rogers in London and Oxford where B.R. seemed as much at home as in New York and Connecticut. The meeting began at the small, Dickensian Anderton's Hotel in Fleet Street, where Rogers always stayed. Then to the Golden Cross in Oxford, "one of the properest inns in all England"; an evening at a British music hall; and, next day, a long visit at the venerable Oxford University printing house, where the Lectern Bible was under way.

In the First World War many Canadians lost their lives in the Belgian town of Ypres, which the soldiers called "Wipers." Ten years later the Canadian government built a memorial chapel where their young had died. The king of England wished to present a lectern Bible worthy of the occasion. But no Bible had been printed in England comparable to the Baskerville volume of 1763. The Oxford University Press immediately set about repairing the omission. Rogers, then resident in London and recognized as the foremost living book designer, was commissioned to design a folio Bible in the King James version, in one volume not to exceed 1250 pages. The Oxford people suggested Centaur as their choice of type. Rogers tried several alternate types but came back to Centaur, modified slightly to meet space demands. A year was spent in details of type selection and page design. The story of the making of the Bible was told by B.R. himself in a pamphlet (*An Account of the Making of the Oxford Lectern Bible* [Philadelphia: Lanston Monotype Machine Company, 1936]) printed at the request of the head of the English Monotype Corporation. It is available in most special libraries. One quotation is especially revealing: "I had decided in the beginning that notwithstanding its size of page the composition should not be ponderous or too formal—'monumental,' I believe, is the word for the appearance I wished to avoid. I wanted this book to appear as though I were accustomed to knocking off folios daily, or at least weekly, as mere routine work."

THE
RENAISSANCE
IN
AMERICAN
PRINTING

BRUCE
ROGERS

71

THE

RENAISSANCE

IN

AMERICAN

PRINTING

BRUCE

ROGERS

These four years in England (1928–1932) saw Bruce Rogers' ultimate fruition. Three books, at least, are imperishable. They are *The Odyssey of Homer* (1932), *Fra Luca De Pacioli* (1933), and the Oxford Lectern Bible, published in 1935. All were printed in the Centaur type. *The Odyssey* was printed on a lovely gray paper with Homeric roundels taken from Greek vases, printed in black over gold and requiring six impressions to achieve perfection. The *Pacioli*, a Grolier Club of New York publication, was printed at the Cambridge University Press. The title page in black and red is sheer inspired glory. The present writer was recently responsible for the organization of an extensive exhibition, "Art of the Printed Book, 1455–1955," at the Pierpont Morgan Library in New York. This entailed the handling and review of virtually all of the world's most famous printed books starting with the Gutenberg Bible. It is possible to state with absolute personal conviction that the Rogers books stand with the best, including the masterpieces of the fifteenth and sixteenth centuries and the books of Baskerville, Bodoni, and Didot. Rogers' books are free from preciosity, affectation, and ostentation. Yet his major works are assured and majestic, and contain within their covers intellectual strength and power. The reproductions in following pages, of the Rogers books and others, are only a suggestion of the books themselves. The reader is urged to see and, if possible, to handle the original volumes, which have been widely collected in many American libraries. It is the quality of the paper, the subtlety of incised impression, the interrelation of all component parts—the feel of the book—that constitute the achievements and the rewards of great book design and production.

Bruce Rogers was widely honored in his lifetime by the connoisseurs of fine bookmaking. The latest of many exhibitions was held in April 1970 at the Grolier Club on the occasion of the centenary of Rogers' birth. The literature about his work is extensive. Three bibliographies were published: in 1925, 1936, and 1939. Two books were compiled by the Typophiles; there were exhibition catalogues and articles in typographic journals. He received the medal of the American Institute of Graphic Arts and the great distinction of the Gold Medal of the American Academy of Arts and Letters. Rogers' life and work spanned great years in the history of the printed book. He needed fine printing houses and found them in America and England. He needed the collectors who bought his books and the patrons who gave him commissions or sponsored the projects he himself created. He was fortunate to have been born into an era of typographic growth. To that era he brought his own extraordinary gifts. He was the first great artist-typographer— the forebear of the many typographic designers who have made books for publishing houses and printing establishments since his time.

After returning to the United States, Rogers settled into his home in New Fairfield, Connecticut, with a quarter century of life remaining. He designed some good books for the Limited Editions Club of New York, notably an illustrated, thirty-seven-volume folio Shakespeare (plate 39). He was responsible for another Bible and a few other books, but these should not be compared with his earlier achievements. He carved a figurehead for the sailing ship *Joseph Conrad*, testimonial to his love of the four-master and the sea. And he designed the lettering to be cut in stone for the outside south wall of Hunter College where he climbed the workmen's scaffolding in good weather and bad to oversee the carving. It is pleasant to recall of these late years that every spring some thirty of B.R.'s friends and admirers would make a pilgrimage to his home to bring birthday greetings. The last such gathering was arranged for May 1957. It was first postponed and then canceled. Bruce Rogers died a few days after his eighty-seventh birthday.

FREDERIC W. GOUDY (1865–1947)

Goudy's love of type and typography was passionate, articulate, and indefatigable. In his autobiography he listed and discussed his one hundred twenty-two designs. Not all were complete alphabets; some were never cut and cast into type; a few were reworkings of earlier faces; and Goudy counted roman and italic of the same font as two designs. Nevertheless, count them as you will, the output was extraordinary. His types were widely used during his lifetime. Many were very popular commercial successes. Goudy's enthusiasm for lettering and his expansive joy in type were infectious. His many adherents found him to be a "mellow and lovable man," a natural teacher and an excellent raconteur, especially at dinner functions in his honor. He was the only typographic figure whose fame reached beyond professional circles, sparked no doubt by a reputation for "the mostest." Goudy was hailed as the most prolific type designer of all time by colleagues unaware of the productivity of Giambattista Bodoni. (Bodoni's incredible output may be seen in the two-volume, massive typographic manuals issued by his widow in 1818.) Nevertheless, Goudy's large accomplishments and his colorful personality were highly influential factors in the widespread concern with matters typographic in the first half of the present century.

THE
RENAISSANCE
IN
AMERICAN
PRINTING

FREDERIC
W. GOUDY

Frederic W. Goudy was born in Bloomington, Illinois, in 1865, son of a teacher who had become county superintendent of schools. Fred's interest in letters showed as a boy when, by his own account, he cut out three thousand letters of colored papers and with them mounted Biblical texts on his church walls. After some years as a clerk and bookkeeper in several midwestern towns, he landed in Chicago in 1890, where he continued for a time with office work for his livelihood. At McClurg's bookstore he saw the work of the Kelmscott and other English private presses. As they did for other members of his generation, these extraordinary books fired his imagination and his ambition. In 1895 Goudy set up a small, short-lived printing shop called the Booklet Press, later renamed Camelot. His work attracted W. Irving Way, through whom he met Herbert S. Stone and the job of producing the exciting Stone & Kimball *Chap-Book* for one year. Goudy and his compositor set the magazine in Old Style type; the presswork was done elsewhere.

In 1896 Goudy designed his first type. He tells about it in his autobiography: "For want of anything to do, since I was as yet unemployed, one evening in my small bedroom on Michigan Avenue, I drew an alphabet of capital letters in pencil, each letter about five-eights of an inch high; and as letters drawn on paper are useless in themselves, I sent the sheet to the Dickinson Type Foundry in Boston, from which I had earlier purchased type now and then for the Camelot Press. As the drawing took less than an hour to do, I asked if the drawing was worth five dollars; and to my great surprise, in the course of a week or two, a letter of acceptance came enclosing a check for ten dollars. . . . Later the Foundry added a lower-case to my capitals, but by whom it was drawn I do not know." The type was called Camelot.

In 1899 Goudy set up as a free-lance designer. He received commissions for book covers and lettering from Herbert S. Stone & Co., the *Inland Printer* magazine, and from Thomas B. Mosher. He built up a considerable clientele in Chicago with lettering for advertising—for the Marshall Field department store; Hart, Schaffner & Marx; Kuppenheimer Clothes; and others. Three types—Pabst, Powell, and Village—grew directly out of this commercial lettering.

74

Goudy's second venture in printing, called the Village Press, was in the sacred handcraft ideal inspired by the English Arts and Crafts Movement. He was joined by Will Ransom, a young student from the Art Institute, who later became a staunch, producing individual in the typographic community. The third working member was Fred's wife, Bertha Sprinks Goudy, an adept craftswoman and musician who became a fast and dependable compositor, co-worker, and faithful companion, with a vital share in the Goudy progress through the years. Two small books were produced at the Village Press, then the Goudys and their equipment moved to Hingham, Massachusetts, near Boston. Nine books were produced during two years in Hingham, then the next move was made to New York, where a small plant for general printing was set up, with Everett Currier as partner. After two years of some growth, everything was lost in a disastrous fire in 1908. That ended printing as a livelihood. Thereafter Goudy devoted himself to his drawing board for letter design and to type cutting, casting, and sale.

In 1909 Goudy made the first of several trips to Europe, where he visited the great repositories of manuscripts and early printed books, met famous men in his field such as Emery Walker, and was able to study the inscriptional letters on European monuments, especially the Trajan column in Rome. During these years when Fred and Bertha kept the Village Press alive on a tiny press in a small New York apartment, Mitchell Kennerley, preparing to publish H. G. Wells' *The Door in the Wall*, asked Goudy to design the book. Unable to find a typeface acceptable to himself, Goudy designed a special sixteen-point size and named it Kennerley Old Style. When cut in a full series by Robert Wiebking in Chicago, the type was cast for Goudy by the American Type Foundry and offered for sale in fonts by Goudy's newly established Village Letter Foundery. The Forum type, an inscriptional titling letter, was also completed at this time. Kennerley and Forum became Goudy's first substantial successes. The Caslon Letter Foundry in London bought the English and Continental rights and Goudy was on the road to fame. The Lanston Monotype Company in Philadelphia cut Kennerley for their typecasting machines. A lifetime relationship was thus begun. Goudy later became the Lanston Art Director and, in due course, was responsible for a number of successful types.

From 1916 to 1924 Goudy taught lettering at the Art Students League in New York. During this period he started a handsome periodical, *Ars*

THE
RENAISSANCE
IN
AMERICAN
PRINTING

FREDERIC
W. GOUDY

THE

RENAISSANCE

IN

AMERICAN

PRINTING

FREDERIC

W. GOUDY

Typographica, printed at the Marchbanks Press in New York, and wrote two excellent books, *The Alphabet* (1918) and *The Elements of Lettering* (1922). Both books were superbly printed by Rudge and published by Mitchell Kennerley. In 1942 a combined one-volume edition, revised and enlarged, was issued by the University of California Press, set in the private type Goudy designed for the Press, logically called University of California Old Style (plate 40). Renamed Californian, the type later became available on Monotype. This book (also issued in paperback) traces the origins and development of the alphabet and type, with copious, lucid illustrations. It is unreservedly recommended to students. In 1940 the University of California Press had published Goudy's *Typologia*, subtitled "Studies in Type Design and Type Making, with Comments on the Invention of Typography, the First Types, Legibility, and Fine Printing." Shortly before Goudy's death, the Typophiles published a two-volume autobiography, *A Half-Century of Type Design and Typography, 1895–1945*, which includes a description by Goudy of all his designs and a bibliography of his extensive writings, compiled by George L. McKay. The *Bibliography of the Village Press* was handsomely issued in 1938 by Melbert B. Cary at his Press of the Woolly Whale in New York.

In 1923 the Goudys moved to Marlboro-on-Hudson, on the west shore of the river in the fruit belt of New York State, where he bought an old mill on a falling stream. It was a romantic spot with excellent working space. Here at the Village Letter Foundery, Goudy thrived for fifteen productive years. In addition to many alphabetical designs, Goudy built his own precision tools and developed delicate pantographic machines which made it possible to cut matrices in all sizes from his hand-cut patterns. The type was then cast and sold. In 1939 Goudy suffered his second disastrous fire when the mill burned to the ground. The flames consumed hundreds of drawings and patterns and thousands of matrices. What did not burn fell into the stream below.

Goudy's late years were full of the recognition that gladdened his heart. He received honorary doctorates from Syracuse University, Mills College, and the University of California. There were retrospective exhibitions of his types and books by the American Institute of Graphic Arts and the Grolier Club; medals from the A.I.G.A., the American Institute of Architects, and the Ulster Society; awards from several schools of journalism; and several festschrift books for a succession of birthdays. His friendships and his admirers were legion.

Paul A. Bennett, leader of the Typophiles and the editor of its many invaluable publications, wrote of Goudy: "His most prolific years spanned the decades from 1911 to 1932, when he completed sixty-seven designs and produced at least two dozen good, popular types. Among these were Kennerley, Lanston, Goudy Old Style and New Style; the Forum and Hadriano titling letters; Goudy Modern and Open, Deepdene, Village No. 2, Medieval, Goudy Text, and Deepdene Text; the Garamont and Italian Old Style faces for Monotype; the Cloister Initials for American Type Foundry, and several private faces, including the Franciscan for the Grabhorn Press and Companion Old Style for *Woman's Home Companion*."

THE

RENAISSANCE

IN

AMERICAN

PRINTING

FREDERIC

W. GOUDY

Favorites are dethroned by the fickle winds of fashion that sweep through type design, as they do through other, more familiar areas of human activities. Advertising faces must be bizarre and striking. Highly successful when they first appear, or when resurrected from the past, novelties are cast aside as soon as they become common currency. Book faces, on the other hand, must be calm, familiar, easy to read, and free from eccentricities. Differences in the design of type for books are extremely subtle. Letter for letter variations are scarcely perceived, especially in small sizes. The essential character and quality of a typeface can be seen only in the mass; that is, on an entire page of type. To the average layman, ease of reading is the sole criterion; only professionals normally recognize variations in design. Yet the potential beauty in bookmaking, for all to see, lies in the design of type and *in the competency and artistry of its handling.*

An exhibition, "Fifty Books of the Year," has been held annually for more than fifty years by the American Institute of Graphic Arts in New York; then traveled throughout the country. The selections have been, on the whole, the best American books, typographically, chosen for excellence of design and manufacture by representative juries which change each year. The catalogues have been indexed with entries for typefaces and manufacturing processes. From these data it is clear that a handful of classic typefaces from the past have most successfully survived the fundamental changes from hand to machine composition and, at this writing (1976), to photoelectronic film composition which is of great importance in book production. The top type performers have been those that have most persistently weathered the centuries: Bembo, Garamond, Janson, Caslon, Baskerville, Bulmer, and Bodoni. The most

THE
RENAISSANCE
IN
AMERICAN
PRINTING

FREDERIC
W. GOUDY

frequently used book faces designed during the present century have been Cheltenham, Caledonia, Palatino, and Times Roman, and, most recently, Optima, Univers, and Helvetica. The Goudy types have not fared well in this competition, in part because his types were available chiefly for hand composition and on the Monotype machine, whereas American commercial book production was almost exclusively limited to the Linotype. However, these "Fifty Books" represented the work of the most discriminating trade-book designers and the smaller printers of special books, many of whom were partial to Monotype composition. In addition to the classic types, contemporary Monotype faces seen with some frequency were Centaur (Bruce Rogers), Perpetua (Eric Gill), Lutetia (Van Krimpen), and a scattering of others. Goudy's Kennerley, Goudy Old Style, and Italian Old Style, which were seen occasionally, were more successful in the twenties and thirties for advertising, magazine, and job printing. His best book faces, judged by their continued appearance among the "Fifty Books," are Deepdene and Goudy Modern. They have contrasts and crispness which, in these years, have been more welcome than the softer old styles. The Forum and Hadriano titling letters and Goudy Text (a gothic face) have also been of great value. Goudy Modern has had the accolade of choice by Sir Francis Meynell for three of his hundred Nonesuch Press books, and for books by other distinguished printers including the Grabhorn and Allen presses on the West Coast. Edwin and Robert Grabhorn (as will be seen in later pages) were especially enthusiastic about the many Goudy types they used with considerable frequency and with great variety and interest. Many of the Goudy faces have a rugged, non-commercial quality, which appeals to the producer of books in the private press manner, and especially to those who are committed to the handpress.

There are extensive collections of Goudy's work in many libraries. Among them, the New York Public Library is well supplied, as is Vassar College with its Kennerley collection; the very complete Cary collection is held by the Grolier Club in New York; and Goudy's own working library is in Washington at the Library of Congress. A "Goudy Society" with a substantial membership continues to honor the name, as does the Rochester Institute of Technology which awards a "Goudy Medal" each year to distinguished practitioners of typography, European and American.

WILL BRADLEY (1868–1962)

Will Bradley was an extraordinarily talented practitioner of the varied arts of the book in America. He began as a printer's apprentice, then
became a trade compositor, and soon thereafter a free-lance designer.
A typographer of marked originality, he owned and operated a printing
shop and acted as editor and publisher of his own magazine. He designed typefaces and printers' type ornaments, made illustrations for
books and magazines, and painted posters when poster-collecting was
much in fashion. He was the art editor of several American magazines
and art supervisor for Hearst publications and motion picture serials.
He wrote and directed his own motion picture, *Moongold*. He was the
author of published plays, short stories, and a novel.

When a delivery boy, Will Bradley spent his first earnings for a miniature printing press. His father, a cartoonist on a Lynn, Massachusetts,
newspaper, died early from wounds received in the Civil War. After her
husband's death Will's mother took the boy to Ishpeming, a Michigan
mining town, where he went to school for a few more years. At twelve
years of age, with no funds in sight for an art education, he asked to be
allowed to go to work and earn money for the eventual realization of his
dream to become an artist. Will's mother reluctantly agreed. The lad
got a job at the local newspaper. In Bradley's altogether charming and
engrossing *Memories* which will be here much quoted, he tells about
the start of his career in 1880: "You are put to work washing up a Gordon [press]. Then you receive your first lesson in [hand] feeding. There
is power, a small engine mounted on an upright boiler, for the newspaper press. The two jobbers are kicked [foot power]. Having half an
hour of leisure you learn the lay of a lower case beside the window
where you can proudly wave to the schoolchildren as they are going
home to their noon meal. You are now a working man—wages three
dollars a week." The hours were from seven in the morning until six at
night. By the time he was fifteen he was "spoken of as foreman, and
receiving fifteen dollars a week—a man's wages in the 1880's."

At seventeen young Bradley headed for Chicago and the larger world.
There he worked in the printing plants of Rand McNally and of Knight
& Leonard. At the latter establishment he was moved out of the composing room to the office as a full-time typographic designer. The new
invention of photoengraving made possible the reproduction of pen-

79

THE
RENAISSANCE
IN
AMERICAN
PRINTING

WILL
BRADLEY

and-ink drawings. The first halftone plates appeared. Both new processes were used to advantage by Bradley. At twenty-one he set up as an independent designer in Chicago with a studio in the new Caxton building. He bought a foot-operated Golding press but the demands for his designed work prevented him from enjoying the newly bought fonts of his beloved Caslon type. However, just then a young bookkeeper in Chicago named Fred Goudy, who felt the urge to print, gratefully took over the press and equipment. Meanwhile Bradley was making friends and customers and entering the cultural life of a rapidly expanding city that was about to startle the country with the Chicago World's Fair.

Again from Bradley's *Memories*: "Recognized now as a period of ornamentation and bad taste, the Nineties were nevertheless years of leisurely contacts . . . and certainly a friendly Bohemianism seldom known in the rush and drive of today. . . . Eugene Field has just returned from a vacation in Europe and in his column, *Sharps and Flats*, Chicago is reading the first printing of *Wynken, Blynken and Nod*. Way & Williams, publishers, have an office on the floor below my studio. Irving Way, who would rather barter his last shirt for a first edition, his last pair of shoes for a volume from the Kelmscott Press of William Morris, is a frequent and always stimulating visitor. . . . 'Will,' says Irving, 'be over at McClurg's some noon soon, in Millard's rare book department, the "Amen Corner." Field will be there, and Francis Wilson, who is appearing at McVickar's in *The Merry Monarch* and other collectors. Maybe there'll be an opportunity for me to introduce you—and Francis Wilson might ask you to do a poster.'"

Success followed quickly. Bradley had an exhibit at the World's Fair. In addition to book design for Stone & Kimball and Way & Williams, he designed covers for *Harper's Weekly*, *Harper's Bazaar*, *Vogue*, and other magazines. He painted a series of beautiful advertisements for Ault & Wiborg inks, a twenty-eight-sheet playbill for Charles Frohman, and posters for many occasions. Commissioned to design a new cover for the *Inland Printer*, a trade magazine which then covered cultural aspects of printing as well as its sales and profits, Bradley made the revolutionary suggestion of a different cover each month. Twelve were accepted and printed. From one of the covers that contained a panel of lettering, the American Type Founders Company, then under the enlightened presidency of Robert W. Nelson, cut and cast a new typeface called Bradley. It was widely copied. This was the beginning of a very fruitful relationship that lasted for many years and was responsible for other typefaces and a host of decorative florets, ornaments, and type cuts that could soon be found in the cases of almost every printing house in the country. Bradley edited and designed many mailing pieces at Nelson's bidding in 1904 and 1905, including the famous American Type Founders' Chap Books. These gay little booklets showed lively uses of type and ornament which had widespread, if rather temporary, influence on American typography.

THE
RENAISSANCE
IN
AMERICAN
PRINTING

WILL
BRADLEY

In 1895 Bradley established the Wayside Press in Springfield, Massachusetts (plate 28). His printer's device was a dandelion leaf, "a wayside growth." The purpose was to publish a magazine, *Bradley, His Book*, entirely of his own editing and design and printed under his immediate supervision. He had studied colonial American printing at the Boston Public Library's Barton collection and found it "void of beauty-destroying mechanical precision, the most direct, honest, vigorous and imaginative America has ever known—a sane and inspiring model that was to me a liberal education." Bradley's work showed this influence in the bold use of large capital letters for display, in his avoidance of conventional rectangular composition, and in the joyous, youthful innocence which (to the present writer) characterizes much of Bradley's work. Seven issues of the magazine were completed. They were an ambitious undertaking, each of sixty-four pages with sixteen pages of advertisements. The masthead called *Bradley, His Book* "A Magazine of Interesting Reading Interspersed with Various Bits of Art." The promise was more than fulfilled. However, commissions for printed matter, including a first specimen book of Strathmore papers, flooded in, and Bradley found it difficult to say no. An attempt at plant expansion, with increased press equipment and personnel, was too great to be managed, and almost broke Bradley's health. He tried consolidation with the University Press in Cambridge, but this, too, proved to be unsatisfactory. Bradley had, he said, learned his lesson. Thereafter he devoted himself to the more manageable drawing board.

In the thirty-five full years that remained before his retirement, Bradley was a very active, innovative, and dynamic force in magazine layout and design—an area in which American influence was felt throughout the world. He was associated in various capacities, as artist and as art editor, with *Ladies' Home Journal*, *Good Housekeeping*, *Collier's Weekly*, *Cosmopolitan*, and others. A close relationship was later established with William Randolph Hearst that absorbed all of Bradley's time as typographic and art supervisor of the Hearst chain of newspapers, magazines, and motion pictures.

A retrospective exhibition of Bradley's work in its many aspects was held at the Huntington Library in San Marino in 1951. That library and the Metropolitan Museum of Art in New York each hold large collections. The Typophiles published *Will Bradley: His Chap Book* (New York, 1955), which contains Bradley's amplified *Memories*, first printed by Grant Dahlstrom in 1949 at the Castle Press in Pasadena where, in the later years, Bradley occasionally enjoyed the nostalgia of again putting type in the stick. In the active years Bradley developed his ideas and carried out his designs right at the typecase. He made layouts on paper only when his plans were executed outside his own domain. His work was full of gusto, with youthful and joyous exuberance and opulent color. He was said to be as American as the Declaration of Independence. In any event, he was, by his own words, a happy man. His work shows it.

CARL PURINGTON ROLLINS (1880–1960)

A small boy who stole away to watch the printing of the local newspaper in West Newbury, Massachusetts, where he was born; who set up a table-model press in the attic at age twelve; who was business manager of his high-school paper; and who was later stirred by William Morris, should hardly have become anything but a printer. Brought up in a conservative New England background, Carl Purington Rollins read Kropotkin and Ruskin and exchanged Republican Party principles for socialist-craft ideals and convictions. He attended Harvard University, but after three years became impatient for a start in printing. His first love—printing—would sustain him through a long life. In his mature development he gave back to his craft and to his generation a cultivated, heightened respect for workmanship and scholarship. Leaving Harvard he found a job with Heintzemann, the best press in Boston after Merrymount. In the Heintzemann plant he met Henry Lewis Johnson, J. M. Bowles, and soon formed friendships with Updike, Rogers, Dwiggins, and the other talented young men who were already adding to the new excitement in typography.

At the turn of the century, Edward P. Pressey, a graduate of the Harvard Divinity School and a Unitarian minister, felt the call to establish a rural utopian community. In his zeal for a simple and rewarding life, Pressey set up a colony in Montague, Massachusetts, dedicated to spiritual values, to the arts and crafts, and to the beauty of the earth. It was called New Clairvaux after the twelfth-century abbey of Clairvaux founded by Saint Bernard. Schooling and a small magazine were started. Funds were raised to build a shop on the bank of a stream that furnished waterpower for furniture making, basketry, weaving, and printing. Carl Rollins joined Pressey at New Clairvaux in 1903. He liked the countryside with its hills and streams and cultivated valley farms and soon participated in New Clairvaux activities. But he found the vision and the reality too far apart. Utopianism failed here as it had at Brook Farm and other communal societies.

During this period Rollins lost the sight of one eye and was advised to give up printing. He made a trip to Europe. On his return he tried a few jobs which entailed less eye strain, but decided, finally, to gamble his remaining eyesight on the craft that continued to be his absorbing passion. In 1907 he returned to Montague and bought the Dyke mill, which happened to contain an old chaise. In a letter to a friend, Rollins exulted: "a mill, a mill pond, and a chaise—o blessed Trinity." A cooperative craft group without religious or educational involvements was set up, but only printing survived. The Dyke Mill, Incorporated, became The Montague Press. Type and presses were added and commissions were solicited from Boston and New York. Meantime, in Montague, Carl married a schoolteacher who, looking back fifty years later, wrote of these beginnings: "Carl began to establish a reputation as a printer, and colorful days followed. Personalities in the printing world and the book world found their way to Montague. . . . Carl and I were married in December of 1915 and lived in a house that Carl had built when he bought the mill. They were lively days of work and play. From the presses run by water power came work that attracted attention. Pieces were reproduced in such magazines as *Printing Art*. Everything from advertising for the local fish dealer to Francis Thompson's 'Hound of Heaven' was given careful attention and appropriate treatment. . . . Bruce Rogers printed two or three books there, and found the conditions congenial. . . . The Montague Press did not do too badly financially— it was out of the red now and then—but as the first World War wore on, the demands for fine printing began to dry up." Here, in 1918, the Yale University Press stepped in. Rollins accepted the offer to take

THE
RENAISSANCE
IN
AMERICAN
PRINTING

CARL
PURINGTON
ROLLINS

83

THE

RENAISSANCE

IN

AMERICAN

PRINTING

CARL

PURINGTON

ROLLINS

charge of their manufacturing department. His type and presses went with him to New Haven to become the nucleus of the Printing Office of the Yale University Press. A year later Rollins was formally appointed to the post created for him, Printer to Yale University (similar to those at Oxford and Cambridge in England), with the rank of professor.

Rollins stayed at Yale. During the next thirty years he designed the books published by the Press and was responsible for the University's catalogues, brochures, broadsides, bookplates, diplomas, tickets, etc. To all of this, Rollins gave forthright, urbane distinction. He had made the mental adjustments needed for the transition from the hand to the machine processes by which university books and ephemera were produced. An address by him on this subject in 1932 closed with these brave words: "The great fabric of commercialism may crumble away, but the love of reading for pleasure and information and edification will continue. And to restore to the production of reading matter some of the artistic and aesthetic qualities it now lacks, and more, to give human beings pleasure in their work, we must bring about harmony between the hand, which is as old as Adam, and the machine, which in its present development is only a few decades old. We must preserve the machine so far as it is useful, but no farther. We must dominate it and not let it dominate us."

Then in 1958 after his career was behind him, he faced the forces that were transforming his beloved craft. The direct incised impression of letterpress printing, with its subtle, tactile values, was being supplanted by the flat (and often too thin) lay of ink of offset printing. In an affirmative attitude, and without sympathy for sentimental antiquarianism, Rollins predicted that the graphic artists of the future would cope with their new media as did the craftsmen of the past with theirs: "I believe that it is a demonstrable truism that the best work is the result of man's working in his own times, with which he is familiar through long and intimate association, and in which he is cognizant of the spirit of his contemporaries."

At Yale Rollins met the academic community on its own level. He conducted an undergraduate course in bibliography. He was a typographic consultant to the Rutgers University Press, lectured at the University of California and elsewhere, as well as at Yale. For some ten years he wrote a lively, witty, and informative weekly column, "The Compleat Collector," for *The Saturday Review of Literature*, with reviews of the books and reports on the activities of the spirited typographic world through which he moved. He wrote widely and wrote well. Furthermore, Rollins was an excellent designer who, as Printer to Yale, produced a vast amount of work. His typography was solid, mature, and pleasing, with strength and sensitivity. A very knowledgeable English typographer mentioned Rollins' "extraordinarily successful use of Caslon type, to better effect than any of his contemporaries that I can call to mind." His profound respect for literature evoked a logical and forthright clarity in his handling of type. In upholding these typographic virtues and making them evident, Rollins' impact was wide and clear, especially on the many university presses from coast to coast that became a vital force in American publishing. The high standards of bookmaking maintained by these learned presses bear a large measure of debt to the inspiration of Carl Rollins.

A few of Rollins' own favorites among his large book production are *Old Houses of Connecticut* by Bertha Trowbridge (1922) and *Horace Walpole's Correspondence* (1937), both published by the Yale University Press; Stevenson's *A Lodging for the Night*, Grolier Club, New York (1923); Thoreau's *On the Duty of Civil Disobedience*, from his own handpress At the Sign of the Chorobates (1928); Whittier's *Snowbound* (1930) and several other volumes for the Limited Editions Club, New York; and *Wine Making for the Amateur* (plate 43) by R. Seldon Rose (1930), for the members of the Bacchus Club in New Haven. Dartmouth, Yale, and the Grolier Club held exhibitions of Rollins' work. Yale conferred an honorary Doctorate of Letters on her adopted son in 1949, and the American Institute of Graphic Arts awarded its medal in recognition of Rollins' contributions to craftsmanship and scholarship in printing.

THOMAS MAITLAND CLELAND (1880–1964)

T. M. Cleland was one of the "heroic generation" of designers and printers born between 1860 and 1890 who played their different roles in the shifting typographic scenes of the years ahead. Son of a physician, Tom Cleland grew up in the Chelsea district on the west side of New York. He attended kindergarten in an upstairs room of the ornate, mid-Victorian Grand Opera House on Eighth Avenue and Twenty-third Street, built by the financial buccaneer James Fisk at the height of his gaudy career. This building with its large auditorium may have had a profound influence on a sensitive boy whose ultimate career as an artist was compounded of a romantic and histrionic temperament tied

THE
RENAISSANCE
IN
AMERICAN
PRINTING

CARL
PURINGTON
ROLLINS

THE
RENAISSANCE
IN
AMERICAN
PRINTING

T. M.
CLELAND

to an exquisite sense of craft and the capacity for unremitting labor. At fifteen Tom quit school to attend an art academy which he left within a few months to take a job in a small printing shop where he learned to set type and run a press. But after working hours the young man who would not stay in school burned with enthusiasm for the opera and for books. The pageantry of Wagnerian music and Arthurian idylls especially touched his soul. One day, having spent several hours gazing at a Kelmscott Chaucer in Scribner's bookstore window on Fifth Avenue, he was invited in by a kind young clerk. Here a new friend (it was Lewis Hatch, who later opened his own excellent bookshop) introduced Tom to the glory of illustrated books from private presses. The old Lenox Library opened the way to illuminated manuscripts and early printed masterpieces. During these growing years Tom brought orders to his employer for printed matter which he designed and embellished. And in the parental basement he set up a foot-operated press for privately printed books. One of these, Tennyson's *Lady of Shalott*, attracted some admirers in Boston who urged Cleland to establish his press there, in Cornhill, a street already associated with trade in books and that gave the press its name. After printing three small books, the Cornhill Press closed for lack of support. Its chief benefit to Cleland was the start of a friendship with D. B. Updike that nourished a lifetime of personal and professional association.

Cleland returned to New York where he was commissioned by the Bruce Type Foundry (later absorbed by the American Type Founders) to design an ornamental typeface that was baptized Della Robbia. Although quite successful as to sales, Cleland later was ashamed to acknowledge its paternity. Meantime the professional theatre exerted its pull, and Cleland won a scholarship for the American Academy of Dramatic Arts. On completion of the course, and after a period of not very successful stage and ballet design and production, the graphic arts drew him back once again to his drawing board as a free-lance artist, and to the printing press. In 1904, during a trip to Europe, Cleland succumbed to the romantic ornament of the Italian and French Renaissance and to the opulent rococo decoration of the eighteenth century, which dominated all his succeeding work. Cleland's architectural sense of space probably stemmed from the British brothers Adam.

In 1907–1908 he assumed the art-editorship of *McClure's* magazine which he promptly redesigned. Then followed years when Cleland

86

emerged as a gifted artist adept in drawings for commerce that expressed "irreproachable elegance." During a period of great industrial expansion and wealth, Cleland produced elaborate catalogues, brochures, and advertisements for expensive automobiles; menus and wine lists for high-priced hotels and restaurants; a miscellany of bookplates, Christmas cards, calendars, etc., for collectors; typographic ornaments and decorative initial letters for typefounders; and, among much other work, a remarkable *Grammar of Color* for the Strathmore Paper Company and posters and catalogues for the Metropolitan Museum of Art. Much of this output was set in type and printed on Cleland's own presses. The major pieces were collected and celebrated in a sumptuous, colorful, quarto volume, *The Decorative Work of T. M. Cleland*, issued in 1929 after "five years of preparation and labor" at the Pynson Printers in New York. Despite the acclaim with which this substantial volume was greeted, it marked the end of Cleland's career in advertising. The exquisite labor and craftsmanship that he had poured into commercial art landed in thousands of wastebaskets. He sold his printing equipment and planned to spend future efforts on less ephemeral workmanship.

In the late 1920's, as Art Director of *Fortune* magazine, Cleland was responsible for its sophisticated appearance. Among other assignments involving periodical design, his most stimulating experience came with the typographic planning and direction in 1939–1940 of the newspaper *P.M.* Cleland's first complete book illustration may be seen in *The Life and Opinions of Tristram Shandy*, with line drawings, issued in 1930 by the Limited Editions Club for its subscribers. A close, collaborative relationship with George Macy, Director of the Club, resulted in seven more books illustrated by Cleland in various media including watercolor. Books were also designed and illustrated for the Overbrook Press, including a charming *Sentimental Journey* in 1936 (plate 41) and a plush *Manon Lescaut* in 1958.

Cleland's deepest instincts lay in the past when privileged and elegant people lived in elegant houses. He was an eighteenth-century artist-craftsman in everything he touched, including the letters he wrote with his beautiful calligraphic hand. He was intolerant and contemptuous of modern art and defended his convictions about current bookmaking, with stinging sarcasm and pungent wit, in two public addresses. *Harsh Words*, spoken before the American Institute of Graphic Arts in New York in 1940, was printed in the same year by the Typophiles. "Progress

87

in the Graphic Arts," a speech at the Newberry Library on the occasion of the opening of a Cleland exhibition in 1948, was printed in the Library's *Bulletin* of 1949, and then reprinted during the following year by the Overbrook Press in Stamford, Connecticut.

In a review of Cleland's work in the *Fleuron* No. VII (London, 1930), D. B. Updike wrote: "Just as an actor sees the dramatic possibilities in the part he is to play, so Cleland sees the decorative possibilities in the particular school of decoration in which he is, like an actor, for the moment 'cast.' He seizes, therefore, the most outstanding characteristics of the style that he has chosen to work in, and to make them 'carry across the footlights' he slightly exaggerates them. The result is usually charming. It amuses those who know, astonishes those who do not, and delights both the one and the other."

WILLIAM ADDISON DWIGGINS (1880–1956)

Dwiggins was a painter and wood-carver, a writer, calligrapher, typographer, and printer, and during the first twenty years of his professional career a very successful designer for advertising. Dissatisfied with advertising's waste and impermanence, he turned to the book, its design, decoration, and illustration, both for trade publications and limited editions; and to the design of type. He wrote tales of fantasy and adventure. With his fertile pen he fought for higher standards of integrity and workmanship in book publishing and book production. He pleaded for good taste in the graphic arts with, for example, proposals for a new approach to the design of American postage stamps and toward a reform in the appearance of the paper currency. Withal, Dwiggins was a gentle, a modest, and a social being, with a delicious sense of whimsy which leavened his professional work and his many avocational activities.

William Addison Dwiggins was born in Martinsville, Ohio, in 1880, the son of a country doctor of Quaker background, and the grandson on his mother's side of an itinerant Baptist minister who, according to family legend, traveled across Ohio with a printing press. At nineteen years of age, thanks to an uncle's generosity, young Dwiggins went to Chicago for an education in art. He attended the Frank Holme school, where he studied lettering under Goudy and became interested in printing. Until 1903 he did miscellaneous artwork for advertisers in

Chicago, then returned to Cambridge, Ohio (his mother's birthplace), and there opened a small press which soon proved inadequate as a source of livelihood. In 1904 the Goudys, who had moved to Hingham, Massachusetts, invited Dwiggins and his new wife to join them.

Hingham, where they settled for life, soon became home for the Dwigginses. Meantime Dwiggins obtained some commissions from advertising agencies in Boston and rented a small studio in Cornhill. Through the Boston Society of Printers he met Updike, Rollins, and other congenial colleagues in this hub of typographic activity. Dwiggins prospered, and the many-sided characteristics of later years were already to be seen. John Goss, who shared a studio with Dwiggins for some years in Boston before World War I, wrote that Dwiggins "had a great appreciation of Oriental design, French and Italian etchings, Pillemont and Piranesi. Most of his work was in black and white, small drawings, decorations, and lettering with little chance to use colors, but it was at about this time [1915] that he made the two very beautiful illustrations for *The Fabulist*, done with stencils in several colors. . . . He also made a few woodcuts . . . printed in black, and a print in three or four colors of a kind of Tibetan subject with figures. This was one of those that he called 'graphic responses to verbal stimuli,' cut on the side of the plank with knife and gouges. I think that most of the work was done in Hingham, as his time in Boston was taken up with his many commissions."

C. Chester Lane, Director of the Harvard University Press, enlisted Dwiggins' help on several occasions. When Lane left for service in the army, the Syndics of the Press appointed Dwiggins acting director during Lane's absence. Work for advertising accounts continued into the early 1920's, but before finally turning his back on that mercurial world, Dwiggins wrote and illustrated an excellent manual, *Layout in Advertising*, published in 1928 by Harper and Brothers. The book ran into several editions and was reissued in 1948.

In 1923 Dwiggins made calls on several New York publishers. Frederic G. Melcher, editor of *Publishers' Weekly*, himself an aficionado of fine printing, took Dwiggins to meet Alfred A. Knopf. From this meeting grew an extraordinarily fruitful relationship between publisher and book designer that gradually consumed half of Dwiggins' working time for the rest of his life, and that had a stimulating effect on American trade-book production. Altogether, Dwiggins designed almost three

THE
RENAISSANCE
IN
AMERICAN
PRINTING

W. A.
DWIGGINS

THE
RENAISSANCE
IN
AMERICAN
PRINTING

W. A.
DWIGGINS

hundred books with the Borzoi publisher's mark. The first such Knopf book was Willa Cather's *My Mortal Enemy*, published in 1926. It delighted the author.

Dwiggins was a highly literate person with respect for the dynamics of language. His handling of text was, therefore, clear and conservative. But he believed that books should be decorated. His ornamentation usually consisted of mechanical abstractions in floral patterns built up from intricate celluloid stencils he had cut. It has been said that these floral designs grew only in Dwiggins' mind, not in anyone's well-tended garden. Other admirers have used such descriptive terms as "rhythmic repetition," "space music," or "classic forms reduced to geometric essentials." They were best seen on book jackets and bindings, with more restraint needed for title pages and chapter openings. The hand-lettered, ornamented Dwiggins' bindings are especially handsome and appropriate. This visual exuberance did not please all authors. Mr. Knopf, occasionally caught between an irate author and a stubborn designer, favored the designer where possible. A few of the many Knopf books characteristically of Dwiggins' design are: *Collected Poems of Elinor Wylie* (1933); *Supplement One: The American Language* by H. L. Mencken (1936); *The Sea of Grass* by Conrad Richter (1937); Goethe's *Faust* (1941); and *Kristin Lavransdatter* by Sigrid Undset (1946). There were, also, books for several other publishers. Two noteworthy volumes were done for Random House: Stevenson's *The Strange Case of Dr. Jekyll and Mr. Hyde* was designed in 1929; H. G. Wells' *The Time Machine* (1931) (plate 44) has a daring double-spread title page combining many of Dwiggins' stenciled patterns. There were enchanting title pages for two books by Archibald MacLeish in 1926: *Nobodaddy*, published by Dunster House in Cambridge, and *Streets in the Moon*, issued by Houghton, Mifflin; also, among many others, an Edgar Allan Poe for the Lakeside Press, Chicago, (1930); *Travels of Marco Polo* for the Printing House of Leo Hart in Rochester, New York (1933); and *One More Spring* by Robert Nathan printed and published by the Overbrook Press in 1935. *One More Spring* was illustrated with chapter headings of highly stylized human figures, with rather mystical or abstract backgrounds, printed in the cool colors that blend well with type. A selective checklist of Dwiggins' writings and the books he designed and illustrated, compiled by Dorothy Abbe and Rollo Silver, is included in a two-volume chapbook, *Postscripts on Dwiggins*, published by the Typophiles in 1960, with essays on the many phases of Dwiggins' career by fourteen of his contemporaries. The several quotations in the present text have been drawn from these *Postscripts*. An appreciative essay on Dwiggins by Philip Hofer, with a generous group of illustrations in color, appeared in *The Dolphin* No. II (1935).

THE
RENAISSANCE
IN
AMERICAN
PRINTING

W. A.
DWIGGINS

The eight books that Dwiggins designed and decorated and illustrated for the Limited Editions Club are among his principal achievements. In them one immediately recognizes the hand of a person for whom books were a deep and joyous experience. Dwiggins resisted the temptation to make large books. These were twelvemos and octavos, made to be read, with an irrepressible flow of appropriate ornamentation and illustration. The first, Daudet's *Tartarin of Tarascon*, was completed in 1935, the last, Meredith's *The Shaving of Shagpat*, in 1955. The three-volume edition of Balzac's *Droll Stories* (1931), in a handy 5½-by-8-inch format, is especially enjoyable. In retrospect, George Macy, Director of the Club, wrote with good reason: "If there is a series of heavens to which books may go, I think each copy of this book will eventually be assigned to the topmost of these heavens. It represents, to me, the complete successful consummation of the arts of the book. The stories themselves chuckle. In this edition, the translation chuckles; the typography chuckles; the decorations chuckle."

In discussing Dwiggins' work, George Salter, himself a distinguished European graphic artist who became an American citizen, wrote: "Dwiggins' work has always impressed me as more truly American than the work of any other graphic artist in this country. It is without visible signs of foreign influence. There is no traceable movement leading to him. Cultures of the past and cultures of distant lands find their way into his work but as they become tangible images their stylistic expression becomes Dwiggins. . . . The shape of his ornament glides from illustrative through decorative to abstract form, and it then goes further, to concrete letter form. Thus the cycle closes itself. There is, in fact, very little separation in his expression. An abstract ornament turns into a human figure before one's eyes." To this may be added Dwiggins' own statement about himself, expressed through the pen of Hermann Püterschein: "He [Dwiggins] creates an illusion of machines. But his machines are a masquerade. There are men inside them."

In *Layout in Advertising* Dwiggins had written that "Gothic capitals are indispensable, but there are no good Gothic capitals, the type found-

THE
RENAISSANCE
IN
AMERICAN
PRINTING

W. A.
DWIGGINS

ers will do a service to advertising if they will provide a Gothic of good design." ("Gothic" was a term curiously designating sans-serif type.) Harry L. Gage of the Mergenthaler Linotype Company was quick to respond. He wrote to Dwiggins: "What do you mean by good design? And having defined it, would you like to illustrate it? And if so, would you like to see it cut for Linotype?" Dwiggins accepted the challenge. A few weeks later trial characters were submitted and accepted. This exchange brought about the successful sans-serif series known as Metro-black and Metrolite, and the beginning of a very congenial and productive twenty-seven-year relationship with the Linotype organization, particularly with C. H. Griffith, Director of Typographic Development. Eleven type designs were cut as experimental fonts, and an assortment of type ornaments, known when completed as Caravan Decorations. Two of the typefaces that reached the market, Electra and Caledonia, were very widely used in book production and for general printed matter. In the year 1947, for example, ten of the A.I.G.A. "Fifty Books of the Year" were set in Caledonia. It has continued to be a strong favorite. Caledonia stems out of the rugged eighteenth-century Scotch Roman and the more sophisticated Bulmer designed by William Martin about 1790. With its classical background intact, the contemporary virtue of Caledonia lies in the added skills of a twentieth-century graphic artist, designed with the Linotype expressly in view. The italic is especially successful, overcoming many of the difficulties inherent in the Linotype machine in adapting conventional italics to its mechanical functions. A few sentences from Caledonia's articulate designer may well be quoted from the brochure that introduced the type. Dwiggins said: "About the 'liveliness of action' that one sees in the Martin letters, and to a less degree (one modestly says) in Caledonia: that quality is in the curves—the way they get away from the straight stems with a calligraphic flick, and in the nervous angle on the underside of the arches as they descend to the right. The finishing strokes at the bottoms of the letters, cut straight across without 'brackets' making sharp angles with the upright stems, add 'snap' to many of the old 'modern face' designs—and why not Caledonia." In Dwiggins' type designs a practiced eye can see the lively "flick" of the calligrapher. In his calligraphy one finds the discipline of type. This reciprocal relationship buttressed all Dwiggins' extensive lettering, whether for stationery, announcements, or magazine covers, such as for *Harper's* and *The Atlantic Monthly.*

Dwiggins' pen was a graceful accomplice to an active mind. His extensive correspondence with publishers Knopf and Macy, as well as with Linotype's Griffith, was a running, articulate commentary on the daily work in hand. In addition to fanciful stories, he wrote on the "Shapes of Roman Letters," "The Structure of a Book," "A Primer of Printers' Ornament," to name but a few of the many excursions into the highways and byways of the printed word that appeared in trade papers, typographic journals, and literary magazines. He also published through the exclusive Society of Calligraphers, founded by himself, along with eighteen members he appointed. Dwiggins was scribe, secretary, and absolute factotum. With unabashed nepotism, he installed as president his fictitious alter ego Hermann Püterschein, who then officially signed the Transactions of the Society. Dwiggins and L. B. Siegfried together conducted and wrote about an "Investigation into the Physical Properties of Books." There were, also, books by Dwiggins, in addition to *Layout in Advertising. Paraphs* by "Hermann Püterschein" (1928) and *Millennium I* (1945) were both published by Knopf; *Toward a Reform of the Paper Currency* was published for subscribers by the Limited Editions Club in 1932. The interested reader is referred to the check list of writings in the *Postscripts* already mentioned, and to another Typophile Chap Book, *MSS BY WAD*, "Being a Collection of the Writings of Dwiggins on Various Subjects." A bibliography of the books designed by Dwiggins was compiled by Dwight Agner, printed and published by him at the Press of the Night Owl, Baton Rouge, Louisiana (1974).

THE
RENAISSANCE
IN
AMERICAN
PRINTING

W. A.
DWIGGINS

Prodigal imagination found expression in the wonderful twelve-inch-high puppets Dwiggins carved for the marionette theatre he built in the basement of his studio, and in the joyous productions there given for friends and neighbors. Every detail of production—lighting, costumes, and music—was done with professional skill. Even the tickets of admission were designed and printed by Püterschein-Hingham, the private press operated by Dwiggins and Dorothy Abbe, on the floor above. Mrs. Dwiggins, who made the puppets' costumes from her husband's designs, wrote of these extracurricular activities: "Of course the Manuscript Club made its home around the big fireplace in the little theatre for many years, the theatre's own business hummed constantly, many other groups met upstairs . . . here was the setting, for nineteen years, of a man who loved his work so much that no day was long enough." In *The Dwiggins Marionettes* (New York: Harry N. Abrams, 1970) Dorothy Abbe, apprentice, associate, and member of the Dwiggins house-hold for ten years, has provided a fine record in a handsome book of 240 pages, with more than 400 illustrations, of the enchanted world of the miniature actors and actresses created by Dwiggins. The proscenium and the stage with the marionettes and related appurtenances now have a permanent home in the Boston Public Library.

Dwiggins was awarded an honorary Master of Arts degree by Harvard University and was the recipient of the medal of the American Institute of Graphic Arts. There were many exhibitions. The principal record exists in the extensive collection in the Boston Public Library. Here in the Dwiggins Room may be seen the fruits of the work of an abundant life.

RUDOLPH RUZICKA (1883–)

Rudolph Ruzicka is one of the several versatile artists born in the nineteenth century who devoted their talents to the arts of the book. Book design and illustration, calligraphy and lettering, bookplates and inscriptions, and three completed typefaces were among Ruzicka's gifts that added luster to fine printing in America. Born in Bohemia in a family with a craft background, Rudolph was brought to Chicago by his parents in the early 1890's. Totally without English, the Czech boy of eleven was put into the bottom grade, but, aided by an active mind and his early capacity to draw, he was pushed through seven grades in three years. Three years was all the American schooling enjoyed by a youngster who was later esteemed as a learned humanist by all who have known him. When thirteen years of age, he attended drawing classes on Saturday afternoons at Hull House. At fourteen he went to work at a commercial engraving house, cutting on wood. His evenings were spent in classes at the Chicago Art Institute.

In 1903 Ruzicka moved to New York and worked for a time in an advertising agency. Off hours were spent wandering along the East River where he found interesting subject matter in the picturesque life of the waterfront. In his apartment, nearby, he set up a press for the printing of his wood engravings in black-and-white and in color. The press had become an essential part of the equipment that went with him wherever he might move. He spent as much time, he has said, over press, paper, and ink as on design, drawing, and engraving.

In 1907 Ruzicka first met Daniel Berkeley Updike in New York. A few years later the meeting was repeated in Updike's office at The Merrymount Press in Boston. A professional friendship of great importance to both men was then begun which lasted for thirty years. The beautiful New Year's cards already mentioned in the pages about Updike were begun in 1912 and continued until 1942. Never forgotten, they were gathered together in 1975 and made into an attractive book, appropriately entitled *Boston*, with a descriptive and historical text by Walter Muir Whitehill, published in Boston by David R. Godine.

Ruzicka's first important contribution to book illustration came in 1915 when, after two years of preparation, he completed thirty colored wood engravings for the Grolier Club publication *New York*. The volume also contained a scholarly historical treatise by Ruzicka on color printing from wood engravings, and "Prose Impressions of the City" by Walter Prichard Eaton. Two hundred fifty copies were printed from type and from the original wood blocks on French handmade paper, and three copies with progressive proofs on Japanese vellum. Except for the ten full-page illustrations that were printed in Paris, the edition was produced by the De Vinne Press in New York. The significance of the publication was noted by Henry W. Kent of the Metropolitan Museum, then President of the Grolier Club: "This book was planned with the purpose of showing, by example, the beauty and appropriateness of woodcuts in color and as a matter of illustration. Its issue came at a time when the photo-mechanical processes were claiming an over-emphasized importance . . . we must keep in mind the fact, that, except for revivication by this new form of printing in color, the use of the woodcut in books was on the decline, hard-pressed at first by the less exacting forms of the graphic arts, the etching and the lithograph, which during the last part of the nineteenth century became the popular mediums for use by artists. . . ."

The volume on New York inspired the members of the Carteret Book Club of Newark, New Jersey, to commission a similar publication. Ruzicka justified their hopes that he would find beauty and some grandeur where most people saw only industrial blight or, perhaps, nothing. In a generous quarto volume entitled *Newark: A Series of Engravings on Wood* (plate 33) with the text again by Walter Pritchard Eaton, there were five full-page illustrations with color, printed by hand by Ruzicka, for the edition of two hundred copies. Type and twelve black-and-white engravings were produced by Updike. Among the many other

THE
RENAISSANCE
IN
AMERICAN
PRINTING

RUDOLPH
RUZICKA

THE
RENAISSANCE
IN
AMERICAN
PRINTING

RUDOLPH
RUZICKA

Ruzicka books of these decades, a few may be selected for mention. *Fountains of Papal Rome*, in wood engravings, was issued by Charles Scribner's Sons in 1915. Two publications celebrating the fiftieth anniversary in 1916 of Vassar College were the joint effort of Ruzicka and Updike. Copper engravings were made to illustrate *The Fables of Jean de La Fontaine* (1930) for the Limited Editions Club. When William A. Kittredge of the Lakeside Press in Chicago invited Ruzicka to design and illustrate Thoreau's *Walden*, the artist moved to Concord, Massachusetts, with his family for several months. From this close acquaintance with Walden Pond and its environs came an octavo edition of one thousand copies with thirty-three black-and-white brush drawings reproduced by photoengraving, printed and published by the Lakeside Press in 1930.

Ruzicka's very beautiful bookplates, many of them engraved on wood, are eloquent expressions of the skill and felicity of his lettering and design. Medallions also came from his workshop. These talents were recognized by C. H. Griffith of the Mergenthaler Linotype Company who commissioned Ruzicka to provide designs for a new book type. The face, called Fairfield, was completed and issued in 1940. It is a classical alphabet stemming from the personal calligraphy of the designer. Ten years later a somewhat heavier version came along as Fairfield Medium. In 1951 Mergenthaler issued Primer, another typeface from Ruzicka's drawings. Primer is an even-colored type, full-bodied, rather traditional in feeling, with reduced contrast between thick and thin strokes, intended primarily for high-speed production of books, magazines, and newspapers.

Rudolph Ruzicka, still at work at this writing and full of honors, continues his distinguished career in Hanover, New Hampshire, in close relationship with the Dartmouth College Library where, in 1968, the Friends of the Library published a portfolio, *Studies in Type Design*, by Ruzicka.

Until the present mid-century, the production of metal type and printing by direct impression were still major printing processes. But during the next quarter-century (1950–1975), photoelectronic type composition and offset printing have made such enormous technological advances that, at this writing in 1976, printing from type metal is rapidly becoming obsolete. However, it should be emphasized that despite the revolutionary changes that have occurred, the twenty-six characters of the alphabet remain the essential and fundamental historical constant on which printing depends and by which civilization survives. The letters of the alphabet are wonderful and complex forms. They were first written, then drawn by hand for production into type. There have been no fundamental changes in basic letterforms since the tenth century. So long as some men will pursue the intangibles, and so long as the artist-craftsman will not blindly accept whatever is at hand, so long will individual letterforms yield to subtle changes in the pursuit of beauty and of function. In the spirit of this long tradition, artists of the book, in the period we have been discussing, produced new typefaces on both sides of the Atlantic. The American designers, as we have seen, were Bradley, Rogers, Goudy, Cleland, Dwiggins, and Ruzicka.

JOHN HENRY NASH (1871–1947)

Almost alone, John Henry Nash carried the torch for fine printing in California during the first two decades of the present century. Throughout his career he produced large and elaborate books inspired by medieval illuminated manuscripts and by the grandeur of early printed folios. He was at work in a period that he himself helped to create, when the collecting and patronage of sumptuous books and ephemera rewarded the maker and enhanced the buyer thereof. He was a dedicated craftsman. He was, too, an extraordinary promoter—of lavish printing and of himself—successful in both areas.

Nash was born in Canada, the son of a mechanical engineer who had hoped the boy would follow in the paternal footsteps. But youthful inclination ruled otherwise, and Nash was apprenticed in the Toronto printing house of James Murray & Company. A career that would later stay on course was interrupted for three years when Nash became a professional bicycle rider and covered much of Canada and the United States. He returned to Canada to work as a compositor for another few years, then emigrated to Denver, Colorado, for a few months and arrived in San Francisco in 1895. As a compositor, his first job was with the Hicks-Judd Company. During the next twenty-one years Nash worked in a number of San Francisco's printing establishments. He was employed twice by the Stanley-Taylor Company. There were short-lived partnerships in the Twentieth Century Press and the Blair-Murdock Company. In between came an arrangement with Paul Elder and

97

THE

RENAISSANCE

IN

AMERICAN

PRINTING

JOHN

HENRY

NASH

the Tomoyé Press for the production of gift books to be sold, together with pottery, jewelry, and antiques, in Elder's retail store. After the earthquake and fire of 1906, Elder and Nash moved their operations to New York for three years, where Nash met De Vinne and formed a close bond with Henry Lewis Bullen, Director of the American Type Founders' excellent library and museum. Bullen became an ardent and outspoken Nash admirer.

After returning to San Francisco and a breakup with Elder, Nash's most productive relationship was begun in 1911 with the firm of Taylor and Taylor, Inc., themselves excellent printers. With the new corporate name of Taylor, Nash & Taylor, Nash became vice-president in charge of the "Fine Work Department" which gave him substantial scope and the opportunity to advance his own name. After four years, the partnership ended under stress and strain of personalities. Nash made one more brief connection (with the Blair-Murdock Company) before he set up on his own. These years of Nash's development and his later years of success are covered in Robert D. Harlan's full-length volume, *John Henry Nash: The Biography of a Career*, published by the University of California Press in 1970.

Finally at age forty-five, in 1916, Nash set up his own printing office and composing room. During the years that followed he added a very extensive selection of type for hand-setting. He never established a pressroom, preferring always to have presswork done in outside plants where, however, he achieved excellent workmanship by direct supervision. In this, as in other areas of production, Nash was aided by his remarkably competent chief shop assistant, Joseph FauntLeRoy. Established on his own, success came quickly. Several of the San Francisco booksellers and a number of bibliophiles and collectors commissioned books. Large business enterprises, such as the Zellerbach Paper Company, valued printing with an aura of elegance and were willing to pay for it. As the years of recognition brought substantial financial rewards, Nash built a library of masterpieces of printing from the fifteenth century to the contemporary English private presses, which he displayed elegantly in a handsome room in his printing office.

Nash was one of the founding members of the Book Club of California which came into existence thanks to an unsuccessful attempt to include an exhibition of books in the Panama-Pacific-International Exposition. The Club has been a boon to California printers and an institution of importance in the cultural life of the West Coast. Eight of the Club's first ten books were designed and printed by Nash. Its second publication was Edwin Markham's *The Man with the Hoe* (1916). With only fourteen pages of text, Nash produced a tall, thin, and elaborate book in three colors on a heavy handmade paper, with large floral borders surrounded by other ruled borders. Nash's own copy bears the inscription from the author: "My congratulations: you have enfolded the Hoe-man in a glory of print, a raiment of kings."

In 1914 Nash requested and received permission from T. J. Cobden-Sanderson, master of the Doves Press in England, to reprint *The Ideal Book*. This romantic and reverential text by Cobden-Sanderson, which propounds precepts for the book beautiful, fell in with Nash's own exalted ideas. In 1916 on his own premises, Nash completed *The Ideal Book* in folio size, printed in the new Cloister Light Face type from the American Type Founders Company. Under the influence of the austere Doves Press books, Nash's typography was elegant and restrained. Cobden-Sanderson responded to the copy he received with unstinted praise ("I am enchanted with it") in a letter to Nash that was printed by the Book Club of California in its prospectus to members. The episode gave Nash international status. Thirteen years later Nash again expressed his homage in an across-the-seas exchange with a volume, *Cobden-Sanderson and the Doves Press*, subtitled "The History of the Press and the Story of Its Types Told by Alfred W. Pollard; the Character of the Man Set Forth by his Faithful Scribe Edward Johnston. With the Ideal Book or Book Beautiful by Thomas James Cobden-Sanderson, and a list of the Doves Press Printings." Again the example of the Doves Press provided Nash with the model for a volume that added significantly to his reputation.

Nash had an evangelical attitude toward printing. He considered it a major art comparable to sculpture and painting, and he thought of himself as an artist on that level. He could make elephant folios of slight and insignificant texts for delighted patrons. He found clients among men of great wealth who accepted him on his own evaluation and gave him regal patronage. In 1914 while still part of Taylor, Nash & Taylor, he had printed the first volume of the catalogue (for the bookseller John Howell) of the library of Charles W. Clark. It was completed by Nash in his own printing office, in seven volumes, competently bibliophilic, and generously supported by the collector. Nash's

THE
RENAISSANCE
IN
AMERICAN
PRINTING

JOHN
HENRY
NASH

THE

RENAISSANCE

IN

AMERICAN

PRINTING

JOHN

HENRY

NASH

chief patron and benefactor was William Andrews Clark, Jr., who, with his brother Charles, was heir to a Montana copper fortune. A Phi Beta Kappa graduate of the University of Virginia, Clark was a patron of the arts who built a fine, selective library, primarily in English literature, now handsomely housed in the William Andrews Clark Library, University of California in Los Angeles.

Clark entrusted Nash with the production of a catalogue which ultimately involved twenty substantial quarto volumes. They are a credit to the collector and to the zealous printer. But the real bonanzas for Nash were the annual Clark Christmas books made from one of the collector's favorite rare first editions. The start was made in 1922 with Percy Bysshe Shelley's *Adonais*. The pattern that was followed required Nash to provide a facsimile of the original. To this was added an elaborate quarto volume on the finest handmade paper, with an engraved portrait, an introductory text by Clark, some bibliographical data, and a large-size resetting of the original in type. The two volumes were inserted in a sturdy compartmented case. The series reached its extravagant height in 1929 with John Dryden's *All for Love*, from the Clark library, said to contain the finest Dryden collection in America. The usual procedure was followed except for the addition of sixteen color plates of murals from Clark's library. Nash's invoice, reproduced in the Harlan biography, shows a charge of $37,500—for 250 copies. Clark thoroughly enjoyed the production of these sumptuous books (as well as ephemera) which enshrined his name. As evidence of Clark's public approbation, the first of the Christmas books was dedicated by him "To John Henry Nash, whose Preeminence in the Art of Typography is internationally known, whose finished works are unexcelled, whose devotion to his art should be emulated by all in the craft, whose knowledge of printing should be a source of inspiration for others to acquire, and which should be conducive to their renewed efforts in behalf of the typographical art. . . ."

A commission from the Grolier Club in 1921 was welcome recognition that Nash's reputation had become nationwide. He was selected as one of six of the "most prominent" American designer-printers to produce a book of their own choosing. The others came from the east: Goudy, Gilliss, Cleland, Rollins, and Rogers. Nash's choice was Maurice Hewletts' *Quattrocentisteria*. The edition was in the typical Nash manner—which is what the Club expected and why he was among the chosen.

Starting in 1923 Nash labored continuously over his best work, a three-volume edition of Dante's *Divine Comedy* (plate 42) which he completed and himself published in 1929. The translation was by another Californian, Melville Best Anderson of Stanford University, who contributed an introduction which constituted a fourth volume. Nash apparently approached this undertaking with uncommon humility, aware that this should become his *magnum opus*. In his sumptuous prospectus he stated: "For more than five years now, I have been reverently turning the pages of the great poet, striving always to make this presentation of his masterpiece a monument alike to him, to his translator, and to the printing art. It has been an experience rich in intellectual rewards." The Dante pages are nine by fourteen inches, set in Cloister Light Face type, with thin blue printed columnar rules in the manner of early printed books in which scribes drew rules, usually in red, to simulate earlier manuscript volumes. Nash's Dante is an admirable performance in the private press tradition of tall books, magnificent paper, vellum binding, and superb workmanship throughout.

Newspaper tycoon William Randolph Hearst wished to have a memorial volume made to honor his mother, Phoebe Apperson Hearst. Nash was the obvious choice as printer. Opulence was desired and Nash delivered it in 1928 at a charge of forty thousand dollars for an edition of one thousand copies of a rather slim book. Some five years later, during the depth of the Depression, Hearst ordered a matching volume about his father, and at a matching price. It is revealing as an insight into Nash's life style that a personal friendship developed with Hearst as it had with William Andrews Clark, Jr.

With the close of the prosperous twenties, the stock-market crash in 1929, the drop in copper prices, and the spread of the Depression, Nash joined the rest of the world in greatly curtailed activities. Although many years remained to him and many books were to be done, Nash's best and most characteristic work had been accomplished. Through the thirties he produced four books for the Limited Editions Club, a few more volumes for Clark and for the Book Club of California, the second biography for Hearst, a bibliography of his own press compiled by his librarian Nell O'Day, and other commissions. He spent the years from 1927 to 1942 at the University of Oregon, where he received an honorary degree, taught his gospel of elegant printing, and saw a press established in his name. Despite all this he felt himself exiled from his

THE
RENAISSANCE
IN
AMERICAN
PRINTING

JOHN
HENRY
NASH

THE

RENAISSANCE

IN

AMERICAN

PRINTING

JOHN

HENRY

NASH

favored urban setting in San Francisco. On his return to California, his library was bought by admirers for the University in Berkeley. During his last years Nash was made welcome at the press of Lawton Kennedy where the old pro again enjoyed putting his hand to type.

In appraising the work of John Henry Nash one must acknowledge a large body of craftsmanship on a very high level. Although he was a contemporary of the men who made typographic history in Boston, he was not influenced by them. Nash drew his inspiration from the past. His work was essentially derivative, with a style of his own that was, at best, a too-lush interpretation of tradition. The mark of a great talent is the capacity to be inventive, to make some original contribution of value to one's own time and to future practitioners, whether of design, of scholarship, or otherwise. This Nash did not do. He confused pomp and ostentation with beauty. He made monumental books for clients who were pleased to mistake size and ornamentation for quality and originality. Nevertheless, Nash was a valued member of his community. His lusty passion for elegant printing was infectious and brought response from collectors, librarians, booksellers, industrialists, and others. And he widened paths for a new generation of dedicated designers and printers.

WILLIAM EDWIN RUDGE (1876–1931)

William Edwin Rudge started work at the age of eleven in his father's small printing shop in crowded downtown New York City. That was in 1887 when type was still set by hand, the job presses were foot-operated, and the light came from kerosene lamps. The new boy was the "printer's devil." Thirty-three years later he would open a handsome modern plant in his own attractive low, stone building, surrounded by grass and trees in Mount Vernon outside of New York, where he received international recognition. There he provided ideal working conditions for Bruce Rogers during eight years of a close relationship which produced books (plate 38) that became part of America's typographic history. And of great importance to the succeeding generation, Rudge generously welcomed into his employ a considerable number of serious young men who wished to pursue typography as a career. Later known as the Rudge alumni, the Rudge "graduates" spread out into printing and publishing, where they carried with them the ideals and devotion to workmanship they had found in Mount Vernon.

In the 1890's, young Rudge worked for his father until the latter's death. At the same time he continued his education at night, including a three-year engineering course at the Cooper Union. These were years of phenomenal growth in American industry. The Rudge firm grew along with them. During the first decades of the new century and after several moves to larger quarters in New York City, Rudge settled into considerable prosperity with the cylinder presses and Linotype machines he had acquired. Rudge's growing reputation for a craftsmanlike approach brought him into contact with a group of men at the National Arts Club whose interests went beyond the commercial rewards to be found in the new technological advances. This Graphic Group, as it was called, opened new horizons for Rudge. Included were printers and designers Hal Marchbanks, Norman T. A. Munder, and F. W. Goudy; illustrator F. G. Cooper; art director Cyril Nast; and editor and historian of printing John Clyde Oswald. When, in 1914, President Wilson asked the National Arts Club to select American books to be sent to the Leipzig International Book Exhibition, the Club appointed a representative jury of leading practitioners. At an exhibition of American printing held in 1920 at the Club, books and promotional pieces from the Rudge plant won much praise. During that same year Rudge opened his superb printing house in Mount Vernon. This was a most fortunate move with the boom period of the 1920's ahead—a decade that proved to be highly receptive to large projects of scholarly and elegant books, with publishers, institutions, and collectors eager to promote such undertakings. Rudge himself was publisher of many of the books he commissioned and printed.

THE
RENAISSANCE
IN
AMERICAN
PRINTING

WILLIAM
EDWIN
RUDGE

William Edwin Rudge was neither a professional designer nor an academic scholar. He was an entrepreneur with an innate sense for quality, a printer who took great pride in his calling. Although Rudge was successful, it is a mark of his character and love of craft that business profits were not added to business security. Instead, they went into making his books and ephemera rather better than was quite necessary. His very competent staff of thirty to forty compositors and pressmen was trained to the pursuit of excellence, whether in daily routines or in the several new and experimental processes that were usually under way. Rudge naturally attracted a large and distinguished clientele, and the shop was a work-and-meeting-place for artists and designers.

Herbert Hoover, then Secretary of Commerce, appointed Rudge as

American representative to visit the International Exposition of Modern Decorative Art in Paris in 1925 and to report on its relevance to American bookmaking. Rudge reported that "in composition, processes, and efficiency of book manufacture, the western world was far ahead." However, he lauded European attempts at modern typographic design: "the courage of new ideas inspires its designers and enables them even through their mistakes and extravagances to acquire new confidence, new authority, and the dignity of work which may sincerely be called, *original*." Rudge died in 1931. His sons carried on the name in printing for some years, then turned to other occupations.

DARD HUNTER (1883–1966)

Dard Hunter was an American phenomenon. He was a historian of primitive papermaking who wrote and compiled important scholarly volumes for which he first designed and cast the type, then himself set up and printed the books on a handpress, on paper he had made—all of this on a high level of professional competence. He was also the author of two books that appeared in trade editions published by Alfred A. Knopf, New York: *Papermaking: The History and Technique of an Ancient Craft* in 1947, and an extraordinarily readable autobiography in 1958, *My Life with Paper*.

Hunter was born in Steubenville, a small agricultural and industrial town in eastern Ohio, of a cultivated family that had lively interests in the arts and crafts. His father and grandfather were newspaper editors. After 1900, when the family moved to Chillicothe, Dard's father published the town's daily *News-Advertiser*. Dard's mother and brother wrote for the paper; Dard contributed cartoons and news drawings. He set type when eight or ten years of age, and, among other duties, on Saturdays he helped pour the sugarhouse molasses, bone glue, and gelatin into the iron moulds for press rollers. Pottery, wood carving, and furniture making were other family activities in which Dard participated.

At nineteen, when a student at Ohio State University, Hunter was deeply stirred by Kelmscott and Doves Press volumes. A hope to visit England was premature. But from *The Philistine* magazine he learned about Elbert Hubbard and went to East Aurora in 1903 for a vacation job. At the end of summer the Hubbards invited him to stay on as designer for printed matter. Hunter wanted printing experience and stayed nine years. Although aware of the meretricious part of Hubbard's work, he found much to value and enjoy in this domain of arts and crafts for the people: its books, its music, its lectures, and the concerned visitors who came and went.

At one of the concerts held at the Roycroft chapel, Hunter met a young pianist, Helen Edith Cornell, who became his bride. Together they spent several years of study and work in Europe. Dard attended the Imperial Austrian printing school in Vienna. In London he found employment as a typographic designer with commercial art studios. He arranged to fulfill these duties in the forenoons. Afternoons were spent learning about papermaking, its history and manufacture, which had become his consuming passion, and, clearly, his life's work. Evenings he attended Finsbury Technical College for toolmaking; Saturdays were spent in bookstores along Charing Cross Road, hunting for old and rare books on his favorite subject. He worked in a small paper mill and in the shop of a maker of hand moulds for paper production. He visited the Doves, Eragny, and other famous private presses and later explained in his autobiography: "The work of the English private presses was of keen interest to me, and I felt I should like to attempt something of the kind myself. I was convinced, however, that simply purchasing type from a commercial foundry and buying paper from a paper mill left too many of the vital steps of making books in the hands of disinterested workmen. It was my desire to have my own private press, but I wanted my work to be individual and personal, without reliance upon outside help from the typefounder or paper-maker. I would return to America and attempt to make books by hand completely by my own labor — paper, type, printing."

Returning to the United States in 1913, Hunter found an old stone house in Marlboro-on-Hudson, with a mill dam on a brook which would provide sufficient water to make paper. This was New York State's fruit country and the Hunters grew and sold fruit on the side. With a local wheelwright, Hunter built a very small paper mill, complete with a beater to lacerate rags, a dipping vat, pressure press, and the other appurtenances sufficient for him to turn out a hundred fifty sheets, 16 by 23 inches, per day. He wrote: "I had no helpers in the paper mill. The cutting, dusting, and boiling of the rags was my task, and the beating of the boiled rags also fell to me, and when the stock was finally ready, after days of maceration, I formed the individual sheets of paper in the moulds. Each moist sheet was couched upon

THE
RENAISSANCE
IN
AMERICAN
PRINTING

DARD
HUNTER

THE
RENAISSANCE
IN
AMERICAN
PRINTING

DARD
HUNTER

woolen felting, and lastly the pile of paper and felts, called a 'post,' was pressed in the cumbersome oak-and-iron press. . . . After much of the water had been pressed from the 'post,' the paper was removed sheet by sheet from the felts. We would press the sheets again, one upon another, and finally hang the paper to dry in the attic of the main house across the road."

Since its introduction into Europe in the thirteenth century, paper-making has been an industrial craft. In the hands of adequately skilled individual producers paper has been a creative artifact, when finely made and textured, a joy to touch. In the present era of technological "progress," the craft of such fine papermaking is all but obsolete. Paper made of wood pulp at tremendous speed on huge machines and in-stantly dried on heated rollers is in no way comparable to paper skill-fully made from rags and hung in a loft to be slowly dried by air. Only the name is the same.

In dry weather when there was insufficient water to make paper and in the winter months, Hunter designed his type, cut the punches, and struck the matrices. His information and guidance came from Moxon's *Mechanick Exercises*, published in London in 1683. He made the hand mould for casting type letter by letter. The metal alloy—lead, tin, anti-mony, copper—was melted on the coal stove that supplied heat for the workroom.

After another trip to Europe to visit handmade paper mills and to acquire greater familiarity with their methods, Hunter returned to his ancestral home in Chillicothe, where he spent the next few years in the production of the first of his important books. In 1923 he completed and published *Old Papermaking*. This was followed two years later by *The Literature of Papermaking*. These and Hunter's subsequent books were quartos or folios, in editions ranging from 125 to 200 copies. The pattern called for a scholarly historical text, with illustrations of ancient equip-ment and processes, and with mounted specimens of early papers which Hunter acquired on his extensive travels to remote corners of the world. These books were (and are) of great value to students and historians of paper. Each title, necessarily limited by Hunter's personal production and by the specimens he could collect, sold out on publication. They are available in most large libraries having a special concern for books on the graphic arts.

Paper was still being made by the ancient methods in distant, isolated islands and villages in the Far East. Hunter wrote: "For years I had been interested in the primitive bark papers of the South Sea Islands, and a few foreign-language articles dealing with mulberry-bark *tapa* were in my library." Hunter traveled to Tahiti, to Fiji, Tonga, and the Samoan Islands, where he found natives who beat the inner bark of the mulberry tree into strips of paper, then added decoration. He collected tools and equipment. His autobiography tells in fascinating detail of his many tortuous voyages to areas where he found ancient methods still being used. He found counterparts of block-printed papers that Marco Polo had seen in China in the thirteenth century. The titles of his books are eloquent testimony of his successful adventures. In 1927 he completed *Primitive Papermaking*. This was followed by *Old Papermaking in China and Japan* (1932); *A Papermaking Pilgrimage to Japan, Korea and China* (1935), 370 copies printed and published by the Pynson Printers, New York; *Papermaking in Southern Siam* (1936); *Chinese Ceremonial Paper* (1937); *Papermaking by Hand in India*, again in an edition of 370 copies from the Pynson Printers; and *Papermaking in Indo-China* (1947). Finally, a massive volume of research, *Papermaking by Hand in America* (plate 57), produced with help of his son, was completed in 1950 and dealt, stated Hunter, with "those untiring craftsmen who had so patiently struggled with limited skill and inadequate equipment to manufacture the paper needed by the Colonial printers for their books, pamphlets, newspapers, broadsides, and all sorts of ephemeral work." The book was printed in Chillicothe on paper that had been made at Hunter's mill in Lime Rock, Connecticut. There are 326 pages, 96 facsimiles, 27 early American watermarks, 42 reproductions of old paper labels.

In 1920 while in England, Hunter had bought a small paper mill about to be dismantled. It was shipped to the United States and stored. Hunter had thought he might one day set up this equipment to revive a craft that had all but died after the first papermaking machine was established in America in 1817. In 1926 the enthusiasm of a young Michigan businessman convinced Hunter that a market for handmade paper existed in this country. By coincidence, a papermaking family from England had written to Hunter expressing a desire to emigrate. Hunter yielded and a site was found in Lime Rock, Salisbury, in the northwest corner of Connecticut, lying along a trout brook that flowed into the Housatonic River a mile away. Iron products from this mill, according to local legend had supported the army of the American

THE
RENAISSANCE
IN
AMERICAN
PRINTING

DARD
HUNTER

THE

RENAISSANCE

IN

AMERICAN

PRINTING

DARD

HUNTER

Revolution and made cannon for the northern armies during the Civil War. By the time that the Robertson family had arrived from England and the equipment had become operational, the Depression had set in. The young businessman from the west did not fulfill expectations. The mill had reached production of some three reams of paper per day. But with adverse economic conditions, in a market that would be extremely limited even in normal times, and despite the help of a handful of concerned printers, the experiment was abandoned. Finally the equipment was removed from the mill and permanently set up as an exhibit at the Institute of Paper Chemistry in Appleton, Wisconsin. The eighteenth-century structure that had housed Hunter's worthy attempt was swept downstream in the great flood of 1955 and disappeared.

In 1936 Karl T. Compton invited Hunter to establish the Dard Hunter Paper Museum at the Massachusetts Institute of Technology and to become its curator. Hunter accepted. After sixteen years at M.I.T., the entire paper museum was presented to the Institute of Paper Chemistry in Appleton, which already possessed the equipment from the mill at Lime Rock. Here the tools from ancient times to the present may be seen, with samples of paper in all its manifold uses. In closing his autobiography Hunter wrote: "It is my hope that through the years to come the Paper Museum will be used by students, researchers, and writers, who will find as much pleasure as I have found in the ancient and honorable craft of papermaking."

ELMER ADLER (1884–1961)

Elmer Adler was another of those talented and articulate individuals born in the latter part of the nineteenth century who became printers of stature, and who enjoyed extraordinary related capacities. Adler was a designer, a printer, a collector, an editor, a teacher, a curator, and a publisher. In each of these careers he retained the curiosity and enthusiasm of the amateur with the acquired competence of the professional.

Adler abandoned his formal education when he dropped out of Andover Academy and entered the substantial family clothing business in Rochester, New York, where he was born. Eventually he became advertising manager. But during the years of his application to business, he was also a studious collector who filled the walls of his home with prints and drawings, and the bookshelves with volumes on the history of the book. His concern with typography brought into being a collection of sufficient scope to justify an exhibition, in Rochester's Memorial Art Gallery in 1920, of four and a half centuries of masterpieces of printing. During this same period Adler's responsibilities for sales and promotion involved him in the layout and production of advertising and printed matter. In 1922, at age thirty-eight, he gave up his mercantile affiliations and decided to channel his typographic inclinations, his acquired knowledge of production, and his interest in books into the practical world of printing.

Arrived in New York, Adler set up his press and named it the Pynson Printers in honor of Richard Pynson, the early English printer. His partners were Walter Dorwin Teague, David Silve, and Hubert Canfield, but the work turned out at the Pynson Printers was, from the start and throughout its eighteen years of existence, the personal expression of Elmer Adler. The prospectus (really a manifesto) announcing the opening of the press stated that "... we have founded our organization on the belief that the printer should be primarily an artist—a designer and a creator rather than a mere manufacturer." And further on: "We will do no work in which quality must be sacrificed to the exigencies of time and cost." These promises were kept. No careless job ever came from the Pynson presses. Adler never had the inclination to set type or to run a press, but he had an innate sense of typographic form, with the genius to obtain perfection of composition and superb presswork from his carefully chosen and intelligently supervised shop employees.

Adler's first book was a new edition of Willa Cather's *April Twilights*, published by Alfred A. Knopf in 1923. The author showed her delight in a letter to Adler: "We have set a new standard of relations between writer and printer. The pains you have taken with this volume and the absolutely satisfying result you have achieved have quite revived my interest in the text." Knopf, who commissioned a number of other special volumes produced at the Pynson Printers during the 1920's, also asked Adler in 1923 to design his newly projected literary magazine, *The American Mercury*, with H. L. Mencken and George Jean Nathan as editors. In 1924 Arthur H. Sulzberger, publisher of *The New York Times*, invited Adler to move the Pynson Printers to the new *Times* building on Forty-third Street. Believing that a fine printing office would add luster to a huge newspaper plant, and having commissioned Adler to set up a permanent exhibition, "The History of the Recorded Word," for The

Times, Sulzberger provided generous space for the Pynson shop and office; for Adler's library of books on printing; exhibition space for old and new work; and a room for Adler's weekly seminars on bookmaking and printmaking around a large refectory table. Lucien Bernhard, well-known typographer, among other talents, designed the new quarters that gave Adler an elegant setting which soon became an unofficial cultural center. Adler gave famous teas on Thursday afternoons. He invited artists, writers, publishers, printers, collectors—only friends and celebrities of whom he approved. This was during the era of Prohibition when teacups frequently contained alcoholic refreshment. But to Adler, who neither smoked nor drank, and who had fastidious criteria for people and their ways, tea was tea.

In the lush 1920's Adler joined Bennett Cerf and Donald Klopfer in the work of Random House when that newly established (1925) publishing house imported and sold on this continent the great books of the Nonesuch and other English presses, and when Random House commissioned limited editions among America's special presses. These included, for example, the Grabhorn *Leaves of Grass*, the Spiral Press *Collected Poems* of Robert Frost, and, notably, the Pynson Printers' edition of Voltaire's *Candide* (plate 45). This was probably Adler's most original design, said to have been his favorite. It was copiously illustrated by Rockwell Kent, hand-set in the Bernhard Roman type, and printed, as were all Adler's books, on fine European-made paper. Books were designed and printed for several other publishers, also for learned institutions, and privately printed books for collectors. The Pynson Printers also acted from time to time as its own publishing house as, for example, in *The Decorative Work of T. M. Cleland* in 1929; *Beowulf*, a verse translation by William Ellery Leonard, with lithography by Rockwell Kent; two books for Dard Hunter on papermaking; and, starting in 1930, the remarkable *Colophon*. Altogether, Adler completed more than a hundred books. They are listed in the Will Ransom *Selective Check List of Private Presses*. Adler also designed the usual (his were unusual) ephemera of a printing house: bookplates, announcements, invitations, stationery, etc. Effective advertisements, notices, and labels in Caslon type, which he prepared for a prominent New York men's haberdashery store, are still being repeated without change in design some forty years later. But Adler's most important contribution as a printer, editor, and publisher was *The Colophon: A Book Collector's Quarterly*.

Anyone interested in the adventures to be met in writing, making, and collecting books—in bookmen's talk—will find enormous pleasure in the pages of *The Colophon*. The opening announcement set a course for the magazine that was faithfully followed: "The Colophon's primary concern will be with collected and collectible books,—first editions, fine printing, incunabula, association books, Americana, bibliography and manuscripts. The subject of book illustration will receive attention, and significant examples, whether in copper plate, lithography, or woodcut, will be printed. . . ." *The Colophon* was issued in hard covers, each issue decorated by a different artist. Many of the prominent authors of the time contributed articles, for example in the series "Breaking into Print." Its twenty essays included Americans from Sherwood Anderson to Edith Wharton and three English writers. The articles in each of the twenty volumes issued during the first five years were individually designed as to type, paper, etc. Perhaps half were done at the Pynson Printers; the remainder were distributed among the fine presses in the country (Grabhorn, Harbor, Walpole, Spiral, Lakeside, et al.), with a free hand in production. The result was a bright and lively potpourri of the best printing being done in the United States, with several pieces contributed from Europe. The editors were Elmer Adler, Burton Emmett until his death, Alfred Stanford, John T. Winterich, and Frederick B. Adams, Jr. Prominent bibliophiles were among its backers. But *The Colophon* was born in the Depression, with its first issue in February 1930. In 1935 the format was changed from quarto to octavo, wholly produced at the Pynson Printers with typography by W. A. Dwiggins in his Electra type. In 1939–1940 Adler returned to the original format and plan of assembling sections by different printers. After the Pynson Printers' closing in 1940 the magazine enjoyed postwar reincarnation as *The New Colophon*, published by Duschnes Crawford in New York until 1950, all in a uniform format. Textual continuity was maintained with Adler, Winterich, and Adams as active editors until *The Colophon* passed into typographic and bibliophilic history. The writing, the prints, and the typographic content were of such variety and interest that no brief summary could do the magazine justice.

A review of the eighteen years of the Pynson Printers reveals a felicitous body of work produced within a charmed circle of literature and art. Elmer Adler was blessed with financial security. He used it to superb advantage. As a typographic designer he was uninhibited by the historical traditions with which he was thoroughly familiar. His books and miscellaneous printing were neither tightly bound by the past nor affectedly modern. He displayed a natural and personal typographic versatility, ingenuity, wit, and daring. And, withal, his work remained within the province of readability in debt to literature.

With the closing of the Pynson Printers, Adler accepted an invitation from Princeton to establish a department of graphic arts in the University Library as its curator, also to be consultant in typography to the Princeton University Press. Whereupon Adler rented a three-story house near the campus which he filled from top to bottom with his collection of books and prints brought from New York. This house, at number Forty Mercer Street, became a center for the study and enjoyment of the arts of the book and of printmaking. The large round table from the printing office in New York was again used for seminars when students signed up for voluntary three-hour, eight-week evening courses. Exhibitions were held. Students, faculty, and townspeople were welcomed. Artists were brought to Mercer Street to demonstrate the different techniques of woodcutting, etching, and lithography; typographers talked about design and production; collectors discussed their hobbies; and writers spoke about their special problems. A print-lending club offered students landscapes and still lifes for their walls in competition with their more life-like pinups. Remembering teas and talk and inspiration, one of Adler's students wrote of him, "Somehow, whatever comes within his scope of activity mysteriously takes on the form of adventure." In 1952, after twelve years at Princeton, during which he had exposed many young people to his gospel of "quality and good taste" and had made converts to the respect for books, Adler moved on again. His collections of incunabula, books on the history of printing, illustrated and press books, his prints, and the complete records of the Pynson Printers remain in the Princeton University Library.

Adler's university associations continued for another two years as a visiting lecturer. Traveling in a station wagon loaded with books, he toured to college and university libraries and talked to students and faculty members about the joys of collecting. Many of his experiences made good telling, especially stories such as the long trail in pursuit of the first edition of Stephen Crane's *Maggie: A Girl of the Streets*, published under the pseudonym of Johnston Smith. This and other episodes were printed by Saul and Lillian Marks in a charming pamphlet entitled *An Informal Talk by Elmer Adler at the University of Kansas, April 17, 1953*. It has been included in *Elmer Adler in the World of Books*, a volume organized by Paul A. Bennett, published cooperatively by the Typophiles, the Grolier Club, the Friends of the Princeton University Library, and La Casa del Libro. It is a small but comprehensive volume, with essays by eight of Adler's colleagues on the many phases of his life. Included are illustrations and a selective bibliography from the retrospective exhibition of Adler's work held at the Grolier Club in 1963. An earlier exhibition had been held in 1941 by the American Institute of Graphic Arts.

Characteristically, Adler's last years were spent as a teacher and educator in a wholly new setting. While he was on a vacation trip in San Juan in 1955, at a fortuitous meeting a member of the government of the Commonwealth of Puerto Rico asked his advice concerning the possibility of improving the Island's printing. Adler suggested the building of a library and museum which would collect and show early and modern printing at its best, for the inspiration of local printers. The government accepted his proposal. Adler stayed in Puerto Rico, and with official support and with private help he transformed a building in old San Juan into the handsome and elegant La Casa del Libro. There he brought together a remarkable collection of Spanish incunabula and rare books. La Casa del Libro, now administered by a curator with ongoing exhibitions of interest to a wide public, has become an important asset in Puerto Rico's culture. No more appropriate monument could have been erected to Elmer Adler than a House of the Book—and built by himself.

VICTOR HAMMER (1882–1967)

Victor Hammer was born in Vienna in the oldest part of the city where, as a growing boy, he was profoundly influenced by the architectural forms of the seventeenth century. At age fifteen he did apprentice work in an architect's studio. At sixteen he attended the Academy of Fine Arts. Scholarships in painting, with later professional commissions, took him to Paris and London and elsewhere in Europe. In 1910 he was established in his studio in Vienna as a successful portrait painter. After duty in the war from 1914 to 1917, he returned to work as a painter and sculptor. On seeing European manuscripts of the fourth to the eighth centuries, he was stirred by the beauty and vigor of the rounded uncial letterforms written in medieval cloisters—some in burnished gold on purple vellum. The uncial cast a spell on him that stayed through life. After perfecting his own uncial hand, the next step was type. Punches were cut from Hammer's designs by the German Klingspor typefoundry, called Hammer Unziale. Unhappy with the final result, Hammer never used it. (It was chosen by Elmer Adler for the Pynson Printers' 1932 edition of *Beowulf*.)

In 1922 Hammer moved to Florence. Here, between commissions as a painter, his attachment to language and literature and his sense of craft drew him into the making of books. With the help of a local carpenter, Hammer built his own wooden handpress based on an early model in the Laurentian Library. Paul Koch, son of the famous German type designer, having learned punch-cutting in Offenbach, came to live with the Hammers in Florence where a second, newly designed, uncial typeface was cut under Hammer's immediate supervision. Specimen pages were set in the new type for Milton's *Samson Agonistes*, a title suggested by Bernard Berenson, then a neighbor and friend. This work was interrupted by a commission from Edgar Kaufmann, Sr., to paint two portraits which brought Hammer to Pittsburgh for several months. Edgar Kaufmann, Jr., later came to Florence to study painting with Hammer. With the help of the Kaufmanns, who had seen the *Samson Agonistes* proofs, Hammer was enabled to move his studio to the ample Villa Santuccio, where there would be space enough for family, apprentices, and working presses. In a wall niche by the doorway was the figure of a nameless little saint—"a santuccio of no importance in any hierarchy"—which gave the press its name. The *Samson Agonistes*, completed in 1931, was the first of the Stamperia del Santuccio books. During the next eight years nine were completed. One of these, Hölderlin's *Fragmente des Pindar* was set in Pindar Uncial, a new type from punches cut entirely by Hammer. Books with the imprint of the Stamperia del Santuccio printed in Europe and later in America were beautiful volumes, produced by Hammer and his apprentices in a spirit of medieval religious devotion, by the labor of their hands in intimate relation with type, ink, paper, and presses, toward a goal of heroic perfection. This was pure, personal craftsmanship dedicated, as the colophon always stated, Ad Maiorem Dei Gloriam—To the Greater Glory of God.

Hammer welcomed the opportunity to build a chapel on the estate of the Chateau Kolbsheim in Alsace. On its completion, after two years of construction, the owner stated that the chapel was "Victor's greatest offering to God, and the place where all his gifts as an artist were united: architecture, sculpture, stone-carved letters, painting (his crucifix), the goldsmith's art (his chalice)." Soon thereafter Hammer accepted an appointment to teach painting in the Academy of Fine Arts in Vienna. When the Nazis entered Austria his professorship was suspended. On the advice of influential friends, Hammer and his wife in 1939 left for the United States. Hammer's son Jacob, who had assisted his father in printing, soon followed.

America meant a wholly new start. Wells College at Aurora in northern New York State offered Hammer a position in the art department. The college purchased a handpress and equipment as teaching tools and for the establishment of the Wells College Press. Its first publication, completed in 1941, was *Young Voices: A Book of Wells College Verse*. The preface by its editor, Richard Armour, stated: "Both printing and binding have been done in Aurora and by members of the college community. To Victor and Jacob Hammer, and to the students who have worked as their apprentices must be credited the typographical beauty wrought with a hand press and a meager supply of type. Theirs is the achievement of the craftsman."

A second handpress was acquired, set up in their home in Aurora, where father and son could print independently as the Hammer Press. Despite the limited facilities, Hammer produced seventeen titles. Among them were books by Stéphane Mallarmé, Rainer Maria Rilke, Charles Péguy, Thornton Wilder, and Alarcón's *The Three-Cornered Hat* (1944) with colored woodcuts by Fritz Kredel. Publishers were New Directions, Herbert Bittner, Pantheon Books, and others.

Between teaching and printing, Hammer prepared designs for a new uncial type for which he cut the punches himself directly on the slim pieces of steel without intermediate drawings. With the help of funds raised by R. Hunter Middleton and other members of the Chicago Society of Typographic Arts, the new American Uncial was cast at the Dearborn Type Foundry in Chicago. The type is a vigorous, full-bodied, sophisticated letter, with an archaic sense of history and culture. Hammer did not regard it as an anachronism. He believed it to be an adaptation of old forms to modern use. In the opening sentence of a tract introducing the American Uncial, Hammer wrote: "With this uncial type face I am aiming at a letter form which eventually may fuse roman and black letter, those two national letter forms, into a new unity."

Following an exhibition of Hammer's paintings and books at the Renaissance Society in Chicago early in 1948, Raymond McLain, President of Transylvania University in Kentucky, invited Hammer to come to Lexington as artist in residence, to teach in the art department, and to set up his press at the college. Hammer accepted and was welcomed to his new home in July of 1948 by an unusually receptive group of men and women—trustees, librarians, and students—who were eager to add to their knowledge of calligraphy, type, and bookmaking. The press was first housed on the campus but was soon moved to Hammer's home. Here in 1949, working alone, Hammer completed his American masterpiece, Hölderlin's *Gedichte* (plate 55), a magnificent quarto volume in an edition of fifty-one copies, in the new uncial type, with the imprint of the Stamperia del Santuccio, used for the first time since leaving Europe. The title page is embellished with a metal engraving of the author by Hammer. Otherwise without illustrations, the book depends for its beauty on the rare and subtle elegance of typographic design and proportion, of type on paper, and the perfection of its presswork.

In 1952 a group of Hammer's friends and students founded the Anvil Press in Lexington. Victor Hammer was "honorary advisor" and designer; Jacob Hammer was employed as pressman. Among the books chosen for production and publication were, for example, a tall Pico della Mirandola's *Dignity of Man*, *The Tyndale Gospels*, and Shakespeare's *Sonnets*. The Press still functions at this writing (1976) under the direction of Carolyn Reading Hammer, an early Victor Hammer apprentice, who in 1955 became the artist's wife and co-worker.

After retirement from Transylvania, Hammer continued to design, to print, to paint, and to write. His books show his breadth of familiarity with languages, literature, philosophy, and religion. Some of his late books were done in association with Thomas Merton of the nearby Trappist Abbey of Gethsemane. Among tracts, pamphlets, and books written by Hammer may be named: *Type Design in Relation to Language and the Art of the Punch Cutter* (1943); *A Theory of Architecture* (1952); *Memory . . . a Dialogue in Four Chapters* (1956); *On Classic Art* (1959); *Digressions on the Roman Letter* (1963); *Concern for the Art of Civilized Man* (1963); and *Pieces for an Artist's Testament* (1967). A bibliography of the Hammer printed books appeared in *The American Artist*, December 1955 and January 1956.

THE GRABHORN PRESS

EDWIN GRABHORN (1890–1968)
ROBERT GRABHORN (1900–1973)

When Edwin and Robert Grabhorn came to San Francisco to set up
the Grabhorn Press in 1920, they arrived at the beginning of an opulent
decade in commerce and for the arts and crafts. The West Coast was
already fortunate in the printing of John Henry Nash, Taylor & Taylor,
and a few others. The stage was also set for fine books with bookseller-
publishers, concerned librarians, generous patrons, and ardent collectors. And of the greatest importance was the existence of the Book Club
of California with its large membership of bibliophiles and an active
publishing program of books designed and printed by local fine printers.
To this great decade, the Grabhorn brothers added their own highly
original and productive typographic exuberance.

Edwin Grabhorn had learned to set type and run presses as a teen-
ager in his uncle's printing shop in Indianapolis. From 1909 to 1911 he
worked for a music printer and publisher in Seattle, Washington. When
his employer failed, Edwin tried on his own for six months, then returned to Indianapolis in 1912, to spend a few years in various plants as
a journeyman printer. In 1915, having acquired a supply of Goudy's
Forum and Kennerley types, he set up his own "Studio Press." A review
of the early work produced at the Studio Press shows that the mystery of
human predilection had stirred in the young printer in midwest America a gift for the essential qualities of fine printing. Edwin had become
aware of the craftsmanship of William Morris, of Boston's scholarly
Updike, of the elegance and charm of Bruce Rogers, and of the enthusiasms of Frederic W. Goudy with whom he was already in correspondence. These influences, especially that of Rogers, continued into the
first years in San Francisco, until the Grabhorns achieved their own
maturity of style in the stimulating glow of the Golden Gate. Before the
move to the West Coast, Robert, younger brother by ten years, had
joined Edwin in what became an extraordinarily close relationship during forty-five resplendent bookmaking years.

Survival for the Grabhorns during the first few years depended primarily on advertising and job work for business houses, large and small.
Throughout their existence, as for most printing offices, ephemera was
necessary to sustain the making of less profitable, if more satisfying,

THE
TWENTIETH
CENTURY

THE
GRABHORN
PRESS

books. Late in 1920 the publications committee of the Book Club of California took notice of the new printers with a commission to produce Emma Frances Dawson's *A Gracious Visitation*. This was their first real book, seventy-two pages of hand-set Garamond type on handmade paper, rather conservative in design as were three more books made for the Club during 1920–1921. In 1920 bookseller John Howell commissioned Robert Louis Stevenson's *Diogenes in London*. Then two years later came *The Song of Songs* for the Book Club, with Goudy Antique type printed in black and red, with blue initial letters by Joseph Sinel, and an evocative drawing by Harold von Schmidt. This was the first book to signal Grabhorn originality, their capacity for decorative warmth and color, firmness and depth of presswork. *The Song of Songs* was selected in 1923 by the American Institute of Graphic Arts for its first "Fifty Books of the Year" exhibition, as were more than forty Grabhorn books in the years ahead. The coveted Institute medal, and exhibitions in New York, followed in later years.

The Grabhorn Press was firmly established by 1924 and their fame had spread. Books and ephemera were being designed and printed for publishers, institutions, and private collectors. The Press also published for direct sale many of their own books—for example, *The Book of Ruth*, one hundred fifty copies in 1926, and *Francis Drake & Other Early Explorers along the Pacific Coast*, one thousand copies in 1927. Most loyal of the supporters of the Press, Albert M. Bender, patron of the arts, sponsored and financed some twenty-five Grabhorn items during twenty years of friendship, in addition to those he proposed as chairman of the publications committee of the Book Club of California. Between 1922 and 1928 eleven more titles were printed for the Club, most of them typically large in format. Among the most handsome was a folio edition, *The Letter of Amerigo Vespucci* (1926), enhanced with woodcuts and decorative initials by Valenti Angelo. During six years of close association with the Grabhorns, Angelo's illustrations and initial letters contributed illumination and drama to some of the most beautiful books the Grabhorns ever produced. These included three titles for Random House. The first was Hawthorne's *The Scarlet Letter* in 1928, a tall octavo, 980 copies, with Angelo's woodcuts in color. In the same year a noble folio, deliberately allusive, was *The Voiage and Travaile of Sir John Maundeville*, an edition of 150 copies, set in Rudolf Koch's German *Bibelschrift* (or Jessen type) especially imported for this printing, with Angelo's initials in red, blue, and gold. And in 1930 came 400 copies of *Leaves of Grass* (plate 49) generally considered to be the Grabhorn masterpiece. It is a large and weighty folio of more than four hundred pages, 9½ by 14½ inches, with rugged Angelo illustrations throughout. The type is Goudy's full-bodied New-style, somewhat archaic, which contributed perhaps to a sense of the elemental in Whitman verse. The handmade paper was dampened for printing in two-page forms on a 14-by-22-inch Colts Armory press that shuddered with every heavy impression. The book was an Edwin Grabhorn favorite. In *The Fine Art of Printing*, a speech later printed as a pamphlet in 1933, he wrote that "I would go through any form of hysteria again if we could produce another *Leaves of Grass*." The Grabhorn method was trial and error in the workshop, working over and reworking type and proofs. Layouts on paper were never made. Experiment would go on, different types set up, new proofs pulled, until a satisfactory page was achieved. Again from the above-mentioned essay, here is Edwin Grabhorn's story of the progression of design for *Leaves of Grass*: "Well, the finest book [so announced by the publisher's publicity] had to have the finest type, and the finest type was the latest type. And it had to be a folio in size because for One Hundred Dollars you had to get a folio. We bought 1000 pounds of the finest type; 18-point Lutetia, fresh from a new designer in Holland. And we hired two printers to set this bright new type, and when it was all set, we pulled a proof and started to put grass into it—pale green grass—and it looked like grass and we pulled it out and tried again. Well, every time we tried that bright new type it didn't look right. So we dug up some of the latest theories about suitability, tried again, but it was no use. The brain told us one thing and our eyes another. Meanwhile, 1000 pounds of bright new type and months of labor were tied up with strings and the Master Craftsman was getting worried. He went to specialists for advice. They said: 'Try this new initial or this new picture,' and the Master Craftsman went back to his shop and bowed his head. . . . Then his tired eyes lighted on a dusty case of type, designed by the artist Goudy but the critics had condemned it to the graveyard. Wearily the Craftsman dug it up and set a page of Whitman in it. Then he pulled a proof, and Lo! He saw something that the machine had discarded; he saw strength: he saw the strong vigorous lines of Whitman, born of the soil, without grass. He saw what he had heard whispered before. He saw strong, vigorous, simple printing—printing like mountains, rocks and

THE
TWENTIETH
CENTURY

THE
GRABHORN
PRESS

trees, but not like pansies, lilacs and valentines; printing that came from the soil and was not refined in the classroom. And the printer knew that the limited edition was not a racket as long as he had honesty and sincerity, and reverence for the best traditions of his craft."

THE
TWENTIETH
CENTURY

THE
GRABHORN
PRESS

The Depression that flattened the economy of the entire country hit the West Coast somewhat later than elsewhere. The Grabhorns delivered *The Santa Fe Trail* to the Book Club in 1931, at a time when presses everywhere were standing idle. This book and others on the early history of the west found a welcome reception among historians and bibliophiles. Several volumes of Californiana had already been issued successfully by the Grabhorns in the 1920's. In order to bring work into their shop during the Depression, they catered to this regional patriotism with a series of very inexpensive reprints called "Rare Americana." Limited to five hundred copies, editions sold out quickly and the Grabhorn presses were kept at work. Despite the low prices some of the most memorable Grabhorn books were produced. Among them were such favorites as *The Spanish Occupation of California* (1934) and *Wah-To-Yah & the Taos Trail* (1936) with woodcuts by Mallette Dean (plate 50). Among the artists who were essential participants in the Grabhorn output, Mallette Dean contributed beautiful illustrations in various media—headpieces, tailpieces, and initial letters to some thirty of the Press's successful books. A particularly handsome title page with a woodcut by Dean of the publisher's device was made in 1935 for Robinson Jeffers' *Solstice and Other Poems*. Included in the Grabhorn's Americana series was Meyers' *Naval Sketches of the War in California* (1939) with reproductions in color of paintings in the collection of Franklin D. Roosevelt who provided an introduction. By this time Grabhorn books were being collected in all parts of the United States.

The importance of the Grabhorn Press in the history of American typography and the significance of its work may be seen in the two impressive folio volumes of bibliography documenting and describing its 583 major publications and ephemera. The first volume, compiled by Elinor H. Heller and David Magee, covers the years from the Studio Press in 1915 to 1940. The second volume, compiled by Dorothy and David Magee, takes the Press to 1956. Introductory essays were contributed by Frederic W. Goudy and by Elmer Adler. Both volumes were hand-set and printed at the Grabhorn Press in Franciscan type, the proprietary face of the Press, designed by Goudy. Among the indices prepared by the bibliographers is a tally of body types. The Grabhorns used Lutetia 55 times; Oxford, derived from the early American foundry, Binny & Ronaldson, was used 53 times; Janson, 48; Garamond, 39; Centaur, 36; Franciscan, 27; Kennerley, 20; Goudy Modern, 18; and a miscellany of other faces. If all the different Goudy faces are added together, they reach the surprising total of 130 choices.

During the decade ending in 1961, of the thirty-nine books published by the Book Club of California, nine came from the Grabhorn Press including a bibliography of the Club, its hundredth book. Pages of books were included that had been published earlier by the Club "and thus reminded old members of past achievements," wrote James D. Hart, a former president, "and introduced new members to the distinguished examples of fine bookmaking that local presses had created under the sponsorship of the Book Club." Shakespeare's plays in sumptuous individual volumes were the most important work of the Grabhorn Press during its last period. Starting with *The Tempest* in 1951, one new play was published by the Press each year for direct sale in editions of approximately 180 copies. They were designed in varying formats from square quarto, 11½ by 9 inches, to tall folio, 10 by 15 inches. Types were also different for each title, most of them archaic in origin—Inkunabula, French Lettre Batarde, Koch Bibel Gotisch, and others. All were illustrated by Mary Grabhorn, Edwin's talented daughter, chiefly with beautiful colored woodcuts. The printing was so skillful that the plates had the quality of original, hand-colored prints. The books were, one may suspect, the ultimate Grabhorn effort toward realization of the art of the book.

In a lecture delivered by friend Roland Baughman in 1965, later reprinted in *Heritage of the Graphic Arts*, he stated that "The Grabhorn Press consists of a very few key people—Ed, Robert, Robert's wife Jane, Ed's daughter Mary, and, until 1963, the pressman, Sherwood Grover, who had been with the Grabhorns so long that he was virtually a member of the family. It would be a good guess that ideas germinate freely among that group, so that there may be no way of being certain just *who* happened to be the one to think up a particular design or technique. But in general, Ed is the designer, the idea man, Bob is the compositor and make-up expert, Jane oversees the bindery (while running her own show, the Colt Press), and Mary is a general factotum *cum* artist extraor-

THE
TWENTIETH
CENTURY

THE
GRABHORN
PRESS

dinary. Each one, doubtless, would be quite capable of doing anyone else's job if the necessity should arise."

There was an aura of Bohemianism about the Grabhorns with their lightly carried fame and success. They appeared to be carefree, unconventional, and uncommercial. Actually, they were very hard and devoted workers who led lives according to their own rules, not those made by other people. A few revealing fragments may be quoted from the *Recollections of The Grabhorn Press* (1935) by Gregg Anderson, one of the many articulate young workers who spent valuable learning time with the Grabhorns: "Nobody had to come in and work on Sunday morning, but it was fun. Ed reserved Saturday for his longer book-hunting expeditions, so he would clear out as soon as he could, and then come back Sunday morning to finish up something he had been planning to do all week. Usually the young and eager would come around also. . . . At noon everyone on hand was loaded into the car and driven to some restaurant for lunch, and if by any chance you worked part of the afternoon, Ed took you home for dinner. . . . There was an office in the shop with Oscar Lewis in charge. In keeping with some of the theories Ed had as to the usefulness of offices, it was very small and never used except one or two hours in the afternoon. Its size may be judged more accurately by saying that it was an abandoned wash-room. There was still a bathtub there, a rather legendary bathtub, since no one but Oscar had ever seen it, and he had buried it so deep under old correspondence, bills, and the like, that only an archaeologist could have uncovered it." And a few words among many about the brothers: "When Ed was away the shop went to pieces. When Bob was away Ed went to pieces." In a delicious article in the *Book Club of California News-Letter*, in 1948, Jane Grabhorn wrote about her husband and brother-in-law. Let us extract just a few words: "Ed is what you might call an experimenter and an optimist—the inventor type. Bob is a perfectionist and a pessimist—the professional type, in a sophisticated sort of way. Probably the reason Bob is a pessimist is because Ed is an optimist. . . . I share their amazement every time a book is finished."

The very large body of Grabhorn work was produced on four hand-fed Colts Armory presses with 14-by-22-inch platens. The eventual collection of type was extensive and varied. Most of the books were hand-set; some were printed from Monotype cast by Mackenzie and Harris. Linotype was used sparingly. Edwin and Robert Grabhorn were cre-

THE
TWENTIETH
CENTURY

THE
GRABHORN
PRESS

ative craftsmen who set the type and ran the presses themselves. That is the heart of the matter. Compositors and pressmen were employed but always under immediate supervision. The books show the warmth and vigor and completeness that come only from immediate contact with materials in the workshop. The presswork was often experimental and inventive, especially successful with illustrations and reproductions in color. Edwin Grabhorn's typographic design was vigorous and innovative. Once in full swing, his large and lavish and, occasionally, flamboyant style can readily be recognized as typically Grabhorn. It could have been born and matured only in the American Far West.

THE FOREGOING PAGES have involved the designers and printers who were born before and during the nineteenth century. Their work is, therefore, in some historical perspective. The pages that follow are concerned with the men and women of our own time—the recent past and the still uncertain future.

NEW ENGLAND

Three book groups, the Club of Odd Volumes, the Boston Society of Printers, and the Bookbuilders of Boston, have nurtured the souls of New Englanders who have loved literature and the art of the printed page. The Club of Odd Volumes was founded in 1886 for "the promotion of literary and artistic tastes, the study of the arts as applied to bookmaking," for mounting exhibitions and maintenance of a library. These objectives have been achieved in the Club's building on Mount Vernon Street in Boston where a distinguished membership meets together each month. Their published books, exhibition catalogues, and ephemera reflect the character of the Club—produced in the past by D. B. Updike, Bruce Rogers, and Fred Anthoensen, and currently by Roderick Stinehour and Darrell Hyder.

The Boston Society of Printers held its first meeting in 1905 sparked by the substantial attendance at a series of lectures on typography held at the Boston Public Library and by the warm response to Henry Lewis Johnson's landmark magazine, *The Printing Art*. The purpose of the Society was and still is "the determination and advancement of ideals and standards of printing." Its membership has been an honorable roster of those New Englanders who have been involved in bookmaking.

The Bookbuilders of Boston, as the name implies, is an active group of production people drawn primarily from the several important publishing houses in Massachusetts. It brings together "all those interested in and working on the designing, planning, and actual manufacture of books, and the materials of which they consist." The membership of several hundred participants holds monthly meetings; prominent speakers are invited; and among other activities, this organization sponsors the annual New England Book Show.

Among New England's printers to be especially remembered, the Anthoensen Press in Portland, Maine, was a follower of the precepts laid down by Updike at The Merrymount Press. Fred Anthoensen was born in Denmark in 1882 and was brought to the United States two years later. In 1898 he was apprenticed at the Southworth Press in Portland. First hired as compositor, then as foreman, some twenty years later he became the owner of the company and changed the name to his own. Self-educated through reading, and inspired by *The Printing Art* magazine, Anthoensen built a deserved reputation for the meticulous production of difficult texts for universities, museums, libraries, and other cultural institutions. Anthoensen's books were forthright in design, proofreading was impeccable, workmanship was excellent.

Harvard and Yale universities and their presses have been vital factors in the maturity of American book design. Both presses in earlier days owned their own printing plants, but these were given up when it became more advantageous to buy from large manufacturing printers. The contribution by Yale has already been acknowledged in the earlier pages on Carl Purington Rollins. That erudite tradition has been very well nourished and maintained in the present direction and staff of the Press. Graphic Design and Photography are currently taught in the Yale School of Art under the direction of Professor Alvin Eisenman. He was the typographic designer of the 1954 Yale University Press publication *Early Victorian Architecture in Britain* (plate 58).

During the nineteen-twenties Bruce Rogers was a working advisor to the Harvard University Press. The Harvard Library was actively pursuing the arts of the book. George Parker Winship was in Cambridge, teaching and writing. In a lecture at Gallery 303 in New York in 1966, printed in *Heritage of the Graphic Arts*, Walter Muir Whitehill, doyen and arbiter of the cultivated life in Boston, said, "As a Harvard freshman in the academic year 1922–1923, I wandered into the Widener Room in the Library and encountered George Parker Winship, who had a singular genius for infecting undergraduates with a love of books and printing. I often returned, and as a junior enrolled in Winship's highly individualistic course entitled Fine Arts 5e, History of the Printed Book. It met on Tuesday and Thursday afternoons at three o'clock in the Widener Room, and was conducted with extreme informality. Winship would bring up from the Treasure Room armsful of incunabula, Aldines, French illustrated books of the eighteenth century, products of the Kelmscott, Doves, and Ashendene presses, and simply talk about them in the most offhand manner. Through George Winship I came to know the work of Daniel Berkeley Updike and Bruce Rogers."

Philip Hofer, bibliophile, scholar, and collector, established the Department of Printing and Graphic Arts in the Harvard Library in 1938. The department has grown around Hofer's own extraordinary collection of thousands of the world's great illustrated books, which he has donated to the college. Several extensive catalogues of parts of the collection, compiled by Ruth Mortimer, have already been published. Hofer has arranged many exhibitions and publications along the highways and byways of fine books, past and present. Perhaps the most important was "The Artist and the Book, 1860–1960, in Western Europe and the United States," accompanied by a fully documented and illustrated book as a catalogue of the exhibition, a joint venture with the Boston Museum of Fine Arts where the exhibition was held. The catalogue was designed by the museum's Carl F. Zahn, who has been an important part of New England's typographic landscape.

Because there has been only occasional education in printing on a scholarly level in the United States, most practitioners have made their way by instinct and circumstance. One of the bright spots was the lecture course and workshop in the art and history of the book conducted by Professor Ray Nash in the Art Department of Dartmouth College, Hanover, New Hampshire, from 1937 to 1970. A graduate of Oregon University and a newspaperman, Nash was an associate of the Plantin-Moretus Museum of Printing in Belgium, a lecturer in bibliography at Oxford University in England, and for a decade an editor of a lively small American quarterly magazine, *PaGA: Notes on Printing and Graphic Arts*. The equipment of the Dartmouth workshop consisted of a hand press for letterpress printing, a lithographic press, an etching press, and an interesting assortment of type. The practical shop work and Nash's leadership proved its worth to a number of young men. Alvin Eisenman became a professor in the Yale School of Art; Edward Connery Lathem is now Dean of Libraries at Dartmouth; Sinclair Hitchings is Curator of Prints at the Boston Public Library; David R. Godine established a printing office and a publishing house in Boston with a fine list of belletristic books; and Roderick D. Stinehour founded a superb press along the upper reaches of the Connecticut River.

THE STINEHOUR PRESS

The Stinehour Press, established by Roderick Stinehour in 1950 in the town of Lunenburg in northern Vermont, is at this writing the only fine press in New England with a scholarly staff (headed by C. Freeman Keith) and a plant of sufficient size to be capable of turning out substantial, well-designed books and catalogues that sustain a high degree of craftsmanship (plate 64). Consequently, a large proportion of the cultural institutions of the American northeast, and some from Canada and other parts of the United States, have turned to Stinehour for their publications, of which the present volume is a fair example. Primarily a letterpress house with Monotype machines and small cylinder presses, Stinehour has also installed photocomposition and offset equipment. And there is a very close working relationship with The Meriden Gravure Company for voluminous illustrated volumes, as for example, the superb catalogues for the Pierpont Morgan Library in New York which have won international recognition. An anniversary publication, *Twenty-five Books ... Twenty-five Years ...* (1950–1975), was issued by the Dartmouth College Library to describe their traveling exhibition which celebrated the first quarter-century of the Press. In an introduction Stinehour wrote: "All of us have received our most exacting training on the job. Besides a devotion to the ideals of good bookmaking and to their realization, each individual has a pronounced desire for country living and for personal involvement in a modest, closely-knit working unit. We have grown, over the years, to a group of about forty who join and blend their personalities and talents to make it possible for a small industrial craft enterprise to survive in an economic and business climate that seems more suited to the continued growth of bigness. . . . I do not believe that small organizations such as The Stinehour Press are mere vestiges of a crumbling past, soon to be outmoded by technology. Technology will not only serve the mass culture, but will bend also to comfort the small."

THE MERIDEN GRAVURE COMPANY

The Meriden Gravure Company of Meriden, Connecticut, has played a conspicuous role in extraordinarily sensitive reproduction of works of art and scientific data. The printing was done for many years by collotype. This excellent but laborious process gave way to the mechanical merits of offset printing when the 300-line screen was perfected. Led by E. Harold Hugo, assisted by John F. Peckham and others, The Meriden Gravure Company has attracted the leading university presses, museums, libraries, and learned societies, who have come to value the unusual skills and articulate capacities of this organization. Both Yale and Wesleyan universities have acknowledged Hugo's contribution to bookmaking with honorary degrees in the arts and humanities. (Reproductions in the present volume have been printed at The Meriden Gravure Company.)

THE GEHENNA PRESS

Leonard Baskin is a noted sculptor, wood engraver, and printmaker with, in his own words, "a secondary passion for printing." At his Gehenna Press over the past quarter-century he has designed, illustrated, and printed a remarkable succession of books of considerable erudition and magnitude. Baskin's involvement in printing began with the discovery that William Blake, one of his heroes, had printed his own poems and engravings. When an undergraduate at Yale in 1942, Baskin set in type and printed his youthful verse, *On a Pyre of Withered Roses*, on a student press in Jonathan Edwards College. After duty in World War II, and study in Italy and France, Baskin became an instructor in printmaking at the Worcester Art Museum in Massachusetts. Here in 1951 he printed a small portfolio, *A Little Book of Natural History*, with his engravings cut on linoleum and wood—the first of his bestiaries and the first of his private press publications. In 1953 he moved to an associate professorship in drawing, printmaking, and sculpture at Smith College in Northampton, Massachusetts, where he began to produce books in a local printing shop. Noteworthy from that early period is Hart Crane's *Voyages* (1957), an oblong folio in Perpetua type with Baskin's woodcuts printed on tissues and exotic papers.

In 1962 Baskin was able to set up his own financially backed press in Northampton with several associates, including Harold McGrath as the compositor and superb pressman. This was one's own plant, said Baskin, which would provide "that splendid ambience and unharried quiet in which our books take shape and achieve their final form."

From a large and venturesome program which drew on other artists for certain books, three fine folios may well be selected for mention: Melville's *Encantadas* (1963), with drawings by Enrico Lebrun engraved on wood by Baskin; *The Defense of Gracchus Babeuf before the High Court of Vendome* (1964), which included a series of twenty-one portrait etchings by Thomas Cornell of Babeuf, Marat, Mirabeau, and other leaders of the French Revolution; and currently (1976) the Press is issuing an elephant-folio edition of Shakespeare (plate 68) in individual volumes. Illustrated by Baskin, the page is a massive fourteen by twenty inches, the type is Centaur.

The University of Chicago Press commissioned Baskin to illustrate their special edition of *The Iliad of Homer* (1962), translated by Richmond Lattimore, for which forty-nine heroic drawings were separately printed by The Meriden Gravure Company. Baskin also illustrated a monumental three-volume *Divine Comedy* of Dante with 124 drawings (reproduced by Meriden) that crowded the nine by thirteen inch folio pages. The translation was by Professor Thomas G. Bergin; the books were designed and printed by Martino Mardersteig at the Stamperia Valdonega in Verona, Italy, issued in 1969 by Grossman Publishers, New York.

Although a "wild and passionate admirer" of William Morris, Baskin's acknowledged mentors have been Daniel Berkeley Updike and Carl Purington Rollins, traditionalists both. Two typographic idiosyncrasies are seen throughout Gehenna Press books: ornaments as paragraph separations to achieve a continuous and solid text page; and type set in geometric shapes "to make a pleasing ornament to run a whole length of the page." Baskin's recent books have been large in format, but his ephemera—informal pieces for family and friends—are dainty and joyous confections using typographic fleurons, boxed rules, and other devices in soft and enticing colors. His books have been exhibited and collected by institutions and individuals on both sides of the Atlantic. Baskin's honors have been many, including recognition, with its medal, by the American Institute of Graphic Arts.

THE JANUS PRESS

Since 1954 Claire Van Vliet, a printmaker, has produced more than forty books and substantial portfolios at her own press, finally settled in West Burke, Vermont. She designs and prints and publishes these volumes, most of them illustrated with her own wood engravings, relief etchings, and lithographs, as original prints. The subject matter has been interesting, sometimes rather esoteric, with an apparent liking for Kafka with whom her prints show some affinity. Her typography is colorful, fresh, and forthright. The work is superbly produced on a Vandercook press and an etching press. Type is always handset—usually in Times Roman, Optima, or Spectrum.

Among a considerable number of newcomers in New England are the special presses, all in Massachusetts, of wood-engraver Michael McCurdy at the Penmaen Press in Lincoln; Barry Moser at the Pennyroyal Press in Easthampton; and modest printing houses conducted by Darrell Hyder in North Brookfield, and Michael Bixler in Somerville.

NEW YORK AND THE EAST

New York was a lively place in the nineteen-twenties. Rogers, Goudy, Rudge, Cleland, Ruzicka, and their contemporaries were active participants at the height of their careers. Beautiful books came from the Nonesuch Press in London where, in a great publishing program, Francis Meynell showed that noble books could be done by machine at lower prices for a larger audience. There were great booksellers, like A. S. W. Rosenbach; formidable collectors, like Huntington, Houghton, and Widener, to name but the most famous; and a market for press books that gave fine printing its patronage. New publishing houses sprang up, with entrepreneurs like Bennett Cerf at Random House, that were concerned with good bookmaking. And there were newly established presses with staying power: Marchbanks, Pynson, Harbor, Walpole, Peter Pauper, Hawthorn, Spiral, and others. Carl P. Rollins conducted a spirited weekly column about printed books in the *Saturday Review of Literature*.

The meeting place where the faithful gathered was the American Institute of Graphic Arts with headquarters in New York. Founded in 1914, the A.I.G.A. had more than a thousand members nationwide. Among its numerous exhibitions, the most famous has been the "Fifty

Books of the Year," begun in 1923 and chosen each year thereafter by a different jury. Despite the personal dissatisfactions inherent in selection by jury, the exhibition has, overall, represented the best bookmaking in the United States. It has been a strongly competitive and helpful stimulus. Selections during the first decades were dominated by small, limited editions from the elder statesmen and by their followers among the new fine presses. In succeeding years as the general publishers became more aware of the importance of design, their books were substantial factors in the showings. In recent years the university presses, museums, and other learned institutions have taken the lead. The Institute has sent these annual exhibitions in two or three traveling shows throughout the United States, and one set was sent abroad by the United States Department of State as part of its cultural program. The scope of the A.I.G.A., as its name implies, embraces all phases of graphic communication. Among its many other exhibitions have been those for children's books, printing for commerce, newspaper advertisements, magazine design, record covers, and packaging.

William Edwin Rudge (see page 102) provided rare hospitality in the twenties and thirties to a dozen or more aspiring young men. Frederic Warde, of the Rudge staff, designed books of elegant austerity (plate 47), and completed a typeface based on the work of Ludovico Arrighi, the sixteenth-century Italian scribe and printer. Among the Rudge apprentices were Herbert Simon, who came from England; John S. Fass, Roland Wood, Peter Beilenson, Edmund B. Thompson, and Joseph Blumenthal, who later set up their own offices; and James Hendrickson, Milton B. Glick, Melvin Loos, and others, who became designers and production heads in representative publishing houses.

THE MARCHBANKS PRESS

Hal Marchbanks came from Texas and in 1914 established his printing house in New York City, where he became a member of the group in the National Arts Club that founded the American Institute of Graphic Arts. He attracted Goudy, Oswald Cooper, and other graphic artists to his plant. With its considerable press capacities, the Marchbanks Press turned out a large body of fine work for concerned publishers and for special industrial accounts. After Marchbanks' death, Emily E. Connor carried on the press for many years.

THE
TWENTIETH
CENTURY

NEW YORK
AND
THE EAST

THE HARBOR PRESS

The first of the Rudge alumni to set up were Fass and Wood, who became partners in New York at the Harbor Press in the nineteen-twenties. They produced ephemera and books for, among others, the Limited Editions Club, learned institutions, and private collectors. The book here reproduced, *Arabia Infelix* by Aldous Huxley (plate 46), was printed at the Harbor Press for the Fountain Press, conducted by James Wells, who during the lush twenties induced famous authors to provide him with unpublished short pieces, with the lure of beautiful books in signed limited editions, printed at the best presses. These titles were snapped up by the many new unsophisticated collectors who stopped buying as soon as the Depression dried up their surplus incomes. The Harbor Press survived until the forties when Roland Wood returned to his early love of professional acting. Fass turned to work in the trade, but in his ample spare time pursued his gifts for exquisite craftsmanship at his small and private Hammer Creek Press.

THE

TWENTIETH

CENTURY

NEW YORK

AND

THE EAST

THE PETER PAUPER PRESS

Peter Beilenson forsook his father's diamond business in 1926 and spent the next two years learning to set type and print with Rudge in Mount Vernon, with Goudy at Marlboro-on-Hudson, and with Melbert B. Cary at his private Press of the Woolly Whale. Then Peter bought an eight by twelve Pearl press which he set up in his father's cellar, acquired some Oxford and Original Old Style type, and in 1928 designed and printed a small book, *With Petrarch*, which was promptly bought up by New York booksellers. Although this was his first book, it made the "Fifty Books" selection. "For an imprint," wrote Beilenson, "I set up the words 'Peter Pauper Press' because they expressed how I felt about life at the moment, and the name stuck." The next year appeared the first book with the imprint of the Blue-Behinded Ape, the name used by the Beilensons for their delightfully bawdy books and some of their most spirited bookmaking.

In the fall of 1929, Edmund B. Thompson joined Beilenson in a partnership in suburban New Rochelle as the Walpole Printing Office. With two Colts Armory job presses and the Pearl from Peter's basement, they invited and received commissions during the next three years, after which Thompson found it advisable to move to the quiet of a small town

THE
TWENTIETH
CENTURY

NEW YORK
AND
THE EAST

in Connecticut. Edna Beilenson, who had, meanwhile, been setting Peter Pauper books in type, then became her husband's partner in what was to become a sizeable publishing adventure. After a move in 1935 to larger quarters in Mount Vernon, Peter continued to design and print books for Random House, New Directions, and other publishers. An outstanding Peter Pauper publication was *The Four Gospels* (plate 53) with wood engravings by Hans Alexander Mueller. But the Beilensons' major achievement was the production of the attractive and inexpensive Peter Pauper books, decorative, colorful, varied in design, and usually illustrated, at one and two dollars per copy. Ten or a dozen new titles have been added each year, sold in bookshops throughout the country in a highly successful publishing enterprise.

Peter Beilenson combined a ready wit and a scholarly pen. He wrote a perceptive historical account of printing in the nineteenth century for *A History of the Printed Book* (The Dolphin, 1938); a biography of Goudy, 1939; counsel to beginners in "What Every Young Man Should Know" (The Dolphin, 1941); on the amateur printer, in the Harvard University Press publication *Graphic Forms: The Arts as Related to the Book* in 1949; and a sprightly account of the first ten years of his Press for the Colophon's *The Annual of Bookmaking*, 1938. He edited and printed the A.I.G.A. *Journal* from 1947 to 1950, and its *News-Letter* from 1957 to 1960.

Peter died suddenly in 1962 at fifty-six years of age. His many friends —writers, artists, publishers, and printers—joined to make a Typophile Chap Book, issued in 1964, *The Life and Times of Peter Beilenson and His Peter Pauper Press*, including a checklist of the more than four hundred books for which Beilenson was responsible. At this writing in 1976, Edna Beilenson continues to edit, design, print, and publish the Peter Pauper books. Among other contributions to her craft, Mrs. Beilenson served for two years as President of the American Institute of Graphic Arts.

HAWTHORN HOUSE

After the three years as Beilenson's partner, Edmund Thompson and family moved in 1932, for country quiet, to Windham, Connecticut. In the wing of his newly built modest home, Thompson installed a small printing shop, named Hawthorn House, where he and his wife set type by hand and printed slender books of great charm for a few private collectors, for the Columbiad Club (a group of Connecticut typophiles), and for the Limited Editions Club, New York. Other books bore the imprint of Hawthorn House as publishers—"We have preferred to work new ground, with the feeling that reprints of the classics are being excellently (and adequately) done by others." Among the Hawthorn House published books that show Thompson's sensitive skill with type are *Portraits on Our Postage Stamps* (1933) and *A Printer's Common-place Book* (1937). A checklist of books is included in the article on Hawthorn House in the Colophon's *The Annual of Bookmaking*, 1938. A few years thereafter, with America's entry into World War II, Thompson moved to Washington, to work in the U.S. Army Map Service. He did not return to printing.

THE
TWENTIETH
CENTURY

NEW YORK
AND
THE EAST

THE SPIRAL PRESS

The Spiral Press was established in 1926 by the author of this volume. It survived one depression and one world war before it was liquidated in 1971. The autobiography of a printing house and a checklist of its publications may be found, by anyone so curious, in the published catalogue of an exhibition, *The Spiral Press through Four Decades*, held at the Pierpont Morgan Library in New York in 1966. However, a few pertinent facts may be set down here in the seeming objectivity of the third person singular. At age twenty-eight, after some experience in the business of publishing, stimulated by press books seen on bookstore tables, Joseph Blumenthal made his first direct acquaintance with printing processes thanks to the benevolent generosity of William Edwin Rudge. Further good fortune came during another short apprenticeship at the Marchbanks Press where a meeting with George Hoffman provided the knowledge for setting up a new shop. Equipment began with two platen presses. Small automatic cylinders were soon added. There were three compositors, two or three pressmen, a papercutter, and the office staff for proofreading and keeping of records—and so it remained.

The Spiral Press, like other small fine printing houses, produced work for cultural institutions such as museums, universities, foundations, book clubs, book shops, and art galleries; for special book publishers; and for private individuals and book collectors whose interests and tastes would normally demand printed matter of some distinction. A few escapades into publishing in the private press manner, such as an *Ecclesiastes* (plate 63), illustrated by Ben Shahn, as well as books in normal routines, brought several of America's most prominent graphic artists to the Press. The most remarkable personal relationship came with Robert

133

THE
TWENTIETH
CENTURY

NEW YORK
AND
THE EAST

Frost and his books. The first was Frost's *Collected Poems*, completed in a limited and signed edition of one thousand copies. The volume was set in Lutetia type from which electroplates were made for the publisher's large trade edition. This general procedure was continued until Frost's last book, *In the Clearing*, in 1962. Another important work was *The Public Papers and Addresses of Franklin D. Roosevelt* (1928–1936), designed for Random House, printed by their trade printers, and published in 1938. This brought an inscribed copy from President Roosevelt, who had actually given close personal attention to typographic detail. These were some of the brightest spots among the thousands of jobs that sustained a printing office, that provided a livelihood and made for a good life. An expedition into type design produced the Emerson typeface. First cut by Louis Hoell in Germany from Blumenthal designs, the type was later issued by the Monotype Corporation in London.

Retrospective exhibitions of Spiral Press printing were held at Cornell University (the printer's alma mater) in 1961; at the Pierpont Morgan Library in 1966; at the Royal Library of Belgium in Brussels and at the Meermano-Westreenianum in The Hague in 1968; at the National Library in Edinburgh in 1970; and in 1971 at the Hebrew University Library in Jerusalem.

A commission in 1971 from the Pierpont Morgan Library in New York to organize an exhibition and to select the best printed books of the five centuries since Gutenberg opened the treasured stacks of the Morgan and other great repositories. The exhibition, "Art of the Printed Book: 1455–1955," opened in 1973. An illustrated catalogue with an essay by the present writer was issued in paperback by the Library, in cloth by David R. Godine in Boston and by the Bodley Head in London.

To complete this personal memoir, acknowledgment must be made of the medal of the American Institute of Graphic Arts and honorary membership in New York's Grolier Club and Boston's Society of Printers.

THE TYPOPHILES

Early in the nineteen-thirties a group of typographic enthusiasts—printers, graphic artists, paper manufacturers, bookbinders, librarians, and others—met each week in New York for luncheon. From these enjoyable meetings grew an informal organization called The Typophiles, without officers or dues, under the inspired leadership of Paul A. Bennett of the Mergenthaler Linotype Company, the typographic conscience of his generation. From anniversary dinners, at which the younger Typophiles honored their elders and betters with keepsakes, grew an extensive program of clothbound Chap Books, designed, illustrated, printed, and bound by the leading practitioners in the field. Professionals all, they met and produced as amateurs. Altogether some sixty titles were published between 1935 and 1965, open to subscription. Subjects included some of the byways of typography, such as ampersands and roman numerals. Of the greatest importance are the biographies of the prominent designers, illustrators, and printers that form a unique record of a fertile period. Bennett wrote of these "Adventures in Bookmaking" in the *Penrose Annual*, London, Volume 54 (1960). After Bennett's death, Robert L. Leslie has led The Typophiles.

THE
TWENTIETH
CENTURY

NEW YORK
AND
THE EAST

THE LIMITED EDITIONS CLUB

The first book of the Limited Editions Club was issued in October 1929, the black month in the New York stock market that touched off the Depression. Despite the grim years ahead, George Macy, founder and director, published a volume every month for fifteen hundred subscribers. The titles were chosen from the classics of literature, edited by scholars of repute, illustrated by famous artists (including Picasso and Matisse), designed by the most talented typographers, and produced by the best printers of Europe and America. Macy later established the Heritage Club for an unlimited membership that subscribed to books reproduced from the Limited Editions Club volumes but in smaller formats and less expensive materials. In addition, Macy published some special books such as W. A. Dwiggins' *Towards a Reform of the Paper Currency*, and of great importance, *The Dolphin: A Journal of the Making of Books*, in four splendid folio volumes. Here, too, Macy called on the leading scholars and practitioners in the field.

Macy died in 1956, but the Limited Editions Club and the Heritage Club are producing books in the spirit of the founder at this writing in 1976. The first two-hundred-and-fifty books (1929–1954) were celebrated in an elegant, illustrated bibliography, entitled *A Quarto-millenary*, published by the Limited Editions Club in 1959. Virtually all the contemporary practitioners who have been discussed in the present volume were called on to make books for the Limited Editions Club. Despite the excellence of the many minds and hands that produced books under Macy's patronage and direction, an element of salesmanship was necessary for the success of the program. Adornment, especially of the bindings, was called for in order that the volumes would attract new buyers and hold the membership. It may be suspected that these books, as has been the fate of many books of large and elegant format, were bought, in part at least, for their decorative qualities. Two excellent Limited Editions Club volumes are here reproduced (plates 39 and 51). Since Macy's death the Club's books have been made under the capable supervision of Max Stein during several changes of ownership.

UNIVERSITY PRESSES

The importance of the American university presses has several times been emphasized in these pages. At their annual conventions an impressive exhibition of bookmaking has usually been on view. The average of design and production has been high despite the need for budgetary control. In a choice of the most distinguished of the university press designers, the accolade would, with little doubt, fall on P. J. Conkwright and his thirty years at the Princeton University Press. Typical of the great projects that have been developed at learned presses are the twenty volumes already issued, of the fifty projected, of *The Papers of Thomas Jefferson*. Julian P. Boyd has been the editor, Conkwright the designer, the Princeton University Press the publisher (plate 54). The typeface used, appropriately called Monticello, was cut especially for the Jefferson papers by the Mergenthaler Linotype Company, patterned on an early American Binny & Ronaldson casting in use during the latter years of Jefferson's life.

THE OVERBROOK PRESS

Unlike most private presses which mirror the personality and capabilities of the proprietor, the Overbrook Press was "many streams run into a small river." The Press was established in 1934 by Frank Altschul, a banker and collector whose bibliophilic enthusiasms included a term as president of the Grolier Club. With its own printing facilities, the Press was housed in a remodeled outbuilding on the Altschul estate "amid willows and bird-song on the bank of the Mianus river in the country back of Stamford, Connecticut." Many prominent designers and illustrators were drawn into its activities. The titles were chosen from the classics of literature, with occasional publications representing the proprietor's political convictions. Margaret B. Evans was staff de-

THE
TWENTIETH
CENTURY

NEW YORK
AND
THE EAST

signer and manager, with a full-time pressman for production. Among an impressive list of books are Sterne's *A Sentimental Journey* (1936), with a superb title page by Cleland (plate 41); Stevenson's *The Inland Voyage* (1938), illustrated by Jean Hugo; a folio Shakespeare *Poems* (1939); and a luxuriant *Manon Lescaut* (1958), illustrated by Cleland. A bibliography of the Press, 1934–1959, was published in 1963.

THE

TWENTIETH

CENTURY

NEW YORK

AND

THE EAST

LEXINGTON, KENTUCKY

In a city usually associated with horse racing rather than bibliophilia we find a pocket of typographic enthusiasts who welcomed Victor Hammer (see page 113) to Lexington in 1948, and who were carried forward by his inspiration. Joseph C. Graves, a trustee of Transylvania University, issued several interesting books from his private Gravesend Press for a decade beginning in 1949. A good example is the charming *Aucassin & Nicolette* with woodcuts by Fritz Kredel.

Since Hammer's death his widow, Carolyn Reading Hammer, has led the Anvil Press with occasional publications including an enchanting hand-colored volume, *Kentucky Wild Flowers* by Harriet MacDonald Holladay. Mrs. Hammer has been the typographic designer and, with her associates, responsible for type composition, presswork, and binding, all accomplished by hand. As Curator of the Rare Books Collections of the University of Kentucky Libraries, Mrs. Hammer founded the King Library Press, where she has been guiding students at work on two Washington-type handpresses and the publication of small editions.

JOSEPH LOW

Graphic artist, printmaker, book illustrator, Joseph Low set up his own private press in the 1950's in Newtown, Connecticut, where he could produce and control his own highly individualistic work. In addition to book jackets and book illustration, etc., for publishing houses, he printed and published portfolios of his own prints at the Eden Hill Press in editions of several hundred copies, from linoleum and woodblocks, cut and scraped for texture, and in exotic colors. They were fables and proverbs, usually set in Bulmer type, illustrated with stylized animals and other bizarre creatures of Low's fertile imagination.

America was handsomely enriched by the émigrés who arrived from Hitler's Germany during the 1930's and became citizens of the United States.

THE
TWENTIETH
CENTURY

NEW YORK
AND
THE EAST

Bookmaking received its full share. Among the artists who brought their talents to illustration were Fritz Kredel, Fritz Eichenberg, and Hans Alexander Mueller. Victor Hammer's contribution has already been acknowledged. George Salter was an outstanding calligrapher, typographer, illustrator, and jacket artist. His art classes at the Cooper Union in New York City developed first-rate new talent. Ernst Reichl has been a book typographer in the forefront of a contemporary approach to design. His layout for the Random House edition of Joyce's *Ulysses* was a landmark. From the Bauhaus in Weimar came Herbert Bayer and Laszlo Moholy-Nagy, who were protagonists for asymmetrical layouts and other means of introducing industrial functionalism into American book design.

Several American artists and designers have attempted to correlate book typography with modern art and contemporary design. The most prominent among them were Alvin Lustig, with provocative books for the publisher New Directions in New York; Paul Rand, a very successful advertising artist who designed a few books for Alfred A. Knopf; Marshall Lee, who produced articulately and consistently for several trade publishers; and Merle Armitage, a bold free-lance designer at work on both ends of the continent. The results have frequently been refreshing, but few fundamental changes have occurred. Book design is tied to rigid and inflexible reading habits. The first duty of the book designer is to provide ease of reading, undisturbed by vagaries of design. However, the arrival of photocomposition and offset printing have given the designer new freedoms in the selection and disposition of type, especially in books with illustrated matter. New textbooks, books for children, paperback covers, advertising, promotional literature, etc. — areas outside the province of the present history — have not been bound by the rigidities inherent in traditional book production.

Among New York publishers, Alfred A. Knopf was unique. From the founding of his house in 1915, he has never failed to give his books typographic distinction. The production and design people on his staff were carefully chosen, and Knopf reached out to employ the typographic gifts of the prominent designers and printers in the East. Among them was Warren Chappell, artist, illustrator, and graphic designer, who was responsible for the typography of the Knopf anniversary volume, *Fifty Years*, issued in 1965 (plate 62). Chappell had spent a year in pre-Hitler Germany at the famous workshop of Rudolf Koch. In the United States, among his varied activities in the book arts he designed the successful Lydian type series issued in 1938 by the American Type Founders. He also designed Trajanus for the Stempel foundry in Germany. Chappell is the author of *The Anatomy of Lettering* (1935), *A Short History of the Printed Word* (1970), and *The Living Alphabet* (1975).

Helen Gentry came to New York from the Pacific Coast after an apprenticeship with the Grabhorns and after she had established her own press in San Francisco (1929–1934) where, among other works, she set and printed enchanting, diminutive children's books with woodcut illustrations. In New York she was a co-founder of Holiday House where she designed their books for young people. She was the author, with her husband, David Greenhood, of *Chronology of Books and Printing* (Helen Gentry Press, 1933, and The Macmillan Co., 1936).

Melbert B. Cary, Jr., established the Continental Typefounders Company in New York in the late twenties for the purpose of importing and selling a number of the new and very interesting typefaces produced in Germany during its own typographic revival, and others from the energetic and innovative Deberny and Peignot foundry in France. A good range of Goudy type was similarly distributed. Cary set up his own private press—the Press of the Woolly Whale— and wrote about it for the Colophon's 1938 *Annual of Bookmaking*. A number of attractive books were printed and published, including a definitive *Bibliography of the Village Press* and books on the history of playing cards. Cary's extensive collection of such cards was donated to Yale. The Cary name has been preserved in a memorial fund set up by Mrs. Cary (the Mary Flagler Cary Trust) at the Rochester Institute of Technology, where Professor Alexander S. Lawson has, for many years, taught the art and history of the book to students in the Institute's school of printing. Although most of the Rochester students are primarily interested in techniques and new processes, Lawson has sent many young men on their way with extra appreciation of the cultural values of their craft. Toward this end the Cary endowment's income has been of material help.

The partnership of Bertram Clarke and David Way was joined in 1949 to carry through to completion over the succeeding four years the twelve-volume, illustrated folio catalogue raisonné of the Frick Collection, begun by Porter Garnett. From 1953 to 1970 Clarke and Way built up and operated a sizeable printing plant in New York for the production of fine printing, with Clarke as the very competent and sensitive designer. Since 1970 he has been associated with the Press of A. Colish, once the favorite press of Bruce Rogers and T. M. Cleland. Abraham Colish in 1940 set and printed for the Limited Editions Club the thirty-seven volumes that comprise *The Comedies, Histories, and Tragedies of William Shakespeare* (plate 39).

THE BIRD AND BULL PRESS

The most recent eastern printer of exceptional interest is Henry Morris of North Hills, Pennsylvania, a suburb of Philadelphia. Morris made the moulds, built the beater and other equipment in order to make excellent paper by hand (in his basement) for the books he has printed and published at his private Bird and Bull Press. Morris was born in 1927. After a whimsical choice of printing on entering a vocational high school, Morris became a successful commercial label printer. However, during formative years he had acquired a three-by-five-inch table-top press, a slightly larger foot-treadle press, and fortuitously a single fine page from a fifteenth-century incunable. These possessions must have ignited a receptive typographic imagination. Morris produced his first Bird and Bull book in 1958, in which he used his own first-rate paper. Other books followed in 1961 and 1962. In 1963 came an important volume, *Five on Paper*, "A collection of essays on papermaking, books and relevant matters," by Dard Hunter, J. Barcham Green, John Mason, Henry Morris, and Norman H. Strouse, in an edition of 169 completed copies. This was followed, in 1964, by *The Passionate Pirate*, a biography of Thomas Bird Mosher by Norman H. Strouse. In 1967 Morris again published a valuable edition of paperiana: *Omnibus*, with instructions for amateur papermakers, notes on private presses, and other data, by Henry Morris, with illustrations and paper samples.

Limitation of space permits only briefest mention of some of the many respected workers in the typographic vineyards. Many designers and printers gave vitality to the twenties and later decades. Arthur W. Rushmore, head of design and production at Harper and Brothers, enjoyed the avocation of private printing at his Golden Hind Press in Madison, New Jersey; Richard W. Ellis produced books for the Limited Editions Club and other publishers; Lester Douglas designed and printed in Washington, D.C.; Robert L. Dothard produced in New England; Eugene M. Ettenburg designed in New York, taught at Pratt Institute,

THE
TWENTIETH
CENTURY

NEW YORK
AND
THE EAST

140

and wrote about type and its uses; Paul Standard, New York calligrapher and teacher, held high the torch for fine writing. A recent arrival is Ronald Gordon at his Oliphant Press.

THE MIDWEST

The huge Donnelley organization, printers of national magazines and telephone books, induced William A. Kittredge (1891–1945) to come to Chicago in 1922 to be Director of Design at the Lakeside Press, Donnelley's division for work of special quality. Kittredge, who had been a practical printer and art director in the east, brought typographic purpose to his new position. Along with his other daily duties he designed and printed books for the Caxton Club, the active Chicago group of dedicated bibliophiles; produced several titles for the Limited Editions Club; and initiated four noteworthy editions of American literary classics printed, and published in 1930, by the Lakeside Press: *Moby Dick*, illustrated by Rockwell Kent (plate 48); *Walden*, illustrated by Rudolph Ruzicka; *Two Years before the Mast*, illustrated by Edward A. Wilson; and Poe's *Tales*, illustrated by W. A. Dwiggins. Kittredge also took advantage of the ample Donnelley facilities at his disposal to organize excellent exhibitions in several areas of the arts of the book at the Lakeside galleries.

The Society of Typographic Arts was founded in Chicago in 1927 as a regional counterpart to the New York–based American Institute of Graphic Arts. Annual exhibitions have been held which, owing to the makeup of the membership, have been slanted toward advertising design. A Chicago Book Clinic has held annual exhibitions of regional bookmaking with faithful regularity. Typefounding provided the opportunity for hand punch-cutting in the person of Robert Wiebking, who brought a matrix engraving machine to Chicago when he emigrated from Germany. Wiebking cut some of the early Goudy types and the remarkable Centaur of Bruce Rogers. R. Hunter Middleton, type designer and art director for the Ludlow typecasting machine, has been a prominent figure in Chicago's typographic activities. Middleton has brought together an extraordinary collection of Thomas Bewick's original woodblocks. These he has printed with remarkable clarity and depth in a number of volumes at his own Cherryburn Press. Leonard H. Bahr at his Adagio Press in Harper Woods, Michigan, setting type and printing on evenings and weekends, has turned out interesting work since 1956. Bahr's most ambitious undertaking, currently nearing completion, is a folio edition, *Cobden-Sanderson: The Master Craftsman*, with essays by Norman H. Strouse and John Dreyfus.

One of the few centers in the United States for teaching the arts of the book on an academic level was begun in 1922 when Porter Garnett (1871–1951) was called from a literary environment on the Pacific Coast to an associate professorship in the graphic arts at the Carnegie Institute of Technology in Pittsburgh. Garnett set up the Laboratory Press as a division of the Department of Printing within the Institute's College of Industries. Young men who would spread out into printing plants, advertising agencies, and publishing houses were taught to set type by hand and print on the handpress in the spirit of the masters of the printed book. These worthy efforts were described, and student work of the first five years was reproduced, in a volume, *A Documentary Account of the Beginnings of the Laboratory Press*, printed and issued by the Press in 1927. Among the students who later retained their interest in fine printing were Wilder Bentley, Grant Dahlstrom, Ted F. Gensamer, Frank Powers, and Max Stein. The Laboratory Press was discontinued in 1935. Garnett's own skills as a book designer may be seen in a beautiful *Daphnis and Chloe* (plate 51) handset in Lutetia type (slightly modified at the foundry for Garnett) and printed in 1934 on a handpress for the Limited Editions Club. As already mentioned, Garnett was commissioned to design and produce the catalogue of the great Frick Collection, completed by Clarke & Way after Garnett's death.

THE PRAIRIE PRESS

A salutary tradition was born when Carroll Coleman, a young instructor in English at the University of Iowa, issued the first book of the Prairie Press in 1935. Since then he has printed and published about 175 books of poetry, and some fiction, by contemporary authors. At first regional, Coleman later spread his net throughout the country. *Mortal Summer* by Mark Van Doren (1953) is typical of Prairie Press books and of Coleman's fine craftsmanship (plate 56). His typography has been forthright and legible, with quiet elegance and erudition. Books were usually issued in editions of 500 to 600 copies, rather modest in format and inexpensive, in order that the author's work might reach its reader audience. The Prairie Press has been a modern private press, devoted to a living literary enthusiasm rather than one concerned with elaborate and expensive reprints of the established classics. This attitude has touched a responsive chord among many young college people who, at this writing, are putting new texts into type at small, scholarly, productive, private presses. In 1945 Coleman established the Typographic Laboratory at the University of Iowa and taught several promising students until 1956, when he offered the leadership to Harry Duncan who thereupon moved westward from Cummington, Massachusetts. The books produced by Duncan and his artist-associate Wightman Williams at the Cummington Press rank high among the best work done in the United States during the present century. Since Duncan has become a teacher and practitioner west of the Mississippi, these notes involve him in that area.

THE CUMMINGTON PRESS

The Cummington Press grew out of the romantic enthusiasms of a group of students at the Cummington (Massachusetts) School of the Arts, and its zealous director, Katherine Frazier. From a very slender budget, Centaur type was acquired, also a handpress lacking tympan and frisket which had to be constructed by a local cabinetmaker from specifications in Ringwalt's *American Encyclopedia of Printing* (1871). Painting students had vague hopes of using the press for block printing, and aspiring writers, unaware of the exacting techniques of the handpress, thought they might quickly see their compositions in print.

Harry Duncan was then on a teaching scholarship at the Cummington School. A 1934 graduate of Grinnell College, he held an assistantship in the English department at Duke University. Himself a poet, the path lay open to a professorship. But in his words, "World War II called all in doubt," and after rejection by the army he "began fooling with type and press at Cummington." In 1941 when five leading writers taught at the school, Duncan and some of his associates set up and printed on dampened paper *Incident on the Bark Columbia*, the first book to carry the Cummington Press imprint. Printing had then become a central concern for Duncan. Because he needed more technical experience he spent a brief apprenticeship with Edmund Thompson at Hawthorn House, and received much helpful advice about the handpress from Victor Hammer.

Within another year the Cummington Press printed and published *The Second World* by R. P. Blackmur and *Notes toward a Supreme Fiction* by Wallace Stevens. These books were followed during the next decade by the work of Allen Tate, William Carlos Williams, Marianne Moore, and by the verse of most of the prominent younger American poets. The Press was kept afloat during the war, and several books were issued in 1943. *The Book of Job* (1943), with wood engravings by Gustav Wolf, made the A.I.G.A. Fifty Books exhibition. After the war Duncan was joined by Wightman Williams in an idealistic and fruitful partnership. The press was then housed in the school kitchen, the only building with some heat. Duncan and Williams kept house, cooked, tended the stove, and printed books. Duncan was typographer and compositor, Williams illustrated with drawings and woodcuts. Together, they operated the Washington handpress. *Five Prose Pieces* by Rainer Maria Rilke (1947) is an excellent example (plate 52) of the partners' skills.

The typographic design of Cummington Press books is of a compelling and dramatic simplicity. Eminently readable, Duncan's volumes show the respect for the written word of a sensitive poet turned skillful printer. The books were handset, the early volumes in Centaur, Poliphilus, and Blado types; the later books most often in van Krimpen's Romanée.

After a short-lived move to Rowe, Massachusetts, and Williams' tragic death in an automobile accident, Duncan accepted the invitation to teach typography in the School of Journalism at the University of Iowa. In 1956 he headed west, the Washington handpress close behind in a U-Haul trailer. In 1972 he moved to the University of Nebraska at Omaha where he conducts a workshop with type and presses, and holds seminars in the history of the printed book. Abattoir Editions is the imprint for the books which are produced at the University, reminiscent of the Cummington years.

THE STONE WALL PRESS

A letter from K. K. Merker, a former Duncan student, to the present writer, explains why certain writers and artists have turned to printing: "Since the University of Iowa was the first in the country to establish a graduate degree in creative writing, Harry's presence at Iowa with all of his talents brought a major and spectacular reaction in the writing community. Many writers from the Writers' Workshop became his friends and took his course and, since not all people who want to be Great American Writers can actually make the grade, a number of them, myself included, found that printing was a beguiling substitute. Some used it as a kind of therapy, and others discovered it was their true vocation. Regardless, after Harry's coming, dozens of small presses popped up, most of which disappeared as the proprietors found other interests or careers that were of more importance to them. But some remained and have done important work over the years."

Merker came to the University of Iowa in 1956 as a graduate student in the poetry workshop. The quick transition from poet to practising printer is seen in Merker's own words: "Pretty soon I stopped writing ... purchased type, a Washington handpress, and other equipment, and without much considered thought, found myself to be a printer / publisher. . . . I had absolutely no formal training as a designer, but I had the example of Harry's excellence. . . . The main things I got from him were a sense of craftsmanship, a love for the Washington press, and a decided liking for the types of Jan van Krimpen. From my own sense of the futility of doing otherwise, came a policy of never reprinting work, but only doing original manuscripts." Among the seventy-five excellent books Merker has produced, several have been chosen for national A.I.G.A. Fifty Books shows and regional exhibitions. Two among many are *Sleeping with One Eye Open*, poems by Mark Strand (1964), and *The Stone Wall Book of Short Fictions* (1973).

THE WINDHOVER PRESS

There was countrywide determination among young men and women during the 1960's to work in the handcrafts as opposed to unwelcome industrialism. In response to the desire among college students to study the history of the printed book as a craft, Merker induced the University of Iowa to set up its own press, called Windhover, and he became its director "for the production of books and, primarily for the preservation and dissemination of those skills that go into the creating of a hand-printed book." True to its purposes the Press has completed and issued volumes of translations, essays, fiction, and plays. Its substantial selection of types includes Bembo, Joanna, Emerson, Spectrum, Palatino, Cancelleresca Bastarda, and American Uncial. *Passion Play* by Bernard Shaw, "A Dramatic Fragment," (1971) in Romanée type on Umbria handmade paper has been superbly designed and printed with impeccable craftsmanship. Several students, spread out across the country, have started their own printing and publishing ventures.

145

THE PERISHABLE PRESS LIMITED

Walter Hamady, associate professor of art at the University of Wisconsin, a published poet and professional photographer, has since 1964 designed and printed and published books and ephemera of extraordinary interest and versatility at his private press. Hamady is a graduate of Wayne University, and of Cranbrook Academy of Art where among other matters he learned to make paper. Recipient of a Guggenheim Fellowship in 1969, he studied the production of handmade paper at the few surviving European mills. Much of the Perishable Press Limited work has been printed on the excellent paper (called Shadwell) made by hand by Hamady with his own equipment. Typefounding is at this writing in prospect. Hamady named the Press, he said, "to reflect the human conditions, both perishable and limited."

Among the hundred titles completed during the first dozen years of its existence the Press has printed contemporary writing, including Hamady's poetry and that of his wife who is also a working partner at the Press. Equipment includes a wide range of typefaces, a Vandercook press and an iron handpress. The books are already widely collected and exhibited, with showings at the Grolier Club in New York, the Print Club of Philadelphia, and in the A.I.G.A. Fifty Books. Two volumes among others completed in 1976 may be mentioned: *Guillem de Poitou*, twelfth-century poems translated by Paul Blackburn, with a title-page drawing by Roland Ginzel, set in Tschichold's Sabon Antiqua type; and *Chapter Seven* by H. M. Petrakis, with a title-page drawing by Warrington Colescott, in Van Krimpen's Spectrum type. Some of Hamady's books, as well as those of other midwest college presses, have been aided by grants from the National Endowment for the Arts.

Because Hamady is a poet and an artist who has come to printing free from traditional printing house restraints, his handling of type is fresh and exuberant. His craftsmanship is nothing short of brilliant, especially in the sometimes witty and playful ephemera.

In response to a frequently asked question, Hamady may well have touched on the sometimes compelling attraction of printing: "It is hard to say why printing continues to hold my devotion. Who knows? . . . All I can say is when I am on the press & working at the figgeren things out, etc it fills me with good feelings, that I am trading my energies of my life for something that is extremely worthwhile, for artifacts of communi-

cation that only kindred spirits can fully comprehend with their guts &
heart & mind."

Doyle Moore, a student in the art department at Iowa, with a background in the graphic arts found the printed book to be a vehicle for his
talents and established The Finial Press. He took his Vandercook along
with him when he was engaged to teach in the art department of the
University of Illinois. Moore's typography is bright and experimental
for the books of poetry he issues. The Seamark Press is the serious concern of Kay Amert and Howard Zimmon. Bonne O'Connell studied
with Hamady at Wisconsin, then at Iowa set up her own Penumbra
Press.

CALIFORNIA

The founding of the Book Club of California in San Francisco in 1912
marked the fortunate start of a proud tradition of fine printing on the
Pacific Coast. The early years were in debt to the Taylors and the John-
sons, and to John Henry Nash, especially Nash. The Grabhorns arrived
in 1920. During forty-five years at the Grabhorn Press they were a bea-
con and a dramatic influence for a new generation of artists, designers,
and printers. The several decades starting with the nineteen-twenties
were rich and productive, and witnessed the realization of the four essentials that, according to Jacob Zeitlin, the eminent Los Angeles bookseller, were manifestations of California's emergence from the frontier:
(1) the establishment of great libraries, (2) the existence of a thriving
antiquarian booktrade, (3) the organization of book clubs for the discussion and collecting of books and the encouragement of good printing,
and (4) the presence of a group of printers whose objective was the production of fine books in the tradition of the great printers of the past.

New printers of typographic significance made their appearance in
the nineteen-thirties. Three new supportive book clubs were established, each with social and typographic inclinations of their own. In
San Francisco, the Roxburgh Club began in 1928; in Los Angeles both
the Zamorano Club in 1928 and The Rounce and Coffin Club in 1930
held their first meetings. The latter has sponsored the annual Western
Books Exhibitions since 1939. The great Henry E. Huntington Library
and Art Gallery in San Marino opened its doors in 1928; the William
Andrews Clark Library, in its handsome French Renaissance building,

147

was presented to the University of California in 1934. The Bancroft Library of the University of California in Berkeley is fortunate, at this writing, to have James D. Hart, scholar and part-time printer, as its Director.

THE PLANTIN PRESS

Saul Marks brought to Los Angeles an inborn love of culture and a capacity for immaculate craftsmanship. With his wife, Lillian, he built a printing house of modest proportions, without compromise as to time or commercial advantage. With the naming of his own press in homage to Christopher Plantin, Marks made clear his respect for the historic typographic tradition.

At age eleven, during World War I, in his native Warsaw, Saul was apprenticed to a printing office that had a reputation for excellent workmanship and produced books in Polish, Yiddish, and Hebrew. The alert lad was proud to be directed to set entire books of great literature by hand and to print them on a foot-operated platen press. But in 1921, at sixteen, Saul decided to escape from restrictive Polish anti-Semitism and emigrated to the New World. Although he had found work as a compositor in New York, he enlisted for three years in the U.S. Army, the better to learn English and for much spare-time reading.

After release from the army, there were several years of training in printing plants in Detroit. In 1928 Saul married Lillian Simon, with whom he said he "found it easy to talk at great length about printing." Two years later they moved to the warm climate of Los Angeles where, with unerring instinct, Marks found Bruce McCallister, the first printer in southern California to have been aware of William Morris and the "Revival of Fine Printing." After a false start with the Monarch Press, Marks announced the opening in 1931 of the Plantin Press, with his wife and Kenneth McKay, as his partners. The McKay relationship lasted only a few years.

The first solid encouragement came from Jake Zeitlin who commissioned a catalogue for his bookshop, *A King's Treasury of Pleasant Books and Precious Manuscripts*, and the first Plantin Press book (done in collaboration with Ward Ritchie), *A Gil Blas in California* by Alexandre Dumas, with wood engravings by Paul Landacre, published by the Primavera Press in 1933. The exceptionally fine design and the impeccable execution of Plantin Press work brought commissions for books and ephemera from the several California book clubs, from concerned cultural institutions, bibliophiles, and others. Marks designed and printed many books for the Limited Editions Club in New York, among them the charming *Travels with a Donkey* by Robert Louis Stevenson (1957) with drawings by Roger Duvoisin. Other Plantin Press favorites might include *Unpublished Letters of Bayard Taylor*, printed in 1937 for the Huntington Library, and *The Malibu* (plate 61), essays by W. W. Robinson, California historian, and by Lawrence Clark Powell, then UCLA Librarian. The drawings were by Irene Robinson; the publisher, Dawson's Book Shop, Los Angeles, 1958. There were, also, several "leaf" books in large formats that showed the same certainty of touch as did the smaller volumes.

The earliest Plantin Press printing was done on a Laureate platen press, later replaced by a mammoth Babcock cylinder. This in turn was given up for more manageable presses in a final move to a hillside house on Manzanita Street, which served as family home and workshop. Monotype equipment accounted for most of the type composition, with Lillian frequently at the keyboard. Compositors and pressmen were occasionally employed, but Saul and Lillian with some help from their two sons were the permanent staff. Preferred type faces were Bembo, Centaur, Eric Gill's Joanna, and the narrow Bembo Italic designed by Alfred Fairbank. Marks used type ornament with exceptional skill. And despite the demands of operating a personal press, he found time to conduct a workshop course in "The Art of the Book" at the University of Southern California.

Plantin Press books may be immediately recognized. The typography is of a classical and felicitous clarity that is difficult to describe. Presswork is luminous—sharp and deep. The Plantin Press has been a superb example of scholarship and craftsmanship joined together in the right place at the right time.

THE WARD RITCHIE PRESS

After graduation from Occidental College, with intent to become a lawyer, Ward Ritchie entered the law school of the University of Southern California. But one evening in 1928, on reading the *Journals* of T. J. Cobden-Sanderson (himself an English barrister who abandoned his profession to become the famed master of the Doves Press), young

Ritchie decided he would try printing rather than try cases at the law. Ritchie consulted Bruce McCallister and others for advice, then enrolled in the Frank Wiggins Trade School in Los Angeles.

Even as a tyro, the incipient printer-publisher wrote to some of his favorite poets for pieces to print. He received permission from Carl Sandburg, Archibald MacLeish, Robinson Jeffers, and others, and issued the poems they provided, as pamphlets in editions of about fifty copies each, for friends. "After printing these," wrote Ritchie in a recent letter to the present writer, "with the arrogance of youth I felt capable of challenging the world of type. In the *Fleuron* I had read that a Frenchman, François-Louis Schmied, was creating the book of the future, so I set off for Paris hoping to work for him. I now often wonder how I managed it, but he took me on as an apprentice in the years of 1930 and 1931.

"Jeffers had given me permission to print more of his poems after the *Stars* I had done earlier. On Schmied's Stanhope press I printed *Apology for Bad Dreams* in an edition of thirty copies. On returning to the United States I showed a copy to Elmer Adler who was then editing *The Colophon*. This led to a commission from him to print Jeffers' 'First Book' for *The Colophon* Number Ten. My equipment at that time was quite limited. I had a Washington handpress, a Gally Universal (which I hastily acquired after getting Adler's commission), a couple of cases of 14 point Garamont and some Eve which Ed Grabhorn had let me have. . . . Thus in 1932 The Ward Ritchie Press originated."

The Press began in a barn in the back of his parents' home. With Ritchie's flair for bold and versatile design, his love of literature and art, and his capacity for wide friendships the Ward Ritchie Press soon needed more equipment and type, and a more permanent place for operations. The booksellers, publishers, libraries (plate 65), book clubs, bibliophiles, and others, including the Limited Editions Club of New York, brought their commissions for books and ephemera. Ritchie wrote about the beginnings of his printing house in *The Colophon's* 1938 *The Annual of Bookmaking*.

Gregg Anderson while a young page at the Huntington Library had first introduced Ritchie to the world of printing. Anderson later worked with the Grabhorns, spent a few years in the east, established a friendship with Updike, and landed a job with The Meriden Gravure Company in Connecticut. On his return to Los Angeles in 1935 he joined

Ritchie at his expanding press. In 1940 they became formal partners with the name "Anderson & Ritchie, The Ward Ritchie Press." Tragedy followed. Jake Zeitlin wrote of Anderson after he was killed in World War II: "He was the purest spirit, the most knowing and discriminating among all the printers of our period and his untimely end on the beach of Normandy has deprived us greatly."

"The war brought many complications," wrote Ritchie, "and changed the character of the Press from a small easy-going, semiprivate establishment into one with a great deal of commercial printing along with the books that had previously been our mainstay." The commercial work was conducted by the firm of Anderson, Ritchie & Simon, with Joseph Simon (Saul Marks' brother-in-law) in charge. The Ward Ritchie Press was the publishing imprint which issued Western Americana, cookbooks, and other categories, as well as limited editions. Ritchie withdrew in 1974, having been involved in the production of more than seven hundred books. He has since returned to the one-man handpress that lured him away from the law in his youth.

THE ALLEN PRESS

Lewis Allen's father was the publisher of a newspaper in San Francisco, with a job shop, who gave his son an ancient Gordon platen press. On this, during the nineteen-twenties, the high-school boy produced job printing and a small neighborhood newspaper. After Harvard College and marriage, Lewis Allen, with his wife, Dorothy, established the Allen Press—a private press in every sense of the word. The books, although highly personal, original, and varied in design and production, are in the long tradition of the French illustrated *edition de luxe*. The sumptuous and elegant Allen Press editions have been collected by libraries and bibliophiles throughout the country. The first nine titles were printed on small power-driven platen presses. But thereafter all books have been done on handpresses. The handpress became the *raison d'être* of the Allens. The theme, elaborated in Lewis Allen's admirable book, *Printing with the Handpress* (1969), is that "One of the supreme pleasures available to man is intelligence, discipline, and knowledge guiding the hand to create beautiful as well as intellectually desirable objects; and this pleasure is uniquely inherent in the handpress."

An informal letter to the present writer further reveals the Allens' attitudes toward their work: "The handpress, we believe, has offered us the most satisfactory means for expressing ourselves in book work through hand-craftsmanship. Since the inception of our press in 1939, my wife Dorothy has worked closely with me: typography, choice of texts, color, hand-illumination, rolling ink for second and third colors on a text page, and binding. We believe strongly in accomplishing ourselves all facets of production: selecting the text, typography, hand-setting the types, occasionally illustrating our books, hand-coloring, handpress printing on damped handmade or mouldmade paper, and the edition binding. Up to 1950, this was a spare-time hobby; since then it has been a full-time vocation."

The Allens have produced their editions of usually less than 150 copies on two handpresses: an eighteen by twenty-four Columbian, and a ten by fifteen Albion. They have fifty cases of type, chiefly Romanée, Bulmer, Menhart Unciala, Goudy Modern, and Goudy Thirty. Texts have been chosen from classics and contemporary literature "with sufficient immortality to justify fine materials and countless hours of hard work." Illustrations and much color have been essential components. Typographic design is usually dramatic, with due respect for tradition but not its slave. From the Press's many years of production, three books may be chosen as characteristic: *The Hidden Treasures, or the Adventures of Maitre Cornelius* (1953) by Balzac, with wood engravings by Mallette Dean, "illuminated" in color by Dorothy Allen; *The Fall* (1966) by Camus, with abstract illustrations by Lewis Allen; and Genesis (plate 67), printed from Menhart Unciala type, with illustrations by the English engraver Blair Hughes-Stanton. During the year 1976 retrospective exhibitions of Allen Press books have been held in four leading California libraries.

WILLIAM EVERSON

One of the most skillful and articulate practitioners of the handpress in its current widespread reincarnation is William Everson, formerly Brother Antoninus. From the Lime Kiln Press, the typographic workshop at the University of California in Santa Cruz, Everson, aided by his students, completed a magnificent volume of Robinson Jeffers' poems in 1975. *Granite & Cypress* (plate 70), with a woodcut title-page decoration by William Prochnow, is an oblong folio which preserves Jeffers' long lines without turnovers, set in Goudy New Style type and Castellar initials, printed on dampened handmade paper, with joyous, full-bodied presswork. Pure, unadorned typography is here enhanced by extraordinary craftsmanship.

Everson is a recognized poet with several published books of his own verse. Printing came to him by inheritance when his father, a wandering printer and bandmaster, settled into the small town of Selma in California and opened a printing shop. Before marriage, William's mother had set type in a small town in Minnesota. The son's decisive association with printing came during World War II in a conscientious objectors' camp at Waldport, Oregon, where an official monthly paper was issued, called *The Tide*. A small radical literary group thereupon issued their own underground sheet which they called *The Untied*, in which Everson's poems appeared. An old, worn platen press was found nearby which the writers purchased and on which they printed.

After the war, Everson returned to the San Francisco area, acquired a huge old handpress, and in 1949 printed his first significant book—his own poems, *A Privacy of Speech*. Meantime, he was extremely lucky, he said, to have found a job as night janitor at the University of California Press, where he could watch and perfect his knowledge of printing. On receiving a Guggenheim Fellowship for creative writing, he gave up his janitorial assignment and moved to a Catholic Worker home where he printed *Triptych for the Living* (1951), another collection of his own poems. "Feeling apostolic," he then joined the Dominican order as Brother Antoninus at its House of Studies in Oakland. Here, with religious fervor and the wish to make a contribution to the Catholic church, he began a folio Psalter, the *Novum Psalterium*. Only seventy-two pages were completed. With sponsorship from Mrs. Estelle Doheny, who had bought the printed sheets, a title page and Everson's introduction were subsequently set and printed by Saul Marks at the Plantin Press. The completed volume is an interesting confrontation of dry machine printing and dampened handpress work, both at their superb best.

Everson's career and attitudes were discussed with Ruth Teiser and Catherine Harroun in a highly informative book of interviews, *Printing as a Performing Art*, published by The Book Club of California in 1970. The interested reader is also advised that Everson has written two articles for the Book Club's *Quarterly News-Letter*: "Latter-day Handpress," Vol. XV, No. 2 (1950), and "Printer as Contemplative," Vol. XIX, No. 3 (1954).

ADRIAN WILSON

Adrian Wilson, another incipient poet turned printer and graphic designer, has also contributed significantly to typographic research and scholarship. His introduction to typesetting and printing came via the arts and crafts program at the World War II conscientious objector camp at Waldport, where William Everson and William Eshelman were already at work. Wilson became professionally involved in printing in 1946 when he settled in San Francisco and jointly with his actress-wife, Joyce Lancaster, started a little theater, The Interplayers. He bought a ten by fifteen Colts Armory press and set up shop in the theater lobby, with Caslon and Centaur types. Attractive programs and posters brought larger jobs. In 1952 he acquired a small Kelly cylinder press and moved to a downtown commercial building where a general run of printing was designed and printed for university presses and others, and a first book was produced for the Book Club of California.

When Wilson accepted the assignment of full-time designer for the University of California Press, he continued theater printing at night, and in 1957 completed a major work, *Printing for Theater* (plate 60). Wilson was its author, printer, and publisher, in an edition of 250 copies with chapter headings and binding blocks by Nuiko Haramaki.

After a year of travel and study in Europe, Wilson opened a design and printing studio at One Tuscany Alley in San Francisco, where he has planned books (especially art and photographic volumes) for printing in outside plants. Notable is *Ansel Adams: Images 1923–1974,* in an edition of 28,000 copies, that has received international praise. Wilson prints and publishes limited editions on his own presses, notably children's books written and illustrated by Joyce Lancaster Wilson. An enchanting example is *The Ark of Noah* (1975).

Wilson taught the history of the book at the University of California and has lectured in this country and abroad. He wrote and illustrated an excellent manual, *The Design of Books,* published in 1968 by Reinhold in New York, and later issued in paperback by Peregrine Smith, Salt Lake City. In 1972, on one of his European trips, Wilson made the spectacular discovery of the original layouts, preliminary drawings, and other data for the production of the Nuremberg Chronicle (1493), one of the landmarks of incunabula. Aided in the research by his wife, Wilson completed the scholarship for his book *The Making of the*

154

Nuremberg Chronicle, published in 1976 by Nico Israel in Amsterdam. It is an important addition to the history of the printed book.

THE GREENWOOD PRESS

Designer, printer, and teacher, Jack Stauffacher made his first commitment to matters typographic at age fourteen, in 1934, when he purchased a tiny Kelsey table-model press of a size for printing business cards. Then, some years later, a Chandler & Price platen press provided the opportunity for producing books which during the 1940's won recognition in the A.I.G.A. Fifty Books and regional exhibitions.

In 1950 Stauffacher purchased a complete Janson type series from the Stempel foundry in Germany. Admiration for the seventeenth-century face evoked research into its history which culminated in the text for *Janson: A Definitive Collection* (plate 59), written, printed, and published by Stauffacher. Stanley Morison praised it as "a contribution to learning as well as bibliophily."

A Fulbright grant made possible the study of early Italian printing, with special consideration of the elegant books of Lorenzo Torrentino, printer to Cosimo de' Medici. Stauffacher taught at the Carnegie Institute of Technology from 1958 to 1963, where he resurrected the Laboratory Press. This was followed by three years as typographic director of the Stanford University Press and lectures at the San Francisco Art Institute and elsewhere. The Greenwood Press was reopened in 1966, where Stauffacher has continued with writing, printing, publishing, and teaching.

ANDREW HOYEM / PRINTER

Andrew Hoyem is another designer of fine editions who fits the pattern of the youthful poet and artist who becomes a self-taught scholarly printer. And he is one of the many neophytes in debt to Edwin and Robert Grabhorn for inspiration and technical experience.

Born in Sioux Falls, South Dakota, in 1935, and a graduate of Pomona College, Hoyem joined Dave Haselwood at the Auerhahn Press in 1961 in San Francisco. As a one-man operation, Haselwood had been printing and publishing the avant-garde poets then surfacing in the Bay area. After the relationship of several years was dissolved and after a year at the Grabhorn Press, Hoyem set up his own press (Andrew Hoyem / Printer) early in 1965. When the Grabhorn Press closed late that same year, Robert Grabhorn joined the young printer in a harmonious partnership across two generations, until Robert's death in 1973. Hoyem had taken over all of the Grabhorn Press equipment, including a vast assortment of type for hand composition. The present Hoyem production is accomplished on two platen presses. The staff includes a binder and two young men who, together with Hoyem, set type and run the presses.

Andrew Hoyem / Printer carries on the best tradition of the small fine printing house, combining scholarship and craftsmanship. In addition to attractively designed books, and the general printing which sustains the monthly overhead, several volumes have been issued each year by Hoyem's publishing imprint, The Arion Press. Its first book, which he called *Picture/Poems* (plate 69), is an illustrated catalogue of Hoyem's drawings and writings, published on the occasion of their exhibition in 1975 at the Fine Arts Museums of San Francisco.

Limitation of space does not, unfortunately, permit discussion of other California printers. Admirable books have been done by Wilder Bentley, Lawton Kennedy, Grant Dahlstrom, Jane Grabhorn, Sherwood Grover, and others who have been at work for many years past. The Pacific Coast is showing great vitality among new young practitioners and many new presses. The trend toward smaller operations and scholarly craftsmanship—much of the work done by hand—has been well documented, for example, in the 1976 Western Books Exhibition which contains books by fourteen small presses and publishers, many in the show for the first time. The proliferation of new, small fine presses throughout the country may be seen in the pages of *Fine Print*, an excellent magazine issued in San Francisco, edited and published by Sandra Kirshenbaum, subtitled "A Newsletter for the Arts of the Book."

*   *   *

THE ART OF THE BOOK, one of the slender graces of civilization, works its charms on each new generation. Great changes have occurred since Gutenberg's legacy to mankind spread through Europe in the fifteenth century. If today the inventor of printing, arm in arm perhaps with the scholarly Aldus, were to visit a modern plant, with its photo-electronic type composition and mammoth offset presses, he and his companion would, without doubt, be startled and baffled. But the books in the present collection and the workshops in which they were produced would not be wholly unfamiliar to these distinguished visitors. Indeed, they might well be proud of their productive descendants.

From the early manuscript books, through five centuries of the printed book, the fundamental principles, the eternal verities, have remained constant. The twenty-six letters of the alphabet are still the basic forms with which today's typographic designer fashions his books, as they were for the scribes in the completion of their beautiful volumes on vellum. Despite the vastness and the complexity of today's dissemination of the printed word, the basic craft of bookmaking still pursues its own unyielding ways. Its citadel has been the small, professional fine printing house. A new phenomenon has appeared in the emergence of young printmakers, artists, and writers, who have found fulfillment in type and presses and paper, using, by choice and by necessity, early hand methods. The essential form of the book has not changed; neither, it seems, will the alphabet. Whatever the future, literature and human thought will be preserved, and the book as we have known it will, in all probability, continue as the favored vessel.

THE
TWENTIETH
CENTURY

PLATES

Page sizes are given in inches, width before height. Colonial books vary in size depending on the binder's trim. Exact chronological sequence has occasionally been sacrificed in order to achieve more appropriate grouping or relationship to the text. Margins for a few books have been reduced in reproduction to obtain maximum size of the type area.

All reproductions have been made from books at the Dartmouth College Library, with the following exceptions: plates 3, 5, 8, 10, 12, and 13 have been reproduced from books at the New York Public Library; plates 2 (photostat), 16, and 22 from the American Antiquarian Society; plates 4, 6, 9, 14, 15, and 21 from the Beinecke Library of Yale University; and plate 1 has been reproduced from the Haraszti facsimile published by the University of Chicago Press in 1956.

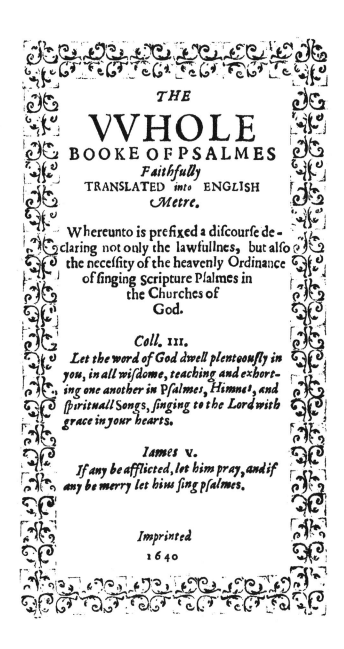

THE
VVHOLE
BOOKE OF PSALMES
Faithfully
TRANSLATED *into* ENGLISH
Metre.

Whereunto is prefixed a difcourfe de-
claring not only the lawfullnes, but alfo
the neceffity of the heavenly Ordinance
of finging Scripture Pfalmes in
the Churches of
God.

Coll. III.
Let the word of God dwell plenteoufly in
you, in all wifdome, teaching and exhort-
ing one another in Pfalmes, Himnes, and
fpirituall Songs, finging to the Lord with
grace in your hearts.

Iames v.
If any be afflicted, let him pray, and if
any be merry let him fing pfalmes.

Imprinted
1640

1 Stephen and Matthew Daye. Cambridge, Massachusetts.
The Whole Booke of Psalmes Faithfully Translated into English Metre.
1640. 5 x 7⅝.

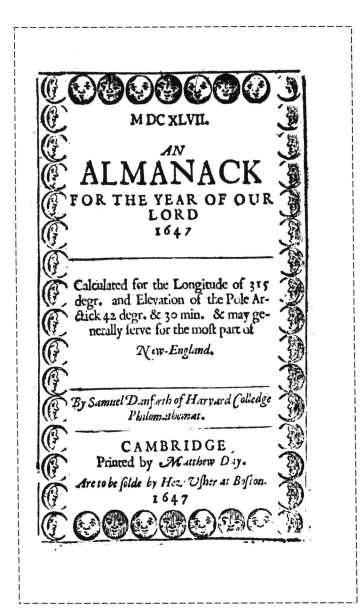

MDC XLVII.

AN
ALMANACK
FOR THE YEAR OF OUR
LORD
1647

Calculated for the Longitude of 315
degr. and Elevation of the Pole Ar-
tick 42 degr. & 30 min. & may generally serve for the most part of

New-England.

By Samuel Danforth of Harvard Colledge
Philomathemat.

CAMBRIDGE,
Printed by Matthew Day.
Are to be solde by Hez. Usher at Boston.
1647

2   Matthew Day. Cambridge, Massachusetts.
An Almanack for the Year of Our Lord 1647. 3⅝ x 6.

MAMUSSE
WUNNEETUPANATAMWE
UP-BIBLUM GOD
NANEESWE
NUKKONE TESTAMENT
KAH WONK
WUSKU TESTAMENT.

Ne quoſhkinnumuk naſhpe Wuttinneumoh *CHRIST*
noh aſoowesit

JOHN ELIOT.

CAMBRIDGE:

Printeuɷop naſhpe *Samuel Green* kah *Marmaduke Johnſon.*

1 6 6 3.

3   Samuel Green and Marmaduke Johnson. Cambridge, Massachusetts.
   Up-Biblum God (The Indian Bible). 1663. 5⅛ x 7½.

A C T S

O F

A S S E M B L Y

PASSED in the

Province of N E VV - Y O R K,

From 1691, to 1725.

Examined and Compared with the Originals in the Secretary's Office.

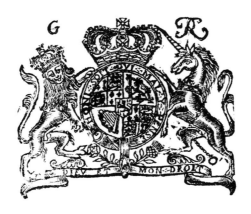

Printed and Sold by *William Bradford*, Printer to the King's moſt Excellent Majeſty for the Province ef *New-York*, 1726.

---

4   William Bradford. New York, New York.
Acts of Assembly Passed in the Province of New-York, from 1691, to 1725.
1726. 7⅝ x 12¼.

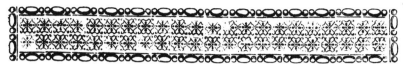

WILLIAM
GOOCH, Efq;
Governor.

ANNO REGNI
GEORGII II,

Regis *Magnæ Britanniæ, Francæ, & Hiberniæ*,
Decimo.

At a GENERAL ASSEMBLY, fummoned to be held at the Capitol, in the City of *Williamf-burg*, on the Firft Day of *Auguft*, in the Ninth Year of the Reign of our Sovereign Lord CEORGE II, by the Grace of God, of *Great-Britain, France*, and *Ireland*, King, Defender of the Faith, *&c.* And from thence continued, by feveral Prorogations, to the Fifth Day of *Auguft*, in the Tenth Year of His faid Majefty's Reign, and in the Year of our Lord, 1736.

CHAP. I.

An Act, for laying a Duty upon Liquors imported by Land; and better fecuring the Duty upon Slaves; and for other Purpofes therein mentioned.

I. ✤✤✤✤✤✤✤✤✤ HEREAS, by an Act of the General Affembly, made at   Recital of
a Seffion held in the Fifth and Sixth Years of His prefent former Acts.
W Majefty's Reign, a Duty or Cuftom of Three Pence, was laid
upon every Gallon of Rum, Brandy, and other diftilled Spirits,
and Wine, imported or brought into this Colony, from any
Port or Place whatfoever, except from *Great-Britain*, to be
paid by the Owner or Importer thereof: And by a former Act, made at a
Seffion of the General Affembly, held in the Twelfth Year of the Reign of
       B   the

5 William Parks. Williamsburg, Virginia.
[Virginia Colony, General Assembly.] *Anno Regni Georgii II*. 1736.
8⅜ x 13.

A
COLLECTION
OF
CHARTERS
AND OTHER PUBLICK ACTS
RELATING TO THE
Province of *PENNSYLVANIA*,

VIZ.

I. The ROYAL CHARTER to *WILLIAM PENN*, Efq;

II. The firft FRAME of Government, granted in *England*, in 1682.

III. LAWS agreed upon in *England*.

IV. Certain CONDITIONS or CONCESSIONS.

V. The ACT of SETTLEMENT, made at *Chefter*, 1682.

VI. The fecond FRAME of Government, granted 1683.

VII. The CHARTER of the CITY of *PHILADELPHIA*, granted *October* 25. 1701.

VIII. The New CHARTER of PRIVILEGES to the Province, granted *October* 28. 1701.

PHILADELPHIA:

Printed and Sold by *B. FRANKLIN*, in *Market-Street*.
M, DCC, XL.

M. T. CICERO's
CATO MAJOR,
OR HIS
DISCOURSE
OF
OLD-AGE:
With Explanatory NOTES.

PHILADELPHIA:
Printed and Sold by B. FRANKLIN,
MDCCXLIV.

7   Benjamin Franklin. Philadelphia, Pennsylvania.
Cato Major, or His Discourse of Old-Age by M. T. Cicero. 1744.
5½ x 8⅛.

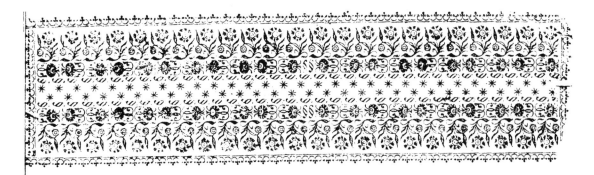

Das erste Buch Mose.

Das 1 Capitel.
Schöpffung der welt.

IM anfang schuff GOtt † himmel und erde. * Joh. 1, 1.3. Col. 1, 16. Ebr. 11, 3. † Pf. 33, 6. Pf. 102, 26.

2. Und die erde war wüste und leer, und es war finster auf der tieffe; und * der Geist GOttes schwebete auf dem waffer. *Pf. 33, 6.

3. Und GOtt sprach: * Es werde licht. Und es ward licht. *2 Cor. 4, 6.

4. Und GOtt sahe, daß das licht gut war. Da scheidete Gott das * licht von der finsternis. *Ef. 45, 7

5. Und nennete das licht tag, und die finsterniß nacht. Da ward aus abend und morgen der erste tag.

6. Und GOtt sprach: * Es werde eine veste zwischen den waffern; und die sey ein unterscheid zwischen den waffern. *Pf. 33,6. Pf. 136,5. Jer. 10, 12.

7. Da machte GOtt die veste, und scheidete * das waffer unter der vesten, von dem waffer über der vesten. Und es geschach also. *Pf. 104, 3. Pf. 148, 4. Jer. 10, 12. c. 51, 15.

8. Und GOtt nennete die veste himmel. Da ward aus abend und morgen der andere tag.

9. Und GOtt sprach: Es samle sich * das waffer unter dem himmel an sondere örter, daß man das trockene sehe. Und es geschach also. *Hiob 38, 8. Pf. 33, 7. Pf. 104, 7.9. Pf. 136, 6.

10. Und GOtt nennete das trockene erde; und die samlung der waffer nennete er meer. Und Gott sahe, daß es gut war.

11. Und GOtt sprach: Es laffe die erde aufgehen gras und kraut, das sich besame; und fruchtbare bäume, da ein jeglicher nach seiner art frucht trage, und habe seinen eigenen samen bey ihm selbst auf erden. Und es geschahe also.

12. Und die erde ließ aufgehen gras und kraut, das sich besamete, ein jegliches nach seiner art; und bäume, die da frucht trugen, und ihren eigenen samen bey sich selbst hatten, ein jeglicher nach seiner art. Und GOtt sahe, daß es gut war.

13. Da ward aus abend und morgen der dritte tag.

14. Und GOtt sprach: Es werden * lichter an der veste des himmels, die da scheiden tag und nacht; und geben zeichen, zeiten, tage und jahre. *Pf. 136, 7. Sir. 43, 2, 9.

15. Und seyen lichter an der veste des himmels, daß sie scheinen auf erden. Und es geschach also.

16. Und GOtt machte zwey grösse lichter; ein groß licht, das * den tag regiere, und ein klein licht, das die nacht regiere; dazu auch sterne. *5 Mof. 4, 19. Hiob 9, 9.

17. Und GOtt setzte sie an die veste des himmels, daß sie scheinen auf die erde,

18. Und den tag und die nacht regiereten, und * scheideten licht und finsterniß. Und GOtt sahe, daß es gut war. *Pf. 104, 20.

19. Da ward aus abend und morgen der vierte tag.

20. Und GOtt sprach: Es errege sich das waffer mit webenden und lebendigen thieren, und mit * gevögel, das auf erden unter der veste des himmels fliege. *c. 2, 19.

21. Und GOtt schüff grosse * walfische, und alerley thier, das da lebet und webet, und vom waffer erreget ward, ein jegliches nach seiner art; und allerley gefiedertes gevögel, ein jegliches nach seiner art. Und GOtt sahe daß es gut war. *Pf. 104, 26.

22. Und GOtt segnete sie, und sprach: * Seyd fruchtbar und mehret euch, und erfüllet das waffer im meer; und das gevögel mehre sich auf erden. *v. 28. c. 8, 17. c. 9, 1.7.

23. Da ward aus abend und morgen der fünfte tag.

A   24. Und

8   Christopher Sower. Germantown, Pennsylvania.
Die Heilige Schrift (Bible in German). 1743. 7¼ x 9¾.

Der
Blutige Schau-Platz,
oder
Martyrer Spiegel
der
Tauffs-Gesinnten,
oder
Wehrlosen Christen,

Welche in dem neunten Jahr-Hundert gelitten haben, von dem
Jahr 800. (nach der Geburt Christi) an
bis zu dem Jahr 900.

Kurtzer Inhalt von den Martyrern dieses
neunten Jahr-Hunderts.

DER Anfang ist eine Wiederholung des vierdten Satzes der Reden Haimonis (auf das Jahr 814.) worinnen gehandelt wird von der Tauff, durch die Bergiesung des Bluts, womit der HErr und alle H. Martyrer seynd getaufft worden.

Hernach folgt (Anno 818.) ein Bericht von der Grausamkeit des Dänischen Tyrannen Regneri, welche er an den Christglaubigen hat ausgeübt: welche Sache (in der Columne) nach der beygefügten Nota, umständlicher erkläret wird.

An dem Rand desselben Spalts wird gemeldet, daß (Anno 826.) die Saracenen in die Römische Eyländer eingefallen seyen, bis in Creta: allwo Cyrillus, der Bischoff der Gemeinde zu Gordina, ist getödtet worden.

Die Tyranney des Bulgarischen Königs, gegen die Christen ausgeübt, wird angeführt um das Jahr 842. und mit Zeugnüssen befestiget.

Eine grose Verfolgung der Glaubigen wird verursachet durch die Streitigkeiten, welche die Könige in Franckenland untereinander hatten, und wird angeführt auf das Jahr 842. zu welcher Zeit auch vorgemeldete Tyranney sich hat zugetragen.

Wir fahren fort in der Verfolgung der Christ-Glaubigen, davon wir (auf das Jahr 850.) eine anführen, welche sehr elendig und jämmerlich gewesen: und ist geschehen zu Corduba, in Spanien, durch die Bosheit der Saracenen.

Unterdessen wird bezeugt, daß dieselbe Verfolgung zu Corduba lang vor dem Jahr 850. ihren Anfang habe genommen, daß sie aber zu derselben Zeit am schwersten und strengsten gewesen seye.

Die elendige Märrer Iohannis, eines Kauffmañs zu Corduba, wird angeführt auf das Jahr 850. welches im Anfang vorgemeldeter Verfolgung geschehen ist.

Hernach folget eine nähere Anmerckung, wegen dem Glauben des gemeldeten Martyrers Iohãis.

Nulilo & Aloida, zwey Geschwister, Christglaubige Jungfrauen, werden in der Stadt Osca um des HErrn Namens willen mit dem Schwerdt getödtet, um das Jahr 851.

Hierauf wird angemercket auf das Jahr 852. an dem Rand, daß zu derselbigen Zeit etlicher Eifer so gros gewesen seye, um als Martyrer zu sterben, daß sie mit groser Menge Christum bekannten, und also der Marter entgegen liefen.   Unter welchen angeführet werden Emilas u. Hieremias, welche beyde um derselben Ursache willen enthauptet wurdẽ; doch wird einem jeden sein Urtheil frey üserlasse.

Aurea eine gottesfürchtige Jungfrau, wird, um des Zeugnuß JEsu Christi willen, nach viel-und schweren Versuchnngs-Proben, enthauptet zu Corduba, Anno 856.

Nachdeme wir eine Nota eingeführt, bereiten wir uns zur Flucht aus den Mahometanischen Verfolgungen, und wenden uns nach Italien und Engeland, allwo ein gröseres und hellers Licht ist aufgegangen.

Hierauf wird (an dem Rand) Hincmarus, Bischoff zu Laudun, angeführt, daß er seye aus Haß des Bischoffs von Rheims und durch ein gewisses Concilium zu Duciacum (um das Jahr 866.) verurtheilt, verdammt, und zuletzt ins Elend verwiesen worden.

Iohannes

---

9   Ephrata Brotherhood. Ephrata, Pennsylvania.
Der Blutige Schau-Platz (The Bloody Arena). 1748. 8¾ x 14.

THE
CHARTER
OF THE
COLLEGE
OF
NEW-YORK,
IN
AMERICA.

Publiſhed by Order of His Honour the Lieutenant Governor, in Council.

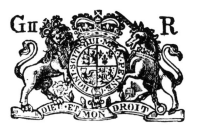

NEW-YORK:

Printed and Sold by J. PARKER and W. WEYMAN, at the New Printing-Office in *Beaver-Street*, MDCCLIV.

10   James Parker. New York.
The Charter of the College of New-York, in America. 1754. 7¼ x 11½.

PIETAS

ET

GRATULATIO

COLLEGII CANTABRIGIENSIS

APUD NOVANGLOS.

BOSTONI-MASSACHUSETTENSIUM

TYPIS J. GREEN & J. RUSSELL.

MDCCLXI.

11   John Green and J. Russell. Boston, Massachusetts.
Pietas et Gratulatio. 1761. 7⅝ x 9¾.

LAWS

OF

MARYLAND

AT LARGE,

WITH PROPER

INDEXES.

Now firſt Collected into One COMPLEAT BODY, and Publiſhed from the Original ACTS and RECORDS, remaining in the *SECRETARY's-OFFICE* of the ſaid

PROVINCE.

Together with *NOTES* and other *MATTERS*, relative to the Conſtitution thereof, extracted from the *PROVINCIAL* Records.

To which is prefixed, THE

CHARTER,

With an *Engliſh* TRANSLATION.

By *THOMAS BACON*, Rector of *All-Saints* Pariſh in *Frederick* County, and Domeſtic Chaplain in *Maryland* to the Right Honourable *FREDERICK* Lord BALTIMORE.

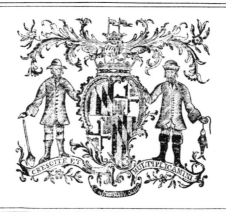

ANNAPOLIS:

PRINTED BY JONAS GREEN, PRINTER TO THE PROVINCE.
MDCCLXV.

12 Jonas Green. Annapolis, Maryland.
   Laws of Maryland at Large. (Compiled by Thomas Bacon.) 1765.
   10 x 16.

not produced as aforefaid, in the fame Manner as directed by this Law with
regard to the Men in any Troop or Company in the County; and the Value
fhall, in the like Manner, be fet, proceeded for, and levied; but it fhall be
paid to the Captain, by the refpective Sheriff, for his own Ufe and Benefit.

IX. **And** to the End that every Perfon fo inlifted or enrolled, at the Time
of their Training, Exercife, or other Duty in the Militia, may improve and
render themfelves fit for Duty and Service, if Occafion fhould require; **Be**
it Enacted, *by the Authority aforefaid,* That every Perfon or Perfons fo inlifted or enrolled, fhall, at the Time and Place of Training, and in the Performance of their Exercife, behave him, or themfelves, decently, and in a
Manner fuitable to the Attention and Care requifite in fuch Exercife, under
the Penalty of One Hundred Pounds of Tobacco, or Ten Shillings Current
Money, for every fuch Mifbehaviour, which fhall be determined by any Two
Field Officers of the County, either upon their own view, or reprefenta-
tion of the Commanding Officer then prefent, and certified by fuch Field
Officers, to the Clerk of the fame County; who fhall, on fuch Certificate,
iffue an Execution, directed to the Sheriff, (or Coroner, if the offending
Perfon fhall be then Sheriff,) to levy fuch Penalty on the Body, Goods, or
Chattels, of fuch Perfon or Perfons fo offending: Which faid Sheriff, or
Coroner, fhall proceed, as is afore-mentioned, and pay the Penalty fo levied,
to the Governor, or Commander in Chief, for the Time being, once every
Year, for the Ufes afore-mentioned.

Perfons to be-have at Muf-ters decently, &c.

Penalty for Mifbehaviour to be deter-mined by two Field Officers.

X. **And be it further Enacted,** *by the Authority aforefaid, by and with the*
Advice and Confent aforefaid, That it fhall and may be lawful, to and for the
Governor, or Commander in Chief, for the Time being, and he is hereby
defired, to nominate and appoint fome fit Perfon or Perfons refiding in each
County, to execute, from Time to Time, fuch Parts of this Act, as is directed to be executed by any Perfon or Perfons appointed by the Governor,
or Commander in Chief.

The Gover-nor defired to depute a Per-fon in each County.

XI. **And be it further Enacted,** That no Servant or Servants fhall from
henceforth continue, or hereafter be Inlifted or Enrolled, in any Regiment,
Company, or Troop, unlefs upon fuch an Emergency as may be judged ne-
ceffary and proper by the Field Officers of the refpective County, or the
major Part of them, for the Inlifting fuch Servant or Servants; any Act to
the contrary notwithftanding.

No Servant to be inlifted in the Militia, unlefs upon Emergency.

XII. **And be it further Enacted,** *by the Authority aforefaid,* That the Sheriff or Coroner, fhall have and receive Thirty Pounds of Tobacco, for every
Execution he fhall ferve or execute, by virtue of this Act, and the ufual
Imprifonment Fee, or Fees due on the Sale of Effects, in cafe of an Imprifonment, or Sale; and the Clerk fhall have and receive Six Pounds of Tobacco
for every Execution iffued by him, in purfuance of this Law: Which faid
Fees fo to be due to the faid Sheriff, Coroner, or Clerk, fhall be levied on
the Body, Goods, or Chattels, of the Perfon againft whom fuch Execution
fhall iffue.

Sheriff's Fee on Execution.

Clerk's Fee.

Leviable on Execution.

XIII. **And whereas,** there are feveral Public Arms now lodged in the feveral Counties in this Province, which may be in a Condition unfit for Ufe,
Be it further Enacted, *by the Authority aforefaid, by and with the Advice and*
Confent aforefaid, That the Colonel of each refpective County, fhall, as foon
as conveniently may be, after the Governor, or Commander in Chief, fhall
require the fame, return to the Governor, or Commander in Chief, a Lift of
fuch Arms which fuch Colonel can find in his County, together with an Account of the Condition fuch Arms are in; and for the Reparation, Amend-
ment, or Difpofal thereof, the Governor, or Commander in Chief, is hereby
defired to give fuch Directions as he may judge moft proper.

A Lift to be made of Old Arms in the feveral Coun-ties,

to be Sold, &c. as the Governor fhall think proper.

E e e 2   XIV. **And**

THE

RIGHTS

OF

COLONIES

EXAMINED.

PUBLISHED BY AUTHORITY.

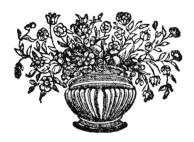

PROVIDENCE:

PRINTED BY *WILLIAM GODDARD.*
M.DCC.LXV.

thence, and digged another well; and faid unto him, We have
and for that they ftrove not: and found water.
he called the name of it Reho- 33 And he called it Sheba:
both; and he faid, For now the therefore the name of the city is
Lord hath made room for us, Beer-fheba unto this day.
and we fhall be fruitful in the land. 34 ¶ And Efau was forty years

23 And he went up from thence old, when he took to wife Judith
to Beer-fheba. the daughter of Beeri the Hittite,

24 And the Lord appeared and Bafhemath the daughter of
unto him the fame night, and Elon the Hittite:
faid, I am the God of Abraham 35 Which were a grief of mind
thy father; fear not, for I am unto Ifaac and to Rebekah.
with thee, and will blefs thee, C H A P. XXVII.
and multiply thy feed for my AND it came to pafs, that when
fervant Abraham's fake. Ifaac was old, and his eyes

25 And he builded an altar were dim, fo that he could not
there, and called upon the name fee, he called Efau his eldeft fon,
of the Lord, and pitched his and faid unto him, My fon: and
tent there: and there Ifaac's fer- he faid unto him, Behold, here
vants digged a well. am I.

26 ¶ Then Abimelech went to 2 And h
him from Gerar, and Ahuzzath am old, I l
one of his friends, and Phichol my death.
the chief captain of his army. 3 Now t

27 And Ifaac faid unto them, thee, thy
Wherefore come ye to me, feeing and thy be
ye hate me, and have fent me field, and t
away from you? 4 And n

28 And they faid, We faw cer- fuch as I lo
tainly that the Lord was with that I may
thee: and we faid, Let there be blefs thee b
now an oath betwixt us, even be- 5 And
twixt us and thee, and let us Ifaac fpake
make a covenant with thee; Efau went

29 That thou wilt do us no venifon, ai
hurt, as we have not touched 6 ¶ And
thee, and as we have done unto Jacob her f
thee nothing but good, and have heard thy f
fent thee away in peace: thou art thy brothe
now the bleffed of the Lord. 7 Bring

30 And he made them a feaft, me favoury
and they did eat and drink. and blefs t

31 And they rofe up betimes before my
in the morning, and fware one to 8 Now
another: and Ifaac fent them obey my vo
away, and they departed from which I co
him in peace. 9 Go n

32 And it came to pafs the fetch me
fame day, that Ifaac's fervants kids of t
came, and told him concerning make then
the well which they had digged, father fucl
B 6

T H E

HOLY BIBLE,

Containing the OLD and NEW

TESTAMENTS:

Newly tranflated out of the

ORIGINAL TONGUES;

And with the former

TRANSLATIONS

Diligently compared and revifed.

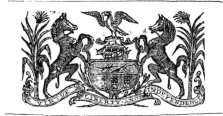

PHILADELPHIA:
Printed and Sold by R. AITKEN, at Pope's
Head, Three Doors above the Coffee
House, in Market Street.
M.DCC.LXXXII.

15 Robert Aitken. Philadelphia, Pennsylvania.
The Holy Bible, Containing the Old and New Testaments. 1782.
3⅜ x 5¾.

THE

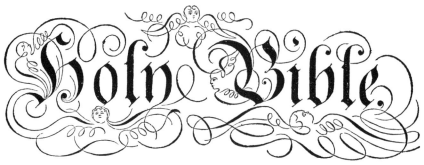

CONTAINING THE

OLD AND NEW

TESTAMENTS:

WITH THE

A P O C R Y P H A.

TRANSLATED

Out of the Original Tongues,

AND

With the FORMER TRANSLATIONS diligently COMPARED and REVISED,

By the fpecial Command of King JAMES I, of *England.*

WITH AN

I N D E X.

Appointed to be read in Churches.

VOL. I.

United States of America.

PRINTED AT THE PRESS IN *WORCESTER*, MASSACHUSETTS,
By ISAIAH THOMAS.

Sold by him in Worcefter ; and by him and Company, at FAUST'S STATUE, No. 45, NEWBURY STREET, Bofton.

MDCCXCI.

16   Isaiah Thomas. Worcester, Massachusetts.
   The Holy Bible. 1791. 8⅞ x 11½.

SONNET XXXVI.

SHOULD the lone Wand'rer, fainting on his way,
    Rest for a moment of the sultry hours,
And tho' his path thro' thorns and roughnefs lay,
    Pluck the wild rose, or woodbine's gadding flow'rs ;
Weaving gay wreaths, beneath some shelt'ring tree,
    The sense of sorrow, he awhile may lose ;
So have I sought thy flow'rs, fair Poesy !
    So charm'd my way, with Friendship and the Muse.
But darker now grows Life's unhappy day,
    Dark, with new clouds of evil yet to come,
Her pencil sickening Fancy throws away,
    And weary Hope reclines upon the tomb ;
And points my wishes to that tranquil shore,
Where the pale spectre Care, pursues no more.

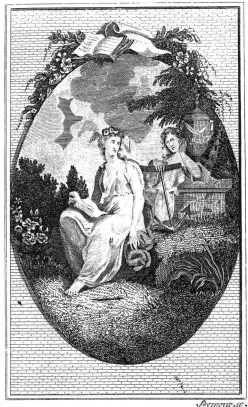

Her pencil sickening fancy throws away
And weary hope reclines upon the tomb.

17   Isaiah Thomas. Worcester, Massachusetts.
Elegiac Sonnets, and Other Poems by Charlotte Smith. 1795. 3⅜ x 5½.

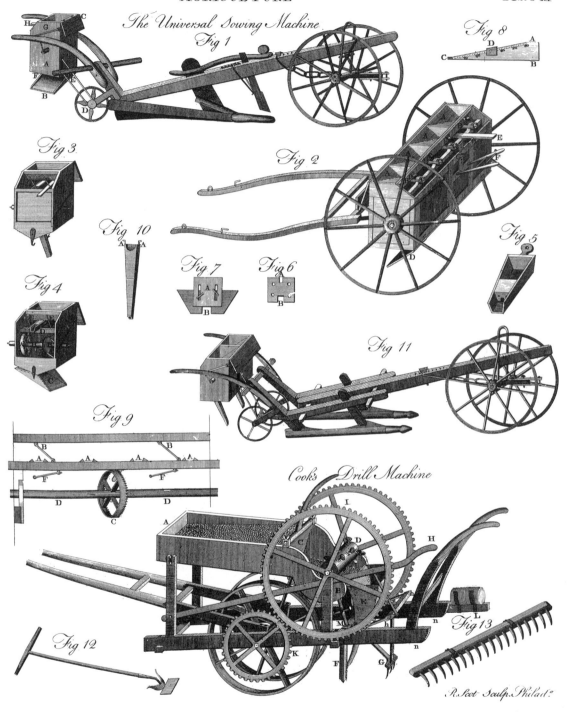

AGRICULTURE

The Universal Sowing Machine
Fig 1

Fig 8

Fig 3

Fig 2

Fig 10

Fig 7

Fig 6

Fig 5

Fig 4

Fig 11

Fig 9

Cook's Drill Machine

Fig 13

Fig 12

Plate IX

R. Scot Sculp. Philad.

18   Thomas Dobson. Philadelphia, Pennsylvania.
*Encyclopædia; or, a Dictionary of Arts, Sciences, and Miscellaneous
Literature.* 1799. 8¼ x 10⅜.

PARADISE LOST,

A

POEM,

IN

TWELVE BOOKS;

By JOHN MILTON,

WITH

A BIOGRAPHICAL AND CRITICAL ACCOUNT

OF THE

AUTHOR and his WRITINGS.

WASHINGTON:

PRINTED FOR MATHEW CAREY,

MARKET-STREET, PHILADELPHIA.

1801.

19   Mathew Carey. Philadelphia, Pennsylvania.
Paradise Lost by John Milton. (Printed for Carey.) 1801. 4⅛ x 6⅞.

Revolving years their ceaseless wanderings led,

And from their sons descending nations spread. 170

These in the torrid tracts began their sway,

Whose cultured fields their growing arts display;

The northern tribes a later stock may boast,

A race descended from the Asian coast.

High in the Arctic, where Anadir glides,

A narrow strait the impinging worlds divides;

There Tartar fugitives from famine sail,

And migrant tribes these fruitful shorelands hail.

He spoke; when Behren's pass before them lay,

And moving nations on the margin stray, 180

Thick swarming, venturous; sail and oar they ply,

Climb on the surge and o'er the billows fly.

As when autumnal storms awake their force,

The storks foreboding tempt their southern course;

From all the fields collecting throngs arise,

Mount on the wing and crowd along the skies;

Thus, to his eye, from bleak Tartaria's shore,

Thro isles and seas, the gathering people pour,

Change their cold regions for a happier strand,

Leap from the wave and tread the welcome land; 190

20 Fry and Kammerer. Philadelphia, Pennsylvania.
The Columbiad by Joel Barlow. 1807. 8⅝ x 10⅞.

SPECIMEN

OF

PRINTING TYPES,

FROM THE

FOUNDERY

OF

Binny & Ronaldson.

PHILADELPHIA.

———•◦◦◦●◉●◦◦◦•———

FRY AND KAMMERER, PRINTERS.
1812.

21 Binny & Ronaldson. Philadelphia, Pennsylvania.
    Specimen of Printing Types. (Printed by Fry and Kammerer.) 1812.
    4⅞ x 8¼.

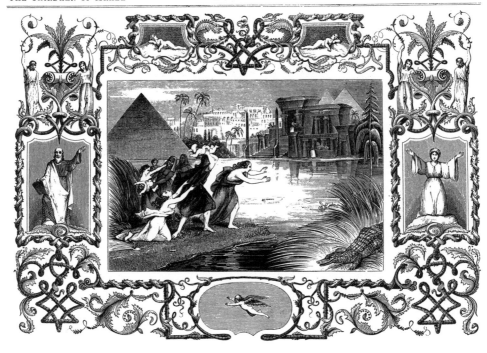

CASTING THE MALE CHILDREN INTO THE NILE

THE SECOND BOOK OF MOSES, CALLED

EXODUS.

CHAPTER I.

1 The children of Israel, after Joseph's death, do multiply. 8 The more they are oppressed by a new king, the more they multiply. 15 The godliness of the midwives, in saving the men-children alive. 22 Pharaoh commandeth the male children to be cast into the river.

NOW ᵃthese *are* the names of the children of Israel, which came into Egypt; every man and his household came with Jacob.

2 Reuben, Simeon, Levi, and Judah,

3 Issachar, Zebulun, and Benjamin,

4 Dan, and Naphtali, Gad, and Asher.

5 And all the souls that came out of the †loins of Jacob were ᵇseventy souls: for Joseph was in Egypt *already*.

6 And ᶜJoseph died, and all his brethren, and all that generation.

7 ¶ ᵈAnd the children of Israel were fruitful, and increased abundantly, and multiplied, and waxed exceeding mighty; and the land was filled with them.

8 Now there ᵉarose up a new king over Egypt, which knew not Joseph.

9 And he said unto his people, Behold, ᶠthe people of the children of Israel *are* more and mightier than we.

60

B.C. 1706.

a Gen. 46, 8. ch. 6, 14

† Heb. *thigh.*

b Gen. 46, 26, 27. ver. 20 Deut. 10, 22.

1635.

c Gen. 50, 26. Acts 7, 15.

d Gen. 46, 3. Deut. 26, 5. Ps. 105, 24. Acts 7, 17.

e Acts 7, 18.

f Ps. 105, 24.

g Ps. 10, 2, & 83, 3, 4.

h Job 5, 13. Ps. 105, 25 Prov. 16, 25, & 21, 30. Acts 7, 19.

i Gen. 15, 13. ch. 3, 7. Deut. 26, 6

k ch. 2, 11, & 5, 4, 5. Ps. 81, 6.

l Gen. 47, 11

† Heb. *And as they afflicted them, so they multiplied, &c*

m ch. 2, 23, & 6, 9. Numb. 20, 15. Acts 7, 19, 34.

n Ps. 81, 6

10 ᵍCome on, let us ʰdeal wisely with them, lest they multiply, and it come to pass, that, when there falleth out any war, they join also unto our enemies, and fight against us, and *so* get them up out of the land.

11 Therefore they did set over them taskmasters, ⁱto afflict them with their ᵏburdens. And they built for Pharaoh treasure-cities, Pithom, ˡand Raamses.

12 †But the more they afflicted them, the more they multiplied and grew. And they were grieved because of the children of Israel.

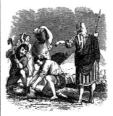

13 And the Egyptians made the children of Israel to serve with rigour.

14 And they ᵐmade their lives bitter with hard bondage, ⁿin mortar, and in brick, and in all manner of service in the field: all their service wherein they made them serve *was* with rigour.

15 ¶ And the king of Egypt spake to the Hebrew midwives (of which the name of one

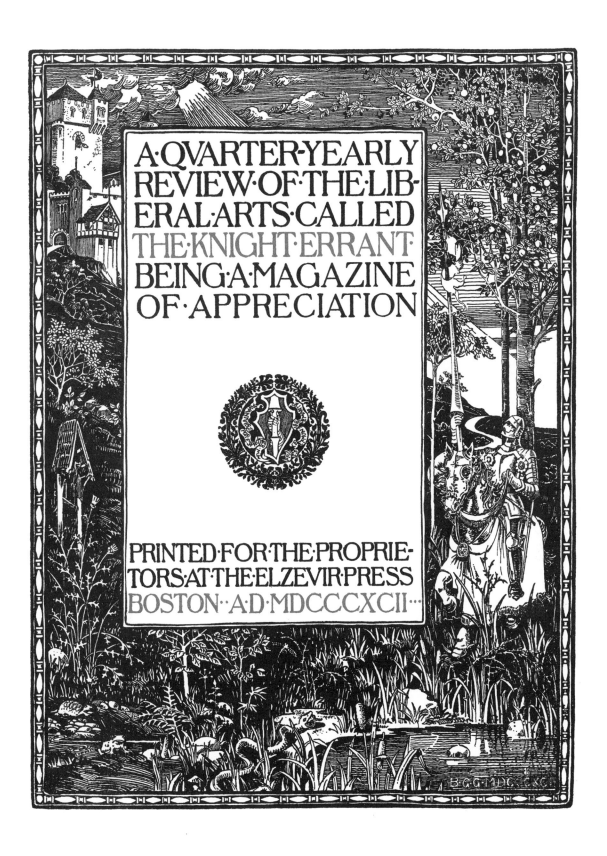

A·QVARTER·YEARLY
REVIEW·OF·THE·LIB-
ERAL·ARTS·CALLED
THE·KNIGHT·ERRANT
BEING·A·MAGAZINE
OF·APPRECIATION

PRINTED·FOR·THE·PROPRIE-
TORS·AT·THE·ELZEVIR·PRESS
BOSTON··A·D·MDCCCXCII···

23   The Proprietors of the Knight Errant Magazine. Boston,
Massachusetts.
The Knight Errant, A Quarter-Yearly Review of the Liberal Arts. 1892.
9⅝ x 12⅛.

borized or moss-agate," *Wright.* Also spelled *arborise.*

arborolatry (är-bo̤-rol'a̤-tri), *n.* [< L. *arbor*, a tree, + Gr. λατρεία, worship.] Tree-worship.

Few species of worship have been more common than *arborolatry.* *S. Hardy*, Eastern Monachism, p. 216.

arborous (är'bo̤-rus), *a.* [< *arbor*1 + *-ous.*] Consisting of or pertaining to trees.

From under shady *arborous* roof. *Milton*, P. L., v. 137.

arbor-vine (är'bo̤r-vīn), *n.* [< *arbor*1 + *vine.*] A species of bindweed. The *Spanish arbor-vine* of Jamaica is an ornamental species of *Ipomœa, I. tuberosa.*

arbor-vitæ (är″bo̤r-vī'tē), *n.* [L., tree of life: see *arbor*1 and *vital.*] 1. In *bot.*, a common name of certain species of *Thuja*, a genus belonging to the natural order *Coniferæ.* *Thuja occidentalis* is the American or common arbor-vitæ, extensively planted for ornament and for hedges. 2. In *anat.*, the arborescent or foliaceous appearance of a section of the cerebellum of the higher vertebrates, due to the arrangement of the white and gray nerve-tissue and their contrast in color. See cut under *corpus.*—**Arbor-vitæ uterinus**, an arborescent appearance presented by the walls of the canal of the neck of the human uterus, becoming indistinct or disappearing after the first gestation.

arbour, *n.* See *arbor*2.

arbrier (är'bri-ėr), *n.* [OF., also *arbreau, arbret, arbriet*, < *arbre*, a tree, beam: see *arbor*1.] The staff or stock of the crossbow.

arbuscle (är'bus-l), *n.* [< L. *arbuscula*, a little tree, dim. of *arbor*, a tree.] A dwarf tree, in size between a shrub and a tree. *Bradley.*

arbuscular (är-bus'kū-lär), *a.* [< L. *arbuscula*: see *arbuscule.*] Resembling an arbuscule; tufted.

arbuscule (är-bus'kūl), *n.* [< L. *arbuscula*, a little tree: see *arbuscle.*] In *zoöl.*, a tuft of something like an arbuscle, as the tufted branchiæ of an annelid; a tuft of cilia.

arbusta, *n.* Plural of *arbustum.*

arbustive† (är-bus'tiv), *a.* [< L. *arbustivus*, < *arbustum*, a plantation of trees: see *arbustum.*] Containing copses of trees or shrubs; covered with shrubs; shrubby.

arbustum (är-bus'tum), *n.*; pl. *arbustums, arbusta* (-tumz, -tä). [L., < *arbos, arbor*, a tree: see *arbor*1.] A copse of shrubs or trees; an orchard or arboretum.

arbute (är'būt), *n.* [Formerly also *arbut*, < L. *arbutus*: see *arbutus.*] The strawberry-tree. See *arbutus*, 3.

arbutean (är-bū'tē-a̤n), *a.* [< L. *arbuteus*, pertaining to the arbutus, < *arbutus*: see *arbutus.*] Pertaining to the arbute or strawberry-tree.

arbutin (är'bū-tin), *n.* [< *arbutus* + *-in*2.] A glucoside ($C_{24}H_{32}O_{14} + H_2O$) obtained from the bearberry (*Arctostaphylos Uva-ursi*) and other plants of the heath family. It forms tufts of colorless acicular crystals soluble in water and having a bitter taste.

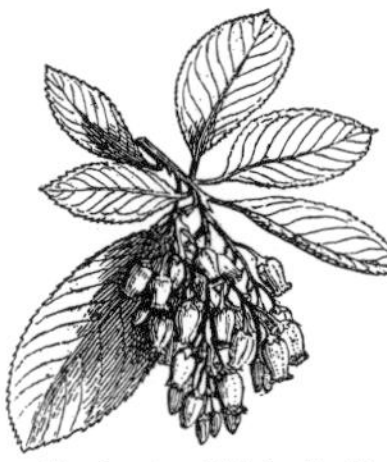

Strawberry-tree (*Arbutus Unedo*).

arbutus (commonly är-bū'tus; as a Latin word, är'bū-tus), *n.* [Formerly also *arbute, arbut* = F. *arbute* = It. *arbuto*, < L. *arbŭtus*, the wild strawberry-tree; prob. akin to *arbor, arbos*, a tree.] 1. A plant of the genus *Arbutus.*—2. The trailing arbutus (see below).—3. [*cap.*] A genus of evergreen shrubs or small trees of southern Europe and western North America, natural order *Ericaceæ*, characterized by a free calyx and a many-seeded berry. The European *A. Unedo* is called the strawberry-tree from its bright-scarlet berries, and is cultivated for ornament. *A. Menziesii* is the picturesque and striking madroño-tree of Oregon and California, sometimes reaching a height of 80 feet or more.—**Trailing arbutus**, the *Epigæa repens*, a fragrant ericaceous creeper of the United States, blooming in the spring, and also known as *May-flower* (which see).

arc1 (ärk), *n.* [Early mod. E. also *ark*; < ME. *ark, arke*, < OF. (and F.) *arc* = Pr. *arc* = Sp. Pg. It. *arco*, < L. *arcus, arquus*, a bow, arc, arch, akin to AS. *earh*, > E. *arrow*, q. v. Doublet, *arch*1.] 1. In *geom.*, any part of a curved line, as of a circle, especially one which does not include a point of inflection or cusp.

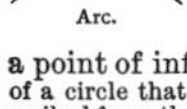

Arc.

It is by means of arcs of a circle that all angles are measured, the arc being described from the angular point as a center. In the higher mathematics the word *arc* is used to denote any angular quantity, even when greater than a whole circle: as, an *arc* of 750°. See *angle*3. 2. In *astron.*, a part of a circle traversed by the sun or other heavenly body; especially, the part passed over by a star between its rising and setting.

The brighte sonne
The *ark* of his artificial day hath ronne
The fourthe part.
Chaucer, Prol. to Man of Law's Tale, l. 2.

3. In *arch.*, an arch. [Rare.]

Turn *arcs* of triumph to a garden-gate. *Pope*, Moral Essays, iv. 30.

Arc boutant (F.), a flying buttress.—**Arc doubleau** (F.), in *arch.*, the main rib or arch-band which crosses a vault at right angles and separates adjoining bays from each other.—**Arc formeret** (F.), the arch which receives the vaulting at the side of a vaulted bay.—**Arc ogive** (F.), one of the transverse or diagonal ribs of a vaulted bay.—**Complement of an arc.** See *complement.* — **Concentric arcs**, arcs which belong to circles having the same center.—**Diurnal arc**, the apparent arc described by the sun from its rising to its setting: sometimes used of stars.—**Elevating arc**, in *gun.*, a brass scale divided into degrees and fractions of a degree, and fastened to the breech of a heavy gun for the purpose of regulating the elevation of the piece; or it is sometimes fixed to the carriage under the trunnions. When secured to the gun itself, a pointer is attached to a ratchet-post in the rear of the piece, and indicates zero when the gun is horizontal.—**Nocturnal arc**, the arc described by the sun, or other heavenly body, during the night.—**Similar arcs**, of unequal circles, arcs which contain the same number of degrees, or are the like part or parts of their respective circles.—**Supplemental arcs.** See *supplemental.*—**Voltaic arc**, in *elect.*, a brilliant band of light, having the shape of an arc, formed by the passage of a powerful electrical current between two carbon-points. Its length varies from a fraction of an inch to two inches, or even more, according to the strength of the current. Its heat is intense, and on this account it is used for fusing very refractory substances. It is also used for illuminating purposes. See *electric light*, under *electric.*

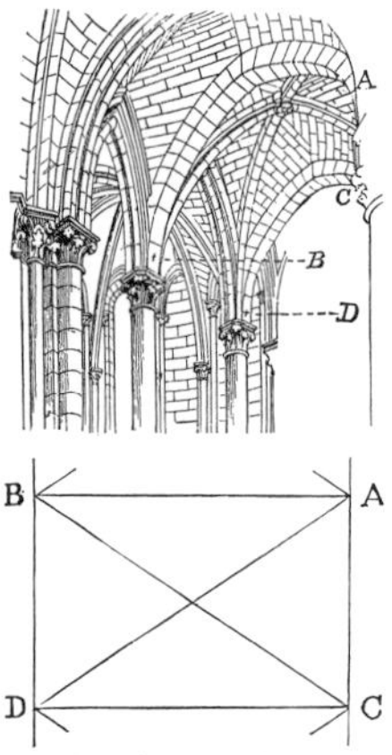

Arcs in vaulting, perspective and plan. (From Viollet-le-Duc's "Dict. de l'Architecture.") *A B, C D*, arcs doubleaux; *A D, C B*, arcs ogives; *A C, B D*, arcs formerets.

arc2†, *n.* Obsolete form of *ark*2.

arca (är'kä), *n.* [L., a chest, box, safe; in eccles. writers, the ark: see *ark*2.] 1. In the early church: (*a*) A chest for receiving offerings of money. (*b*) A box or casket in which the eucharist was carried. (*c*) A name given by St. Gregory of Tours to an altar composed of three marble tablets, one resting horizontally on the other two, which stand upright on the floor. *Walcott*, Sacred Archæol.—2. [*cap.*] [NL.] A genus of asiphonate lamellibranch mollusks, typical of the family *Arcidæ* (which see); the ark-shells proper.

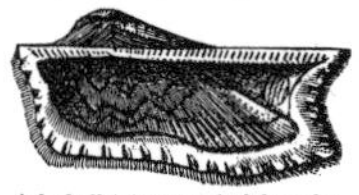

Ark-shell (*Arca noæ*), right valve.

arcabucero (Sp. pron. är″kä-bö-thā'rō), *n.* [Sp., = *harquebusier.*] A musketeer; a harquebusier.

Here in front you can see the very dint of the bullet
Fired point-blank at my heart by a Spanish *arcabucero.*
Longfellow, Miles Standish, i.

Arcadæ (är'ka-dē), *n. pl.* See *Arcidæ.*

arcade (är-kād'), *n.* [< F. *arcade*, < It. *arcata* = Sp. Pg. *arcada*, < ML. *arcata*, an arcade, < L. *arcus*, arc, bow: see *arc*1, *arch*1, *n.*] 1. Properly, a series of arches supported on piers or pillars. The arcade is used especially as a screen and as a support for a wall or roof, but in all architecture since the Roman it is also commonly used as an ornamental dressing to a wall. In this form it is known as a *blind arcade* or an *arcature*, and is also called *wall-arcade.* 2. A simple arched opening in a wall. [Rare.] —3. A vault or vaulted place. [Rare.]—4. Specifically, in some cities, a long arched passageway; a covered avenue, especially one that is lined with shops.

arcaded (är-kā'ded), *a.* Furnished with an arcade.

Arcadian (är-kā'di-a̤n), *a.* and *n.* [< L. *Arcadius, Arcadia*, < Gr. Ἀρκαδία.] I. *a.* 1. Of or pertaining to Arcadia, a mountainous district of Greece in the heart of the Peloponnesus, or to its inhabitants, who were a simple pastoral people, fond of music and dancing. Hence—2. Pastoral; rustic; simple; innocent.—3. Pertaining to or characteristic of the Academy of the Arcadians, an Italian poetical (now also scientific) society founded at Rome in 1690, the aim of the members of which was originally to imitate classic simplicity.

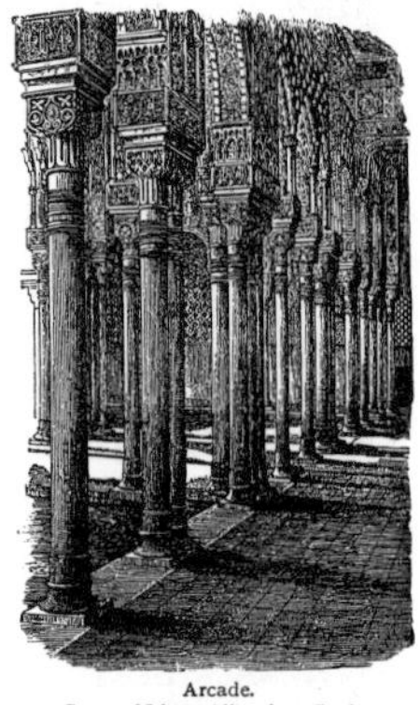

Arcade.
Court of Lions, Alhambra, Spain.

Sometimes written *Arcadic.*

II. *n.* 1. A native or an inhabitant of Arcadia.—2. A member of the Academy of the Arcadians. See I.

Arcadianism (är-kā'di-a̤n-izm), *n.* [< *Arcadian* + *-ism.*] Rustic or pastoral simplicity, especially as affected in literature; specifically, in Italian literature about the end of the seventeenth century, the affectation of classic simplicity.

Arcadic (är-kā'dik), *a.* [< L. *Arcadicus*, < Gr. Ἀρκαδικός.] Same as *Arcadian.*—**Arcadic poetry**, pastoral poetry.

arcana, *n.* Plural of *arcanum.*

arcane (är-kān'), *a.* [< L. *arcanus*, hidden, < *arcere*, shut up, *arca*, a chest. Cf. *arcanum.*] Hidden; secret. [Rare.]

The luminous genius who had illustrated the demonstrations of Euclid was penetrating into the *arcane* caverns of the cabalists. *I. D'Israeli*, Amen. of Lit., II. 294.

arcanum (är-kā'num), *n.*; pl. *arcana* (-nä). [L., neut. of *arcanus*, hidden, closed, secret: see *arcane.*] 1. A secret; a mystery: generally used in the plural: as, the *arcana* of nature.

The very *Arcanum* of pretending Religion in all Wars is, That something may be found out in which all men may have interest. *Selden*, Table-Talk, p. 105.

Inquiries into the *arcana* of the Godhead. *Warburton.*

The Arabs, with their usual activity, penetrated into these *arcana* of wealth. *Prescott*, Ferd. and Isa., i. 8.

2. In *alchemy*, a supposed great secret of nature, which was to be discovered by alchemical means; the secret virtue of anything. Hence—3. A secret remedy reputed to be very efficacious; a marvelous elixir.—**The great arcanum**, the supposed art of transmuting metals.

He told us stories of a Genoese jeweller, who had *the greate arcanum*, and had made projection before him several times. *Evelyn*, Diary, Jan. 2, 1652.

arcature (är'kā-tūr), *n.* [< ML. *arcatura, < *arcata*: see *arcade.*] In *arch.*: (*a*) An arcade of small dimensions, such as a balustrade, formed by a series of little arches. In some mediæval churches open arcatures were introduced beneath the cornices of the external walls, not only as an ornament, but to admit light above the vaulting to the roof-timbers.

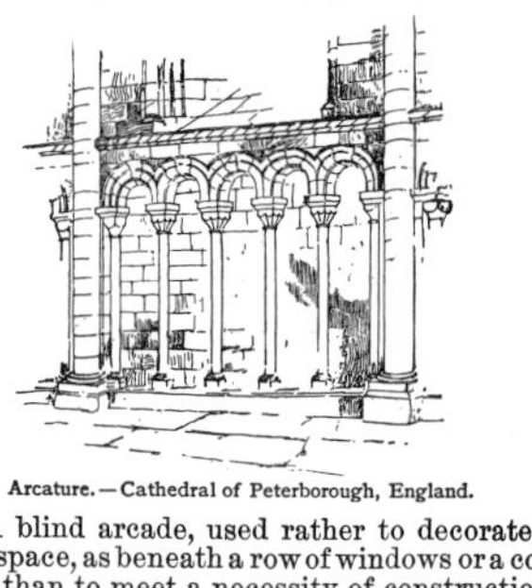

Arcature.—Cathedral of Peterborough, England.

(*b*) A blind arcade, used rather to decorate a wall-space, as beneath a row of windows or a cornice, than to meet a necessity of construction.

arc-cosecant (ärk-kō-sē'kant), *n.* In *math.*, an angle regarded as a function of its cosecant.

24 Theodore Low DeVinne. The DeVinne Press. New York.
The Century Dictionary. 1889–1896. 8⅝ x 11¾.

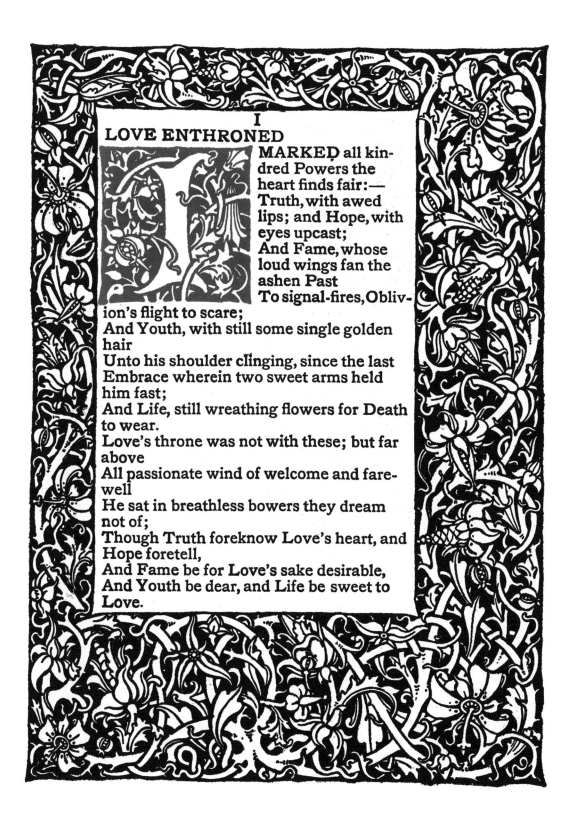

I
LOVE ENTHRONED

I MARKED all kindred Powers the heart finds fair:—
Truth, with awed lips; and Hope, with eyes upcast;
And Fame, whose loud wings fan the ashen Past
To signal-fires, Oblivion's flight to scare;
And Youth, with still some single golden hair
Unto his shoulder clinging, since the last
Embrace wherein two sweet arms held him fast;
And Life, still wreathing flowers for Death to wear.
Love's throne was not with these; but far above
All passionate wind of welcome and farewell
He sat in breathless bowers they dream not of;
Though Truth foreknow Love's heart, and Hope foretell,
And Fame be for Love's sake desirable,
And Youth be dear, and Life be sweet to Love.

25   Copeland & Day. Boston, Massachusetts.
The House of Life by Dante Gabriel Rossetti. (Designed by Bertram Grosvenor Goodhue.) 1894. 6¼ x 8⅝.

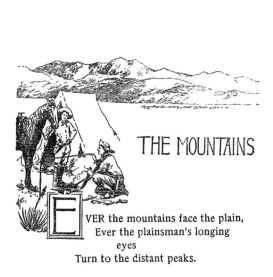

THE MOUNTAINS

EVER the mountains face the plain,
Ever the plainsman's longing
eyes
Turn to the distant peaks.

In the warm mornings, when the lark
Whistles from cool, sage-green, close-curling grass,
When not a cloud stains the sky—
Then the mountains stand forth
Warm, sharply outlined,
Wearing a time-worn cloak of purple rock
And dark green pines.

They draw near the plain,
They seem close, intimate, prosaic.
Every hollow and wrinkle is displayed,
Every rasp and ravage of wind and frost
Is seen, every canon seems emptied
Of its mystery and color.

26 Stone & Kimball. Cambridge, Massachusetts.
Prairie Songs by Hamlin Garland. (Illustrations by H. T.
Carpenter.) 1893. 4⅜ x 6⅜.

Love's Dilemmas

By ROBERT HERRICK

Author of "The Man Who Wins"
"The Gospel of Freedom," Etc.

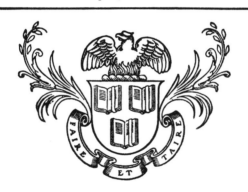

H. S. STONE & COMPANY
CHICAGO *MDCCCXCVIII*

27 H. S. Stone & Company. Chicago, Illinois.
Love's Dilemmas by Robert Herrick. (Designed by Will Bradley.)
1898. 4¾ x 7⅜.

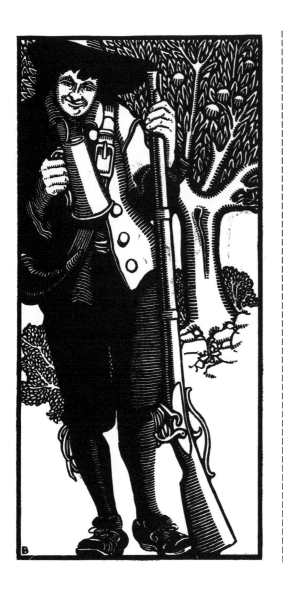

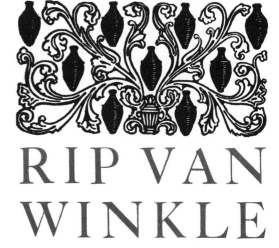

RIP VAN WINKLE

A Posthumous Writing of Diedrich Knickerbocker.

By Woden, God of Saxons,
From whence comes Wensday, that is Wodensday,
Truth is a thing that ever I will keep
Unto thylke day in which I creep into
My sepulchre. —CARTWRIGHT.

WHOEVER has made a voyage up the Hudson, must remember the Kaatskill mountains. They are a dismembered branch of the great Appalachian family, and are seen away to the west of the river, swelling up to a noble height, and lording it over the surrounding country. Every change of season, every change of

28 Will Bradley. The Wayside Press. Springfield, Massachusetts.
Rip Van Winkle by Washington Irving. 1897. 4⅛ x 7⅜.

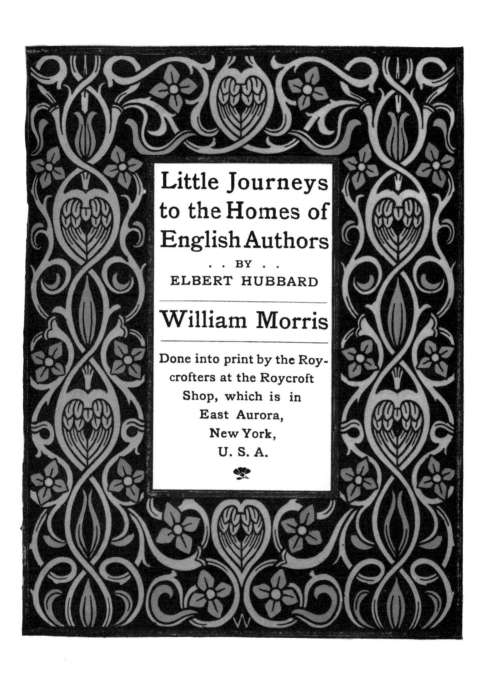

Little Journeys
to the Homes of
English Authors
. . BY . .
ELBERT HUBBARD

William Morris

Done into print by the Roy-
crofters at the Roycroft
Shop, which is in
East Aurora,
New York,
U. S. A.

29 Elbert Hubbard. The Roycrofters. East Aurora, New York.
Little Journeys to the Homes of English Authors: William Morris
by Elbert Hubbard. 1900. 6 x 7¾.

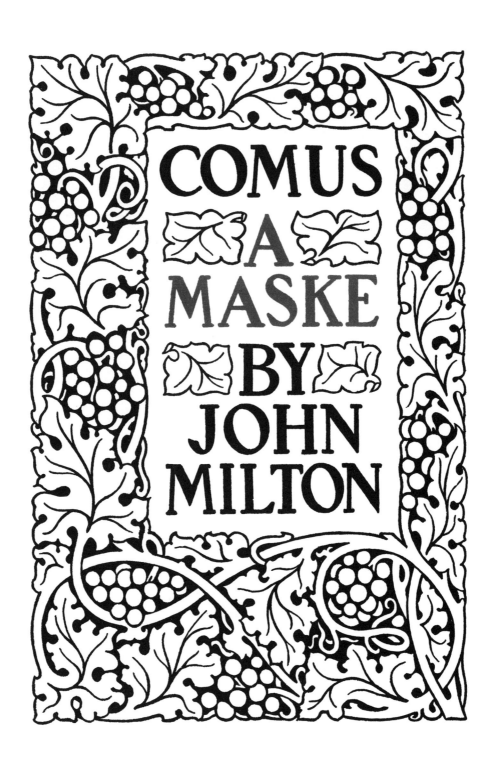

30   Clarke Conwell. The Elston Press. New Rochelle, New York.
      Comus, A Maske by John Milton. 1902. 6½ x 9½.

Dost thou still hope thou shalt be fair,
   When no more fair to me ?
Or those that by thee taken were
   Hold their captivity ?
Is this thy confidence ?   No, no ;
Trust it not ; it can not be so.

But thou too late, too late shalt find
   'Twas I that made thee fair ;
Thy beauties never from thy mind
   But from my loving were ;
And those delights that did thee stole
Confessed the vicinage of my soul.

The rosy reflex of my heart
   Did thy pale cheek attire ;
And what I was, not what thou art,
   Did gazers-on admire.
Go, and too late thou shalt confess
I looked thee into loveliness !

FRANCIS THOMPSON.

LIBER AMORIS
OR
THE NEW PYGMALION
BY
WILLIAM HAZLITT

Portland, Maine
THOMAS B. MOSHER
Mdccccviij

31   Thomas Bird Mosher. Portland, Maine.
    Liber Amoris or The New Pygmalion by William Hazlitt. 1908.
    3¾ x 7.

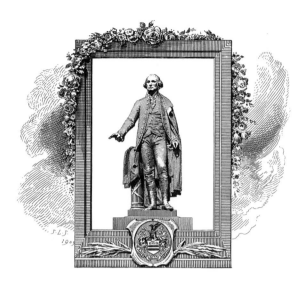

CHAPTER III

 HE first bright little gamin one meets on Wall or Nassau Street, crying the daily papers, can tell the stranger " seeing New York " that Washington's installation as President of the United States, took place in the balcony of Federal Hall, on the thirtieth of April, 1789,—for has he not read and pondered, time and again, the story inscribed on the granite base of the heroic-sized bronze statue of the " Father of his Country " which, on the steps of the Sub-Treasury, stands sentinel over the spot where

39

32   Walter Gilliss. The Gilliss Press. New York.
New York as Washington Knew It after the Revolution
by William Loring Andrews.
(Copperplate engravings by Sidney L. Smith.) 1905. 5¾ x 9.

NEWARK

A SERIES OF ENGRAVINGS ON WOOD BY

RUDOLPH RUZICKA

WITH AN APPRECIATION OF
THE PICTORIAL ASPECTS OF THE TOWN
BY WALTER PRICHARD EATON

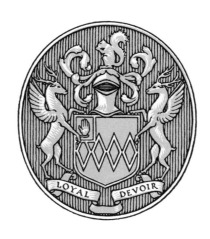

THE CARTERET BOOK CLUB
NEWARK · NEW JERSEY
1917

33 Rudolph Ruzicka. The Carteret Book Club, Newark, New Jersey.
Newark. (Engravings on wood by Ruzicka; text by Walter
Prichard Eaton.) 1917. 9¼ x 12.

Bibliotheca Americana

CATALOGUE OF THE
John Carter Brown Library
IN BROWN UNIVERSITY
Providence, Rhode Island

VOLUME I

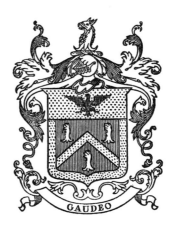

PROVIDENCE
Published by the Library
1919

34 Daniel Berkeley Updike. The Merrymount Press. Boston,
Massachusetts.
Catalogue of the John Carter Brown Library. 1919. 7 x 10½.

THE BOOK OF COMMON PRAYER

and Administration of the Sacraments
and Other Rites and Ceremonies
of the Church

ACCORDING TO THE USE OF THE
PROTESTANT EPISCOPAL CHURCH
IN THE UNITED STATES OF AMERICA

Together with The Psalter
or Psalms of David

PRINTED FOR THE COMMISSION

A. D. MDCCCCXXVIII

35 Daniel Berkeley Updike. The Merrymount Press. Boston,
Massachusetts.
The Book of Common Prayer. 1928. 9⅝ x 13¼.

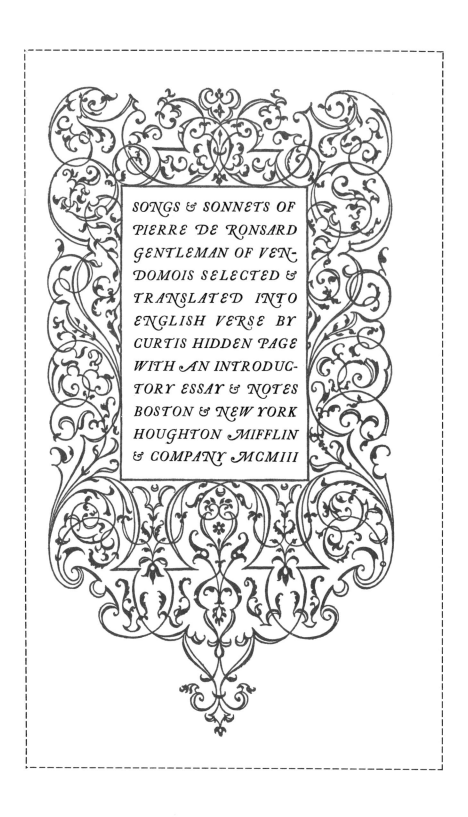

SONGS & SONNETS OF
PIERRE DE RONSARD
GENTLEMAN OF VEN-
DOMOIS SELECTED &
TRANSLATED INTO
ENGLISH VERSE BY
CURTIS HIDDEN PAGE
WITH AN INTRODUC-
TORY ESSAY & NOTES
BOSTON & NEW YORK
HOUGHTON MIFFLIN
& COMPANY MCMIII

36 Bruce Rogers. The Riverside Press. Cambridge, Massachusetts.
Songs & Sonnets of Pierre de Ronsard. 1903. 4½ x 7½.

THE CENTAUR. WRITTEN BY MAURICE DE GUÉRIN AND NOW TRANSLATED FROM THE FRENCH BY GEORGE B. IVES.

I Was born in a cavern of these mountains. Like the river in yonder valley, whose first drops flow from some cliff that weeps in a deep grotto, the first moments of my life sped amidst the shadows of a secluded re, treat, nor vexed its silence. As our mothers draw near their term, they retire to the cav, erns, and in the innermost recesses of the wildest of them all, where the darkness is most dense, they bring forth, uncomplaining, offspring as silent as themselves. Their strength giving milk enables us to endure with, out weakness or dubious struggles the first difficulties of life; yet we leave our caverns later than you your cradles. The reason is that there is a tradition amongst us that the early days of life must be secluded and guarded, as days engrossed by the gods.

My growth ran almost its entire course in the darkness where I was born. The innermost depths of my home were so far within the bowels of the mountain, that I should not have known in which direction the opening lay, had it not been that the winds at times blew in and caused a sudden coolness and confusion. Some, times, too, my mother returned, bringing with her the perfume of the valleys, or dripping wet from the streams to which she resorted. Now, these her home, comings, although they told me naught of the valleys or the streams, yet, being attended by emanations there, from, disturbed my thoughts, and I wandered about, all agitated, amidst my darkness. 'What,' I would say to myself, 'are these places to which my mother goes and what power reigns there which sum, mons her so frequently? To what influences is one there exposed,

37   Bruce Rogers. The Montague Press. Montague, Massachusetts.
The Centaur by Maurice de Guérin. (Translated by George B. Ives.)
1915. 7¹⁵⁄₁₆ x 12.

ANCIENT BOOKS AND MODERN DISCOVERIES

By Frederic G. Kenyon

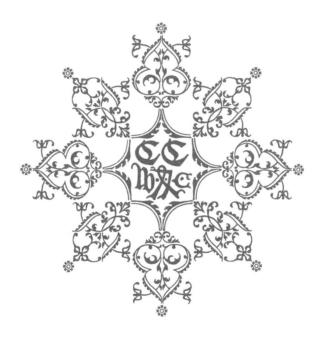

The Caxton Club: Chicago

1927

38   Bruce Rogers. The Printing House of William Edwin Rudge.
Mount Vernon, New York.
Ancient Books and Modern Discoveries by Frederic G. Kenyon. 1927.
9 x 12½.

THE COMEDIES
HISTORIES
& TRAGEDIES

OF

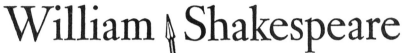

William Shakespeare

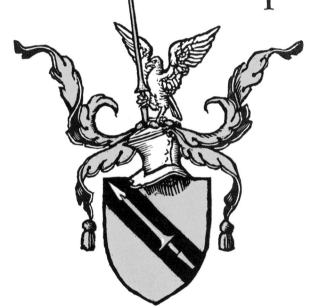

NEW YORK

The Limited Editions Club

1940

39 Bruce Rogers. The Press of A. Colish. Mount Vernon, New York.
The Comedies, Histories & Tragedies of William Shakespeare. 1940.
8¾ x 12½.

[88] is not the best way to develop his individuality. Rather let him get at the underlying form and cautiously work out his own variations. These six drawings show the slight changes necessary to give each letter a different aspect without destroying its harmonious quality or losing the generic likeness. [For another example see the capital 'A' in the word "Alphabet" on the title page of this book.]

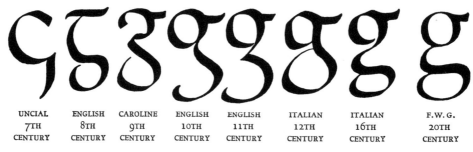

UNCIAL	ENGLISH	CAROLINE	ENGLISH	ENGLISH	ITALIAN	ITALIAN	F.W.G.
7TH	8TH	9TH	10TH	11TH	12TH	16TH	20TH
CENTURY	CENTURY	CENTURY	CENTURY	CENTURY	CENTURY	CENTURY	CENTURY

FIG. 43   DEVELOPMENT OF LOWER-CASE 'g' FROM THE ROMAN UNCIAL

The main reason for the use of drawn lettering is that it is more easily addressed to the artistic sense than are set and fixed type forms, & that it becomes, itself, the decoration of the page. Beautiful letters, as such, are out of place for the text of books, where easy read-ing is the chief desideratum and where symmetry is of less impor-tance. For the decoration of the page, however, the type ready to one's hand does not always serve. Qualities of greater account than me-chanical precision or regularity are needed, making the drawn char-acter necessary; but no license is thereby permitted to the artist to take undue liberties with the proportions of letters. True, the cross-bar of an 'A' or 'H' may be shifted up or down within limits, and so on, but that is not what is meant. It is one thing to disregard tradi-tion, but quite another to go beyond the bounds of moderation. In lettering itself there is not much scope for originality, but there are

40   Frederic W. Goudy. The University of California Press.
Berkeley, California.
The Alphabet and Elements of Lettering by Frederic W. Goudy. 1942.
9⅜ x 12⅝.

[54] good-nature in his eyes he put it into his bosom—and took his leave.

I guard this box, as I would the instrumental parts of my religion, to help my mind on to something better: in truth, I seldom go abroad without it; and oft and many a time have I called up by it the courteous spirit of its owner to regulate my own, in the justlings of the world; they had f⸤ ⸥ ment for his, as I lea⸤ ⸥ till about the forty-fif⸤ ⸥ when upon some mili⸤ ⸥ quited, and meeting⸤ ⸥ with a disappointme⸤ ⸥ of passions, he aband⸤ ⸥ the sex together, and t⸤ ⸥ so much in his conve⸤ ⸥

I feel a damp upo⸤ ⸥ am going to add, tha⸤ ⸥

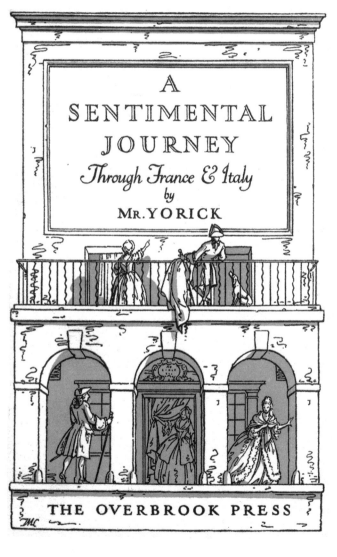

41   T. M. Cleland. The Overbrook Press. Stamford, Connecticut.
A Sentimental Journey Through France & Italy by Laurence Sterne.
1936. 4 x 6.

XV

Seventh Circle: Ring 3. Dante Meets a Great Teacher

Traversing the horrible sand waste upon a dyke of Phlegethon.

LINE 1

Upon the dyke along the red rivulet of Phlegethon the Poets can pass safely, sheltered by certain fumes rising from the stream, as pointed out by Virgil in the last Canto, l. 90.

LINE 9

That is before the snow melts upon the mountains in which it heads. The medieval Duchy of Carinthia extended westward to the headwaters of the Brenta, the river which passes near Padua and flows into the Venetian lagoon.

1 Now bears us over one of the hard banks,
   and fumes above the brooklet, shading well,
   shelter from fire the water and the flanks.

4 As Flemings, who 'twixt Bruges and Wissant dwell,
   fearing the floodtides that upon them run,
   throw up the dyke the ocean to repel,

7 And as by Brenta does the Paduan,
   his villas and his villages to spare
   before Carinthia ever feels the sun:

10 Of like formation those were fashioned there,
   though not so high nor of so broad a base
   the Master made them, whosoe'er he were.

13 We were so distant from the forest chase
   by this, that I could never have descried
   the spot, though backward I had turned my face;

16 And now we met along the margin side
   a company of spirits coming by,
   who each peered at us, as at eventide

19 Beneath new moon, we one another spy;
   and they were puckering their brows at us
   like an old tailor at the needle's eye.

22 By such a family inspected thus,
   well-known I proved to one of them, who caught
   my garment's hem, and cried: "How marvelous!"

25 And when he stretcht his arm, a glance I brought
   to bear so fixt upon his branded hue,
   that his scorcht countenance prevented not

28 His recognition by my inner view;
   and to his visage bending down my head
   I answered: "Ser Brunetto, is it You?"

42 John Henry Nash. San Francisco, California.
   The Divine Comedy of Dante Alighieri. 1926. 9 x 13⅞.
   (Margins slightly reduced.)

Wine Making for the Amateur.

By R. Selden Rose.

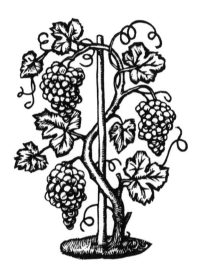

New Haven:
Printed for Members of The Bacchus Club.
Mdccccxxx.

43   Carl Purington Rollins. At the Sign of the Chorobates.
New Haven, Connecticut.
Wine Making for the Amateur by R. Selden Rose. 1930. 7 ¼ x 10.

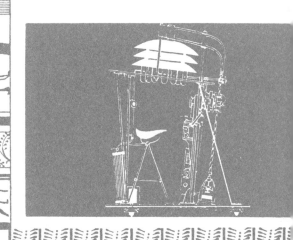

THE

Time Machine

H. G. WELLS

44 W. A. Dwiggins. Hingham, Massachusetts.
The Time Machine by H. G. Wells. 1931. 6 x 9⅛.

N INVENTION

Vith a preface by the Author

ritten for this edition; and

esigns by W. A. Dwiggins

ANDOM HOUSE *New York*

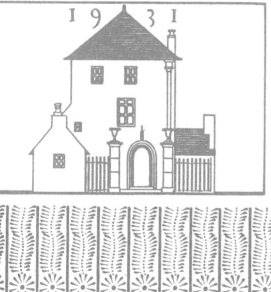

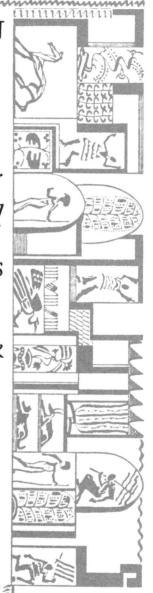

disgusted with everything he possesses? Plato said long ago that the best stomachs are not those which refuse all food." "But," said Candide, "is there not pleasure in criticising, in finding faults where other men think they see beauty?" "That is to say," answered Martin, "that there is pleasure in not being pleased." "Oh! Well," said Candide, "then there is no one happy except me—when I see Mademoiselle Cunegonde again." "It is always good to hope," said Martin. However, the days and weeks went by; Cacambo did not return and Candide was so much plunged in grief that he did not even notice that Paquette and Friar Giroflée had not once come to thank him.

HOW CANDIDE AND MARTIN SUPPED WITH SIX STRANGERS AND WHO THEY WERE

CHAPTER XXVI

ONE evening when Candide and Martin were going to sit down to table with the strangers who lodged in the same hotel, a man with a face the colour of soot came up to him from behind and, taking him by the arm, said: "Get ready to come with us, and do not fail." He turned round and saw Cacambo. Only the sight of Cunegonde could have surprised and pleased him more. He was almost wild with joy. He embraced his dear friend. "Cunegonde is here, of course? Where is she? Take me to her, let me die of joy with her." "Cunegonde is not here," said Cacambo. "She is in Constantinople." "Heavens! In Constantinople! But, were she in China, I would fly to her; let us start at once." "We will start after supper," replied Cacambo. "I cannot tell you any more; I am a slave, and my master is waiting for me; I must go and serve him at table! Do not say anything; eat your supper, and be in readiness." Candide, torn between joy and grief, charmed to see his faithful agent again, amazed to see him a slave, filled with the idea of seeing his mistress again, with turmoil in his heart,

45   Elmer Adler. The Pynson Printers. New York.
Candide by Voltaire. (Illustrations by Rockwell Kent.) 1928.
7½ x 11¼.

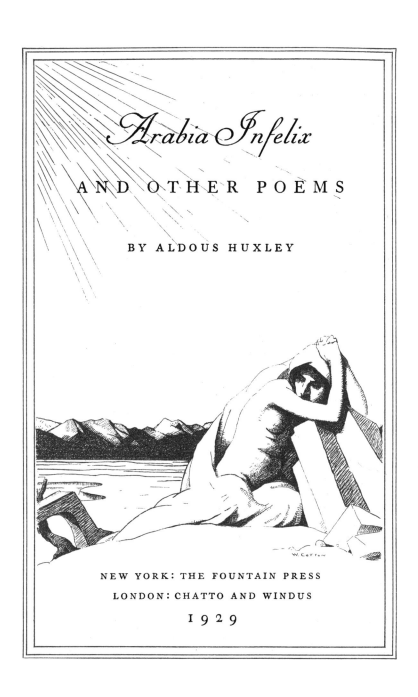

Arabia Infelix

AND OTHER POEMS

BY ALDOUS HUXLEY

NEW YORK: THE FOUNTAIN PRESS
LONDON: CHATTO AND WINDUS

1929

46 John Fass and Roland Wood. The Harbor Press. New York.
Arabia Infelix by Aldous Huxley. (Illustrations by William H.
Cotton.) 1929. 6⅛ x 9¼.

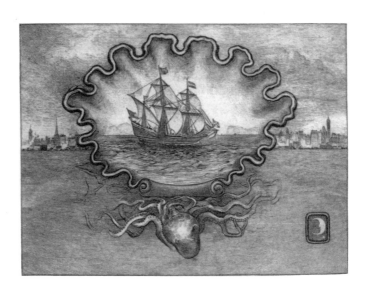

INTRODUCTION

In December, 1894, Mr. William Loring Andrews suggested to several of his fellow members of the Grolier Club the formation of a small club or society for the purpose of issuing a series of engraved views of New York. After considerable discussion a meeting was held on January 2, 1895, which was attended by the following gentlemen: William Loring Andrews, Edward H. Bierstadt, Beverly Chew, Edwin B. Holden, Richard H. Lawrence, and Marshall C. Lefferts. At this meeting it was decided to limit the membership to ten, and subsequently Samuel P. Avery, Charles B. Foote, J. Harsen Purdy, and William F. Havemeyer were enrolled as members. Mr. Chew and Mr. Bierstadt were appointed a committee to draw up Rules and Regulations, and to select a name for the Society. The first subject selected at this meeting for publication was a view of St. Paul's Chapel which Mr. Andrews had already commissioned Edwin Davis French to engrave for his own use.

The first general meeting of the newly formed society was held on January 28, 1895. Mr. Andrews was elected president and Mr. Lawrence was elected to fill the

I X

47 Frederic Warde. The Printing House of William Edwin Rudge.
Mount Vernon, New York.
History of the Society of Iconophiles by Richard Hoe Lawrence. 1930.
8¼ x 11.

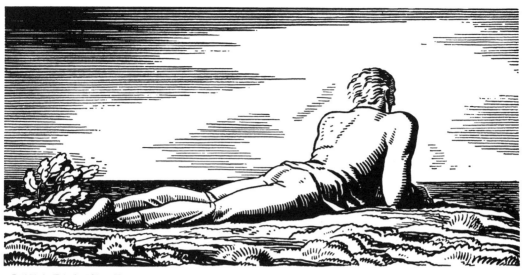

CHAPTER I   LOOMINGS

ALL me Ishmael. Some years ago—never mind how long precisely—having little or no money in my purse, and nothing particular to interest me on shore, I thought I would sail about a little and see the watery part of the world. It is a way I have of driving off the spleen, and regulating the circulation. Whenever I find myself growing grim about the mouth; whenever it is a damp, drizzly November in my soul; whenever I find myself involuntarily pausing before coffin warehouses, and bringing up the rear of every funeral I meet; and especially whenever my hypos get such an upper hand of me, that it requires a strong moral principle to prevent me from deliberately stepping into the street, and methodically knocking people's hats off—then, I account it high time to get to sea as soon as I can. This is my substitute for pistol and ball. With a philosophical flourish Cato throws himself upon his sword; I quietly take to the ship. There is nothing surprising in this. If they but knew it, almost all men in their degree, some

<- I ->

48   William A. Kittredge. The Lakeside Press. Chicago, Illinois.
     Moby Dick by Herman Melville. (Illustrations by Rockwell Kent.)
     1930. 8⅜ x 11½.

[BOOK XXVII.] PRAYER OF COLUMBUS

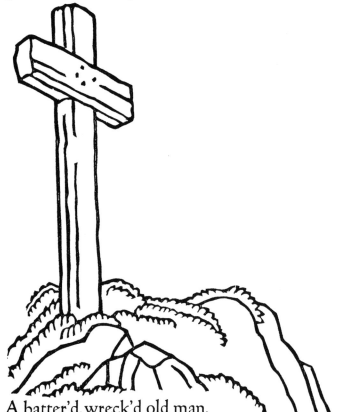

A batter'd, wreck'd old man,
Thrown on this savage shore, far, far from home,
Pent by the sea and dark rebellious brows, twelve dreary months,
Sore, stiff with many toils, sicken'd and nigh to death,
I take my way along the island's edge,
Venting a heavy heart.

I am too full of woe!
Haply I may not live another day;
I cannot rest O God, I cannot eat or drink or sleep,
Till I put forth myself, my prayer, once more to Thee,
Breathe, bathe myself once more in Thee, commune with Thee,
Report myself once more to Thee.

Thou knowest my years entire, my life,
My long and crowded life of active work, not adoration merely;
Thou knowest the prayers and vigils of my youth,
Thou knowest my manhood's solemn and visionary meditations,

330

49   Edwin and Robert Grabhorn. The Grabhorn Press.
San Francisco, California.
Leaves of Grass by Walt Whitman. (Illustrations by Valenti Angelo.)
1930. 9⅞ x 14¾.

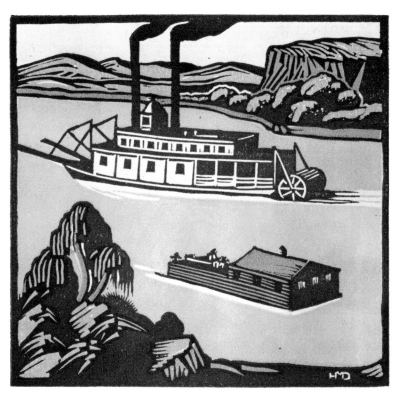

ChAPTER I. from St. Louis to Kansas by Boat. Beginning of the Overland Journey. Description of the Company. hunting Buffalo on the Plains.

HAVING made all necessary preparations, such as laying in a good store of caps, fine, glazed powder, etc.; and having seen the shot towers, French Town, public and private buildings; at the instance of Mr. St. Vrain, our worthy *chef du voyage,* I crammed my purchases, clothes, etc., in my trunk, put it in charge of the porter and walked to the steamer *Saluda* bound for Kansas on the Missouri River, with many kind wishes uttered in my behalf;

50   Edwin and Robert Grabhorn. The Grabhorn Press.
San Francisco, California.
Wah-To-Yah & the Taos Trail by Lewis H. Garrard. (Illustrations by Mallette Dean.) 1936. 6½ x 9½. (Margins slightly reduced.)

THE PASTORAL LOVES OF

DAPHNIS AND CHLOE

BY LONGUS

Done into English, with an Introduction, by

GEORGE MOORE

Illustrated with Etchings by

RUTH REEVES

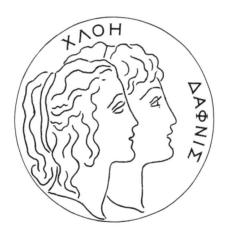

New York

The Limited Editions Club

1934

51   Porter Garnett. Pittsburgh, Pennsylvania.
     The Pastoral Loves of Daphnis and Chloe by Longus.
     (Illustrations by Ruth Reeves.) 1934. 7⅞ x 11¼.

appear from the turn of the path. He understood the still infiniteness of their embodiment; he accustomed himself to see what had taken earthly shape employed so fleetingly and absolutely, that the purposeful consistency of their ways thrust from him every preconception. He was sure they would not notice him were he to move in their midst. A periwinkle standing near him, whose blue gaze he had surely met at some previous time, touched him now from a more spiritual remove, but with such boundless significance as though there were no longer anything to hide. In general he could make out how all objects appeared more distant and at the same time somehow more valid. This may have been due to his own glance, which was no longer directed forward and was becoming tenuous there in the open. He looked back at things as though over his shoulder; and to their existence, locked from him as it was, was added a sweet and audacious flavor as though all were spiced with a trace of the flowers of farewell.—Telling himself from time to time that this could not last, he still did not fear the cease of this remarkable condition, as though from it as from music one might expect only some infinitely just and proper outcome.

All at once his position began to grow irksome. Aware of the trunk, of the lassitude of the book in his hand, he emerged. In the tree a palpable wind now fluttered. It came from the sea. Up the slope the bushes clashed against one another.

followed a bird; he busied himself with a shadow. The very path as it went off and was lost filled him with meditative insight, which appeared to him the purer as he knew himself independent of it. Where else his sojourn was he could not have thought; but that he was only returning to all that was here, that he stood in this body as though deep in an abandoned window looking beyond—of this he was for a few moments so thoroughly convinced, that the sudden appearance of a fellowguest would have been a painful shock, now while his mind was prepared to see Polyxène or Raimondine, or some other departed member of the family

52   Harry Duncan. The Cummington Press. Cummington, Massachusetts.
Five Prose Pieces by Rainer Maria Rilke. (Illustrations by Wightman Williams.) 1947. 8½ x 11⅛.

THE FOUR GOSPELS

OF MATTHEW · MARK

LUKE AND JOHN

With Wood Engravings by

Hans Alexander Mueller

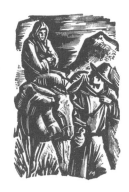

The Peter Pauper Press · Mount Vernon

NEW YORK

53   Peter Beilenson. The Peter Pauper Press.
Mount Vernon, New York.
The Four Gospels. (Illustrations by Hans Alexander Mueller.) 1947.
$7\frac{5}{8}$ x $11\frac{7}{8}$.

THE PAPERS OF
Thomas Jefferson

Volume 1 · 1760-1776

JULIAN P. BOYD, EDITOR

LYMAN H. BUTTERFIELD AND MINA R. BRYAN,

ASSOCIATE EDITORS

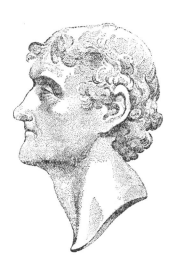

PRINCETON, NEW JERSEY

PRINCETON UNIVERSITY PRESS

1950

54   P. J. Conkwright. Princeton University Press. Princeton,
New Jersey.
The Papers of Thomas Jefferson edited by Julian P. Boyd. 1950.
6⅛ x 9¼. (Margins slightly reduced.)

STIMME DES VOLKS

Du seiest Gottes Stimme/so glaubt ich sonst/
In heilger Jugend; ja und ich sag es noch!
   Um unsre Weisheit unbekümmert
      Rauschen die Ströme doch auch/und dennoch

Wer liebt sie nicht? und immer bewegen sie
Das Herz mir/hör ich ferne die Schwindenden
   Die Ahnungsvollen/meine Bahn nicht
      Aber gewisser ins Meer hin eilen.

Denn selbstvergessen/allzubereit den Wunsch
Der Götter zu erfüllen/ergreift zu gern
   Was sterblich ist und einmal offnen
      Auges auf eigenem Pfade wandelt/

Ins All zurück die kürzeste Bahn/so stürzt
Der Strom hinab/er suchet die Ruh/es reisst
   Es ziehet wider Willen ihn von
      Klippe zu Klippe den Steuerlosen

Das wunderbare Sehnen dem Abgrund zu/
Und kaum der Erd entstiegen/desselben Tags
   Kehrt weinend zum Geburtsort schon aus
      Purpurner Höhe die Wolke wieder.

Und Völker auch ergreifet die Todeslust/
Und Heldenstädte sinken; die Erde grünt
   Und stille vor den Sternen liegt/den
      Betenden gleich/in den Staub geworfen

Freiwillig überwunden die lange Kunst
Vor jenen Unnachahmbaren da; er selbst/
   Der Mensch mit eigner Hand zerbrach/die
      Hohen zu ehren/sein Werk der Künstler.

55 Victor Hammer. Stamperia del Santuccio. Lexington, Kentucky.
    Gedichte by J. C. F. Hölderlin. 1949. 9 x 13.

MORTAL
SUMMER

by

Mark Van Doren

The Prairie Press
IOWA CITY

56   Carroll Coleman. The Prairie Press. Iowa City, Iowa.
Mortal Summer by Mark Van Doren. 1953. 5¾ x 8¾.
(Margins slightly reduced.)

PAPERMAKING BY HAND IN AMERICA

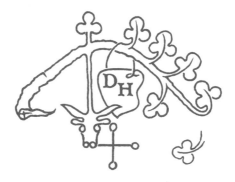

DARD HUNTER

CHILLICOTHE, OHIO
UNITED STATES OF AMERICA
MOUNTAIN HOUSE PRESS
Anno Domini 1950

57 Dard Hunter. Mountain House Press. Chillicothe, Ohio.
Papermaking by Hand in America by Dard Hunter. 1950. 11¾ x 16⅝.

EARLY VICTORIAN

ARCHITECTURE

IN BRITAIN

by Henry-Russell Hitchcock

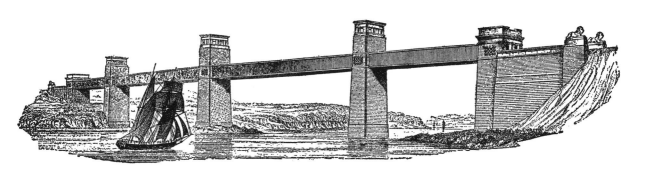

Volume 1: Text

New Haven: Yale University Press, 1954

58   Alvin Eisenman. Yale University Press. New Haven, Connecticut.
Early Victorian Architecture in Britain by Henry-Russell Hitchcock.
1954. 7½ x 10½.

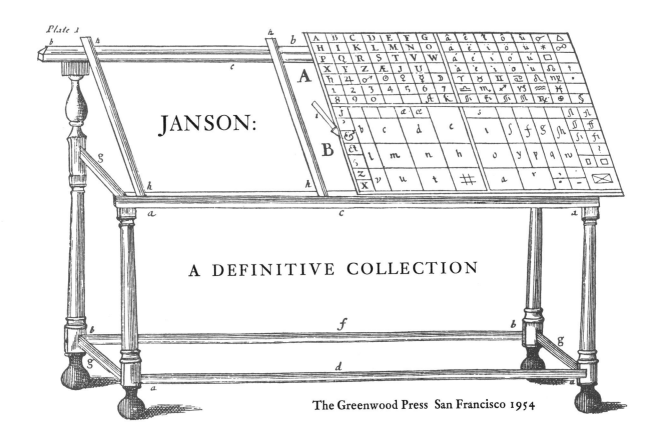

JANSON:

A DEFINITIVE COLLECTION

The Greenwood Press San Francisco 1954

59 Jack Werner Stauffacher. The Greenwood Press.
San Francisco, California.
Janson: A Definitive Collection by Jack Werner Stauffacher.
1954. 9 x 6½.

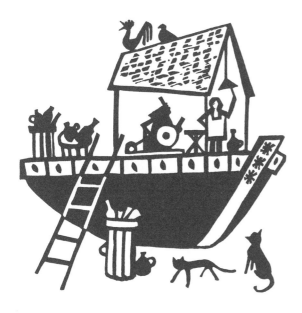

Floating the Press of the Ark

In September 1946, after the inevitable postwar year of vacillation, my wife and I and two friends, Kermit Sheets and Martin Ponch, agreed to meet on a certain day in San Francisco to start a theater. The war years had given us a taste of that peculiar form of romance which culminates in the rising of a curtain. As conscientious objectors, we had been drafted to do "work of national importance"—ditch-digging in North Dakota, privy-building in Florida, snag-felling in Oregon, guinea-pigging in medical experiments throughout the country. For the artists, musicians and writers the historic peace churches which supported the camps for conscientious objectors (The Brethren, The Quakers, The Mennonites), had an ingenious solution—transfer these visionary spirits to one camp where they could stimulate each other and bother no one else. At Waldport, on the Oregon Coast, facilities for a Fine Arts Program were established, spurred by William Everson, poet and printer. After work-project hours there, the musicians

9

60   Adrian Wilson. San Francisco, California.
     Printing for Theater by Adrian Wilson. (Illustrations by Nuiko
     Haramaki and others.) 1957. 10¼ x 15¾.

THE MALIBU

I. Rancho Topanga Malibu Sequit:
An Historical Approach by W. W. Robinson

II. Personal Considerations: *Essays*
by Lawrence Clark Powell

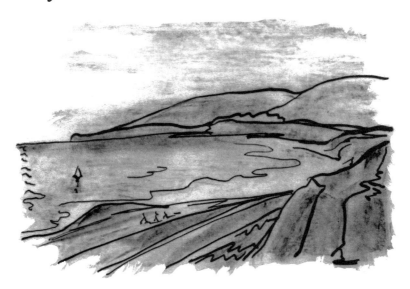

Illustrations by Irene Robinson

Los Angeles DAWSON'S BOOK SHOP *1958*

61   Saul and Lillian Marks. The Plantin Press. Los Angeles, California.
The Malibu by W. W. Robinson and Lawrence Clark Powell.
(Illustrations by Irene Robinson.) 1958. 7¼ x 10⅛.
(Margins slightly reduced.)

Fifty Years

¶ Being a Retrospective Collection of
Novels, Novellas, Tales, Drama, Poetry, and
Reportage and Essays (*Whether Literary,
Musical, Contemplative, Historical, Biographical,
Argumentative, or Gastronomical*)
¶ All Drawn from Volumes Issued during
the Last Half-Century by
ALFRED and BLANCHE KNOPF
Over This Sign and Device

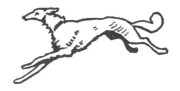

¶ *The Whole Selected,
Assembled, and Edited, with an Introduction
and Sundry Commentaries, by*
Clifton Fadiman

NEW YORK: Alfred·A·Knopf
1965

62   Warren Chappell, designer. Alfred A. Knopf. New York.
Fifty Years edited by Clifton Fadiman. 1965. 6¼ x 9¼.

might manifest them, and that they might see that they themselves are beasts. For that which befalleth the sons of men befalleth beasts; even one thing befalleth them: as the one dieth, so dieth the other; yea, they have all one breath; so that a man hath no preeminence above a beast: for all is vanity. All go unto one place; all are of the dust, and all turn to dust again. Who knoweth the spirit of man that goeth upward, and the spirit of the beast that goeth downward to the earth? Wherefore I perceive that there is nothing better, than that a man should rejoice in his own works; for that is his portion: for who shall bring him to see what shall be after him?

CHAPTER 4 So I returned, and considered all the oppressions that are done under the sun: and behold the tears of such as were oppressed, and they had no comforter; and on the side of their oppressors there was power; but they had no comforter. Wherefore I praised the dead which are already dead more than the living which are yet alive. Yea, better is he than both they, which hath not yet been, who hath not seen the evil work that is done under the sun.

⁋ Again, I considered all travail, and every right work, that for this a man is envied of his neighbour. This is also vanity and vexation of spirit. The fool foldeth his hands together, and eateth his own flesh. Better is an handful with quietness, than both the hands full with travail and vexation of spirit.

⁋ Then I returned, and I saw vanity under the sun. There is one

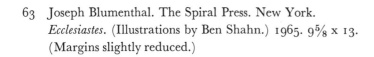

63   Joseph Blumenthal. The Spiral Press. New York. *Ecclesiastes*. (Illustrations by Ben Shahn.) 1965. 9⅝ x 13. (Margins slightly reduced.)

THE VOICE
OF THE WHALEMAN

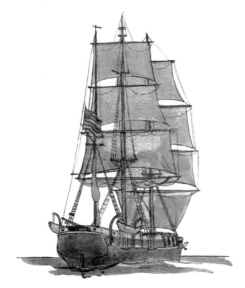

WITH AN ACCOUNT OF THE
NICHOLSON WHALING COLLECTION

BY STUART C. SHERMAN

PROVIDENCE PUBLIC LIBRARY
PROVIDENCE
1965

64   Roderick Stinehour. The Stinehour Press. Lunenburg, Vermont.
The Voice of the Whaleman by Stuart C. Sherman. 1965. 7 x 10.

The
Rocky Mountain Journals
of
William Marshall Anderson

———————————◆•◆———————————

THE WEST IN 1834

———————————◆•◆———————————

EDITED BY DALE L. MORGAN
AND ELEANOR TOWLES HARRIS

THE HUNTINGTON LIBRARY · SAN MARINO, CALIFORNIA

1967

65   Ward Ritchie. The Ward Ritchie Press. Los Angeles, California.
The Rocky Mountain Journals of William Marshall Anderson. 1967.
6¾ x 10. (Margins slightly reduced.)

H.M.S. SULPHUR

at California, 1837 and 1839.

Being the accounts of Midshipman
Francis Guillemard Simpkinson and
Captain Edward Belcher

Edited by
Richard A. Pierce & John H. Winslow

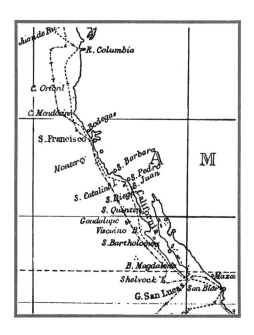

The Book Club of California 1969

66   Grant Dahlstrom. The Castle Press. Pasadena, California.
H.M.S. Sulphur. (The Book Club of California.) 1969. 6⅜ x 9¾.
(Margins slightly reduced.)

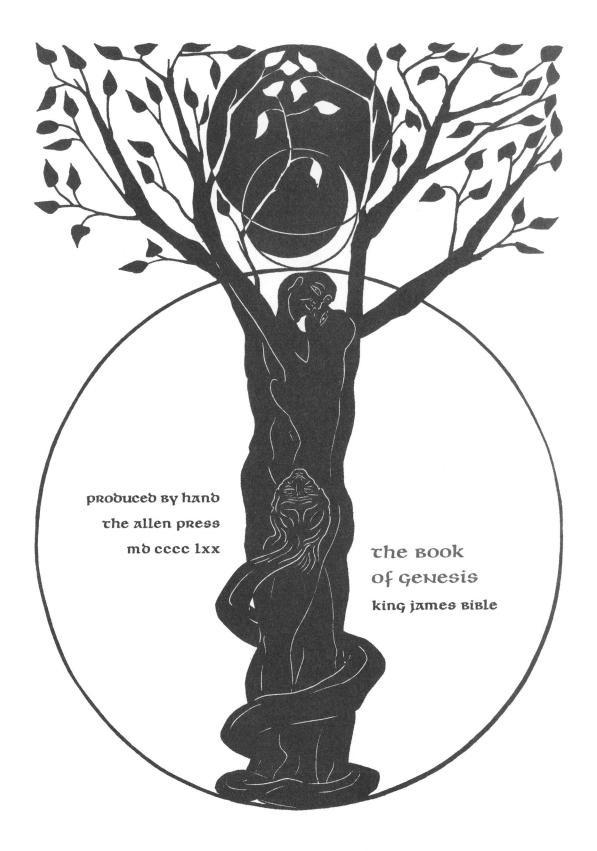

produced by hand
the allen press
md cccc lxx

the book
of genesis
king james bible

67　Lewis and Dorothy Allen. The Allen Press. Kentfield, California.
The Book of Genesis. (Illustrations by Blair Hughes-Stanton.) 1970.
9½ x 12⅞.

That you create our emperor's eldest son,
Lord Saturnine; whose virtues will, I hope,
Reflect on Rome as Titan's rays on earth,
And ripen justice in this commonweal:
Then, if you elect by my advice,
Crown him, and say 'Long live our emperor!'

Marcus With voices and applause of every sort,
Patricians and plebeians, we create
Lord Saturninus Rome's great emperor,
And say 'Long live our emperor Saturnine!'

Saturninus Titus Andronicus, for thy favours done

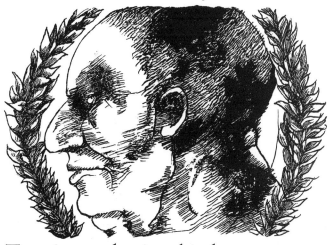

To us in our election this day,
I give thee thanks in part of thy deserts,
And will with deeds requite thy gentleness:
And for an onset, Titus, to advance
Thy name and honourable family,
Lavinia will I make my empress,
Rome's royal mistress, mistress of my heart,
And in the sacred Pantheon her espouse.
Tell me, Andronicus, doth this motion please thee?

68   Leonard Baskin. The Gehenna Press. Northampton, Massachusetts.
Titus Andronicus by William Shakespeare.
(Illustrations by Leonard Baskin.) 1976. 13⅝ x 19⅞.

ANDREW HOYEM PICTURE/POEMS

An illustrated catalogue of drawings and related writings: 1961-1974, prepared by the artist and poet, published on the occasion of an exhibition, January 18 through March 16, 1975, the Fine Arts Museums of San Francisco, California Palace of the Legion of Honor.

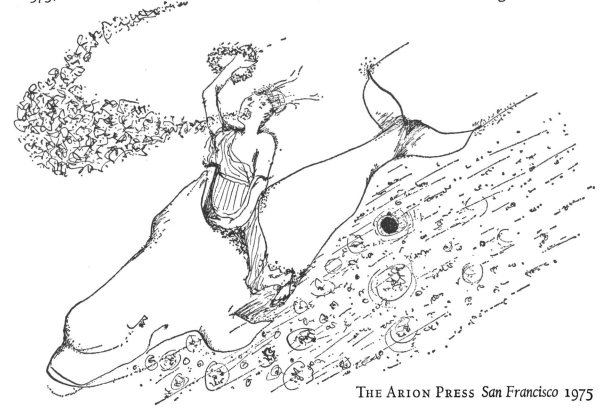

THE ARION PRESS *San Francisco* 1975

69   Andrew Hoyem/Printer. The Arion Press. San Francisco, California.
Picture/Poems by Andrew Hoyem. 1975. 11 ¼ x 11 ¼.

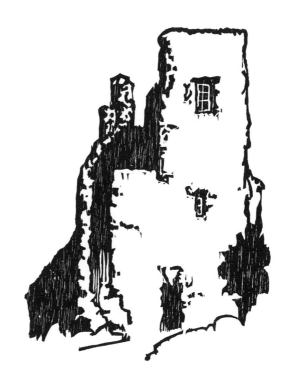

GRANITE & CYPRESS · ROBINSON JEFFERS · RUBBINGS FROM THE ROCK POEMS GATHERED FROM HIS STONEMASON YEARS WHEN SUBMISSION TO THE SPIRIT OF GRANITE IN THE BUILDING OF HOUSE & TOWER & WALL FOCUSED HIS IMAGINATION & GAVE MASSIVE PERMANENCE TO HIS VERSE THE LIME KILN PRESS · THE UNIVERSITY OF CALIFORNIA AT SANTA CRUZ ANNO DOMINI MCMLXXV

70   William Everson. The Lime Kiln Press at the University of California,
     Santa Cruz, California.
     Granite & Cypress by Robinson Jeffers.
     (Illustration by William Prochnow.) 1975. 17 x 12½.

SELECTIVE BIBLIOGRAPHY

Agner, Dwight. *The Books of WAD: A Bibliography of the Books Designed by W. A. Dwiggins.* With a foreword by Alexander Lawson. Baton Rouge: The Press of the Nightowl, 1974.

Allen, Lewis M. *Printing with the Handpress.* Kentfield, Calif.: Allen Press, 1969. (Also published in a trade edition by Van Nostrand Reinhold, New York, 1970.)

American Institute of Graphic Arts. *Catalogue of an Exhibition of the Work of Edwin and Robert Grabhorn of San Francisco.* New York, 1942.

American Institute of Graphic Arts. *WAD: The Work of W. A. Dwiggins Shown by the American Institute of Graphic Arts at the Gallery of the Architectural League.* New York, 1937.

American Institute of Graphic Arts. *The Work of Bruce Rogers, Jack of all Trades, Master of One: A Catalogue.* With an introduction by D. B. Updike, a letter from John T. McCutcheon and an address by Mr. Rogers. New York: Oxford University Press, 1939.

Anderson, Gregg. *Recollections of the Grabhorn Press.* Meriden, Conn., 1935.

The Annual of Bookmaking. New York: The Colophon, 1938.

Balch, David A. *Elbert Hubbard, Genius of Roycroft: A Biography.* New York: Stokes, 1940.

Baughman, Roland O. "The Grabhorns." In *Heritage of the Graphic Arts,* edited by Chandler B. Grannis. New York: Bowker, 1972.

Beilenson, Peter. *The Story of Frederic W. Goudy.* 1939. Reprint. Typophile Chap Book, no. 41. Mt. Vernon, N.Y.: Peter Pauper Press, 1965.

Bennett, Paul A., ed. *Books and Printing: A Treasury for Typophiles.* Cleveland: World, 1951.

Bennett, Paul A. "Frederic William Goudy." In *Heritage of the Graphic Arts,* edited by Chandler B. Grannis. New York: Bowker, 1972.

Bennett, Paul A., ed. *Postscripts on Dwiggins: Essays and Recollections.* By Dorothy Abbe and others. With a selective check list compiled by Dorothy Abbe & Rollo G. Silver. 2 vols. Typophile Chap Books, nos. 35–36. New York: The Typophiles, 1960.

Bianchi, Daniel B. *D. B. Updike & John Bianchi.* Typophiles Monographs, no. 81. Boston: The Society of Printers, 1965.

Binny & Ronaldson. *The Specimen Books of Binny and Ronaldson, 1809–1812,* in facsimile. Conn.: The Columbiad Club; and New Haven: Yale University Press, 1936.

A Bookman's View of Los Angeles. Published for members of the Grolier Club by members of the Zamorano Club, Los Angeles, 1961.

Boston. Museum of Fine Arts. *The Artist & the Book, 1860–1960, in Western Europe and the United States.* Introduction by Philip Hofer. Boston: Museum of Fine Arts; and Cambridge, Mass.: Harvard College Library, Dept. of Printing and Graphic Arts, 1961.

Bradley, Will M. *Will Bradley, His Chap Book*. Typophile Chap Book, no. 30. New York: The Typophiles, 1955.

Bradsher, Earl L. *Mathew Carey, Editor, Author, and Publisher*. Columbia University Studies in English, ser. 2, no. 19. New York: Columbia University Press, 1912.

Cary, Melbert B., Jr. *A Bibliography of the Village Press, 1903–1938*. New York: Press of the Woolly Whale, 1938.

Cave, Roderick. *The Private Press*. New York: Watson-Guptill, 1971.

Chappell, Warren. *A Short History of the Printed Word*. New York: Knopf, 1970.

Cleland, Thomas Maitland. *Harsh Words*. Typophile Chap Book, no. 2. New York: The Typophiles, 1940.

Daniel Berkeley Updike and the Merrymount Press. New York: American Institute of Graphic Arts, 1940.

De Vinne, Theodore Low. *The Invention of Printing*. New York: Francis Hart & Co., 1876.

Duncan, Harry. "The Cummington Press." *New Colophon* 2 (1949), pp. 221–234.

Dwiggins, William Addison. *Mss., by WAD: Being a Collection of the Writings of Dwiggins on Various Subjects*. Typophiles Chap Book, no. 17. New York: The Typophiles, 1947.

Edelstein, David S. *Joel Munsell: Printer and Antiquarian*. Columbia University. Faculty of Political Science. Studies in History, Economics and Public Law, no. 560. New York: Columbia University Press, 1950.

Exman, Eugene. *The House of Harper: One Hundred and Fifty Years of Publishing*. New York: Harper & Row, 1967.

Gilliss, Walter. *Recollections of the Gilliss Press and Its Work during Fifty Years, 1869–1919*. New York: The Grolier Club, 1926.

Goudy, Frederic W. *The Alphabet and Elements of Lettering*. Rev. & enl. Berkeley: University of California Press, 1942.

Goudy, Frederic W. *A Half-century of Type Design and Typography, 1895–1945*. Typophiles Chap Book, no. 13–14. 2 vols. New York: The Typophiles, 1946.

Grabhorn, Edwin. *The Fine Art of Printing*. San Francisco: E. & R. Grabhorn, 1933.

Haas, Irvin. *Bruce Rogers: A Bibliography*. Mount Vernon, N.Y.: Peter Pauper Press, 1936.

Hamill, Alfred E. *The Decorative Work of T. M. Cleland*. New York: The Pynson Printers, 1929.

Hammer, Carolyn R. "Victor Hammer." In *Heritage of the Graphic Arts*, edited by Chandler B. Grannis. New York: Bowker, 1972.

Haraszti, Zoltán. *The Enigma of "The Bay Psalm Book."* Companion volume to *The Bay Psalm Book*, a facsimile reprint of the first edition of 1640. 2 vols. Chicago: University of Chicago Press, 1956.

Harlan, Robert D. *John Henry Nash: The Biography of a Career.* University of California Publications in Librarianship, no. 7. Berkeley: University of California Press, 1970.

Hatch, Benton L. *A Check List of the Publications of Thomas Bird Mosher of Portland, Maine.* Northampton, Mass.: Printed at the Gehenna Press for the University of Massachusetts Press, 1966.

Heller, Elinor Raas. *Bibliography of the Grabhorn Press.* 2 vols. San Francisco, 1940–57. Vol. 2 by Dorothy & David Magee.

Hendrickson, James. "Bruce Rogers." In *Heritage of the Graphic Arts,* edited by Chandler B. Grannis. New York: Bowker, 1972.

Hofer, Philip. "The Work of W. A. Dwiggins." *Dolphin* 2 (1935), pp. 220–55.

Hunter, Dard. "Elbert Hubbard and *A Message to Garcia.*" *New Colophon* 1 (Jan. 1948), pp. 27–35.

Hunter, Dard. *My Life with Paper: An Autobiography.* New York: Knopf, 1958.

Hunter, Dard. *Papermaking: The History and Technique of an Ancient Craft.* 2d ed. New York: Knopf, 1947.

Kainen, Jacob. *George Clymer and The Columbian Press.* San Francisco: The Book Club of California, 1950.

Koenig, Michael. "De Vinne and the De Vinne Press." *Library Quarterly* 41 (Jan. 1971), pp. 1–24.

Kramer, Sidney. *A History of Stone & Kimball and Herbert S. Stone & Co., 1893–1905.* Chicago: Norman W. Forgue, 1940.

Kraus, Joe W. "Messrs Copeland and Day, Publishers to the 1890's." *Publishers Weekly,* 21 March 1942, pp. 1168–71.

Lehmann-Haupt, Hellmut; Silver, Rollo G.; and Wroth, Lawrence C. *The Book in America: A History of the Making and Selling of Books in the United States.* 2d ed. New York: Bowker, 1951.

Littlefield, George E. *The Early Massachusetts Press, 1638–1711.* 2 vols. Boston: The Club of Odd Volumes, 1907.

McMurtrie, Douglas C. *A History of Printing in the United States.* Vol. II. *Middle & South Atlantic States.* New York: Bowker, 1936. Volume I not published.

Munsell, Joel. *Bibliotheca Munselliana: A Catalogue of the Books and Pamphlets.* 1872. Reprint. Burt Franklin Bibliography and Reference Series, no. 290. New York: Burt Franklin, 1969.

Munsell, Joel. *The Typographical Miscellany.* 1850. Reprint. Burt Franklin Research and Source Works Series. Art History & Reference Series, no. 34. New York: Burt Franklin, 1972.

Nash, Ray. *Printing as an Art.* Cambridge, Mass.: Harvard University Press, 1955.

Orcutt, William D. "Frederick Holland Day." *Publishers Weekly,* 6 Jan. 1934, p. 51.

Oswald, John C. *Printing in the Americas.* 1937. Reprint. New York: Hacker Art Books, 1968.

Ransom, Will. *Private Presses and Their Books.* New York: Bowker, 1929.

Ransom, Will. *Selective Lists of Press Books: A Compilation of All Important & Significant Private Presses.* Twelve parts in nine vols. New York: Philip C. Duschnes, 1945–1950.

Richmond, Mary L. "The Cummington Press." In *Books at Iowa* (November 1967).

Roden, Robert F. *The Cambridge Press, 1638–1692: A History of the First Printing Press Established in English America.* Famous Presses, vol. 2. New York: Dodd, Mead, and Company, 1905.

Rogers, Bruce. *Paragraphs on Printing, Elicited from Bruce Rogers in Talks with James Hendrickson on the Function of the Book Designer.* New York: Rudge, 1943.

Rutherfurd, Livingston. *John Peter Zenger, His Press, His Trial and a Bibliography of Zenger Imprints.* New York: Dodd, Mead & Company, 1904.

Shay, Felix. *Elbert Hubbard of East Aurora.* New York. William H. Wise & Co., 1926.

Shipton, Clifford K. *Isaiah Thomas, Printer, Patriot and Philanthropist, 1749–1831.* Rochester, N.Y.: Printing House of Leo Hart, 1949.

Silver, Rollo G. *The American Printer, 1785–1825.* Charlottesville: University Press of Virginia, 1967.

Silver, Rollo G. *Typefounding in America, 1787–1825.* Charlottesville: University Press of Virginia, 1965.

Stein, Max M. "T. M. Cleland." In *Heritage of the Graphic Arts,* edited by Chandler B. Grannis. New York: Bowker, 1972.

Strouse, Norman H. *The Passionate Pirate.* North Hills, Pa.: Bird & Bull Press, 1964.

Teiser, Ruth, and Harroun, Catherine, editors. *Printing as a Performing Art.* San Francisco: The Book Club of California, 1970.

Thomas, Isaiah. *The Diary of Isaiah Thomas.* Edited with an introduction and notes by Benjamin Thomas Hill. Transactions and Collections of the American Antiquarian Society, vols. 9–10. 2 vols. Worcester, Mass.: The Society, 1909.

Thomas, Isaiah. *The History of Printing in America, with a Biography of Printers.* 2d ed. 1874. Reprint. 2 vols. New York: Burt Franklin, 1972.

Thompson, Susan O. "The Arts and Crafts Book." In *The Arts and Crafts Movement in America, 1876–1916,* edited by Robert J. Clark. Princeton, N.J.: Dist. by Princeton University Press, 1972.

The Typophiles, New York. *BR Marks and Remarks: The Marks by Bruce Rogers, et al., the Remarks by His Friends.* Typophiles Chap Book, no. 15. New York: The Typophiles, 1946.

Updike, Daniel B. *In the Day's Work*. Cambridge, Mass.: Harvard University Press, 1924.

Updike, Daniel B. *Notes on the Merrymount Press & its Work . . . With a Bibliographical List of Books Printed at the Press, 1893–1933*. Cambridge, Mass.: Harvard University Press, 1934.

Updike, Daniel B. *Printing Types, Their History, Forms, and Use: A Study in Survivals*. 3d ed. Cambridge, Mass.: Belknap Press, 1962.

Updike, Daniel B. "Thomas Maitland Cleland." *Fleuron* 7 (1930), pp. 133–42.

Updike: American Printer and His Merrymount Press. New York: American Institute of Graphic Arts, 1947.

Van Doren, Carl C. *Benjamin Franklin*. New York: Viking, 1938.

Warde, Frederic. *Bruce Rogers, Designer of Books*. Cambridge, Mass.: Harvard University Press, 1925.

Watts, Steve L. "Will Bradley." In *Heritage of the Graphic Arts*, edited by Chandler B. Grannis. New York: Bowker, 1972.

Wells, James M. "Book Typography in the United States of America." In *Book Typography, 1815–1965, in Europe and the United States of America*, edited by Kenneth Day. Chicago: University of Chicago Press, 1966.

Wells, James M. "Will Ransom." In *Heritage of the Graphic Arts*, edited by Chandler B. Grannis. New York: Bowker, 1972.

Whitehill, Walter M. "Fred Anthoensen." In *Heritage of the Graphic Arts*, edited by Chandler B. Grannis. New York: Bowker, 1972.

Wilson, Adrian. *The Design of Books*. Salt Lake City, Utah: Peregrine Smith, 1976.

Winship, George P. *The Cambridge Press, 1638–1692: A Reëxamination of the Evidence Concerning "The Bay Psalm Book" and the Eliot Indian Bible*. Philadelphia: University of Pennsylvania Press, 1945.

Winship, George P. *Daniel Berkeley Updike and The Merrymount Press of Boston, Massachusetts, 1860, 1894, 1941*. The Printers' Valhalla, vol.1. Rochester, N.Y.: The Print. House of Leo Hart, 1947.

Wroth, Lawrence C. *The Colonial Printer*. 2d ed. Charlottesville, Va.: Dominion Books, 1964.

Wroth, Lawrence C., ed. *A History of the Printed Book, Being the Third Number of the Dolphin*. New York: The Limited Editions Club, 1938.

Zeitlin, Jacob. *Small Renaissance: Southern California Style*. First printed in the *Papers* of the Bibliographical Society of America, Volume 50, First Quarter, 1956. Reprinted for the author, Los Angeles, 1972.

INDEX

Entries include references to persons, presses, business firms, bibliophilic organizations, and book titles. The index was prepared by Virginia L. Close.

246

248

Letterpress composition in the Baskerville type for text,

with Bulmer headings and Perpetua for title display, by

THE STINEHOUR PRESS · LUNENBURG · VERMONT

Plates made by

THE MERIDEN GRAVURE COMPANY · MERIDEN · CONNECTICUT

Reprinted in 1989 by

MERIDEN-STINEHOUR PRESS · LUNENBURG · VERMONT

*

TYPOGRAPHY BY JOSEPH BLUMENTHAL